Lecture Notes in Investment

Investment Fundamentals

World Scientific Lecture Notes in Finance

ISSN: 2424-9955

Series Editor: Professor Itzhak Venezia

This series provides high quality lecture note-type texts in all areas of finance for courses at all levels: undergraduate, MBA and PhD. These accessible and affordable lecture notes are better aligned with today's classrooms and are written by expert professors in their field with extensive teaching experience. Students will find these books less formal, less expensive and also more enjoyable than many textbooks. Instructors will find all the material that they need, thus significantly reducing their class preparation time. Authors can prepare their volumes with ease, as they would be based on already existing, and actively used, lecture notes. With these features, this book series will make a significant contribution to improving the teaching of finance worldwide.

Published:

Vol. 5 *Lecture Notes in Investment: Investment Fundamentals*
by Eliezer Prisman (York University, Canada)

Vol. 4 *Lecture Notes in Market Microstructure and Trading*
by Peter Joakim Westerholm (The University of Sydney, Australia)

Vol. 3 *Lecture Notes in Behavioral Finance*
by Itzhak Venezia (Tel Aviv-Yaffo Academic College, Israel & The Hebrew University of Jerusalem, Israel)

Vol. 2 *Lecture Notes in Fixed Income Fundamentals*
by Eliezer Z. Prisman (York University, Canada)

Vol. 1 *Lecture Notes in Introduction to Corporate Finance*
by Ivan E. Brick (Rutgers Business School at Newark and New Brunswick, USA)

World Scientific Lecture Notes in Finance – **Vol. 5**

Lecture Notes in Investment

Investment Fundamentals

Eliezer Prisman

York University, Canada

World Scientific

NEW JERSEY • LONDON • SINGAPORE • BEIJING • SHANGHAI • HONG KONG • TAIPEI • CHENNAI • TOKYO

Published by

World Scientific Publishing Co. Pte. Ltd.

5 Toh Tuck Link, Singapore 596224

USA office: 27 Warren Street, Suite 401-402, Hackensack, NJ 07601

UK office: 57 Shelton Street, Covent Garden, London WC2H 9HE

Library of Congress Cataloging-in-Publication Data
Names: Prisman, Eliezer Z., author.
Title: Lecture notes in investment : investment fundamentals /
Eliezer Prisman, York University, Canada.
Description: New Jersey : World Scientific, [2021] | Series: World scientific lecture
notes in finance, 2424-9939 ; vol. 5 | Includes index.
Identifiers: LCCN 2020034673 (print) | LCCN 2020034674 (ebook) |
ISBN 9789811219559 (hardcover) | ISBN 9789811220098 (paperback) |
ISBN 9789811219566 (ebook) | ISBN 9789811219573 (ebook other)
Subjects: LCSH: Investments--Mathematical models.
Classification: LCC HG4515.2 .P77 2021 (print) | LCC HG4515.2 (ebook) | DDC 332.6--dc23
LC record available at https://lccn.loc.gov/2020034673
LC ebook record available at https://lccn.loc.gov/2020034674

British Library Cataloguing-in-Publication Data
A catalogue record for this book is available from the British Library.

For any available supplementary material, please visit
https://www.worldscientific.com/worldscibooks/10.1142/11806#t=suppl

Desk Editors: Balasubramanian Shanmugam/Lixi Dong

Typeset by Stallion Press
Email: enquiries@stallionpress.com

About the Author

Dr. Eliezer Zeev Prisman is a Professor of Finance and holds the Nigel Martin Chair in Finance at the Schulich School of Business (SSB) York University. He developed the Financial Engineering Diploma program and was the director of the program for fifteen years. Dr. Prisman's background is in Economics, Statistics and Operations Research. While at SSB, he taught graduate and undergraduate courses, published books and papers in refereed journals besides consulting in various aspects of Finance. He is interested in aspects of modern finance in the Jewish tradition, the use of symbolic and numerical computation for methodological and commercial financial models, arbitrage models, market imperfections and arbitrage.

Contents

Chapter 1

Introduction

Preface

The course begins with an overview of the investment environment in developed markets, followed by a more in-depth analysis of key investment topics. These topics include a modern portfolio theory, asset pricing models, term structure of interest rates, stock and bond portfolio management, and evaluation of portfolio performance. Modern finance extensively uses the concept of arbitrage, or rather the lack of it in financial markets, and the course highlights such uses in different circumstances.

The course takes a hands-on approach with the aid of a software package, Maple, the details of which will be explained during the first lecture. Consequently, most lectures will be divided between a theoretical lecture and a lab — a practical implementation of the theoretical material of the lecture. Most investment brokerages or banks have their own in-house software package that is used to perform the different tasks. The users are familiar with the capability of the software, its basic syntax and have an understanding of what it does. However, the programming code is not exposed to the user who uses an interface. The use of the Maple software in this course simulates, to a certain extent, such a professional environment. After a general and concise review of the investment environment, the course's first unit about the term structure of interest rates and bond portfolio management will be presented.

Investment: The Lay of the Land

This is an introduction to an investment course that focuses on basic models used in the financial industry for investment and decision-making. Institution material is surveyed very concisely, so the reader gets an appreciation of the investment lay of the land. An eLearning unit (no in-class lecture) encompasses reading assignments and self-administrated quizzes complementing the concise introduction. The course makes use of a stock market game. A stock market game gives the students a taste of; trading in the real world, practicing different types of orders as well as introducing conventions common in the investment community. The course targets bachelor students in Business Schools and thus attempts to convey the intuition behind the models while using only basic Mathematics and Statistics. Occasionally, appendixes are added at the end of a lecture to make the arguments more rigorous.

The investment environment is roughly divided into the following areas: Equities (stocks or shares), Fixed Income Securities (Bond Markets, Money Market Accounts, Guaranteed Investment Certificates (GICs) and Term Deposits) and Derivative Securities or Options. While the boundaries between these areas have become fuzzy recently, at this introductory level, it is still applicable. This course covers only Equities and Fixed Income Securities. The fixed income part is dedicated to government bonds only but refers in passing to some attributes of corporate bonds. Hence, one can think about this course as covering risky investments, i.e., stocks, and non-risky investments, i.e., government bonds.

Utilizing stocks is one way for companies to raise funds for their activities. Buying a stock is equivalent to buying a percentage of a firm. However, the owner of a stock enjoys limited liability. Hence in the worst-case scenario, if the company goes bankrupt, the value of the stock will be zero, and stock owners cannot be asked to pay part of the debt. There are different types of stocks, e.g., some give the owner voting rights, and some represent only claims on the firm's assets and dividends. The stocks are issued by firms, usually via an intermediary called an underwriter, in a primary market referred to as Initial Public Offering (IPO). Later, issued stocks are traded between investors in a secondary market, e.g., the TMX in Canada or the NYSE in the U.S.A.

The future price of a stock and its cash flow (dividends) are not guaranteed, hence they are classified as risky assets. In contrast, the cash flow of a government bond is guaranteed and has no default risk, as well as the value of the bond's principle at its maturity. Taking risks and investing in stocks or in other risky assets, may attract investors if a reward is offered for assuming risks, e.g., in terms of higher rates of return relative to risk-free assets. A significant part of this course is dedicated to measuring risks and the risk-return trade off that risky assets should offer.

The risky assets environment is richer and thus requires more institutional material knowledge. Risky assets, in addition to stocks, include some other traded assets in secondary markets, e.g.,

- mutual funds, which are actively managed portfolios of stocks that employ no short positions,
- exchange traded funds (ETF), which are mostly a passive mimicking of certain indexes although recently some hybrid ETFs which employ active trading were introduced to the market, and
- hedge funds which do hold short positions.

The different assets have different schedules of transaction costs and different trading rules. For example, mutual funds are bought and sold based on their prices at the end of the trading day. They trigger higher transaction costs than stocks and ETFs which are traded based on the current market price. There are different types of buying and selling orders, e.g., market orders, limit orders etc. These and other institutional details will be expanded on in the online session in a few weeks. The next three lectures deal with a government bond market since it requires less institutional materials relative to a stock market. The rest of this chapter reviews basic concepts and introduces the notion of arbitrage in preparation for the study of bonds.

The Maple Software: A Preliminary

Maple is a very intuitive symbolic and numeric computation language that allows documentation of the work as part of the process and has excellent visualization tools; 2D, 3D, and animation in 2D and 3D. A Maple document allows linking to the internet, to other documents or to locations within the file and "behind the scene programming" for complex calculations. Generating a Maple file and using it for calculations requires the software. Reading an existing file can be done via the free maple player (click to download the Maple Player). The Maple software (an old version) is installed in the PC lab (room 335). Maple 2019 is **mandatory** for this course and can be purchased for $60 using the discount code in the outline. The lecture files are self-sufficient (there is no need for other sources) and students can alter them, during the lecture or later on, by adding their notes in the file.

A Maple file is divided into text and computation zones.

A text zone facilitates incorporating formulas and mathematical notations, e.g., $\frac{1}{2}\sum_{i=k}^{n} x_i$, a_i, 4^2.

What we have seen so far exemplifies text zones. As seen, text zones can be divided into subsections, as follows.

That can be open or hidden with only the title being exposed. A subsection/section can be generated via the "insert" menu.

The **computation zone** provides direct access to the computational engine via a command line interface that starts with the symbol ">". A command line can be inserted into the document via the insert menu or using the shortcut CTR+j as follows:

CTR+t reverts the command line to a text line.

The Maple syntax is very intuitive and does not require prior programming experience. In the few occasions that complex computations will be required, it will be programmed for you. You will be given the instructions to execute it and an explanation of what it does. A lecture presented via a Maple file has the advantage that it combines the explanations and then immediately the computations in one file. There is no need to switch or split screens from say, Word-to-Excel, etc. Furthermore, it presents an interactive and dynamic-friendly environment allowing readers/instructors to learn/present through hands-on experience, by modifying given examples and recalculating them with ease in real time.

Introduction and Review of Simple Concepts

One of the most basic concepts of finance is *time value of money*. Dollars, like quantities in physics, also have a measure of units other than the magnitude measure. This unit measure is the time at which the magnitude of money is available to you to be used.

Financial markets offer investors the opportunity to invest their money rather than "keeping it idle". If you have a certain amount of money, for example, \$1000, that you do not need now but only in a year, this money can be invested for a year. This course covers both risky and riskless investments. Our starting point is riskless investments, which means that there are no uncertainties about the return of the investment. It is fixed at the time the investment is made, and the likelihood that it will not be realized as promised is zero. While we shall touch on the meaning of "risk-free" investment in the next section, for now let us just take it for granted.

The existence of such risk-free investment possibilities introduces the second dimension (unit) of monies, which is time. Assume that one can get $r\%$ for each dollar invested for a year. If r for example is 10%, then \$1000 today will grow to be \$1000(1.10) or in general to $\$1000(1+r)$. Therefore, \$1000 today is not equivalent to \$1000 a year from today. If one needs \$1000 in a year, one only needs to have $\$\frac{1000}{1+r}$. Given $\$\frac{1000}{1+r}$ today and investing it for a year generates $[\frac{1000}{1+r}](1+r) = 1000$ which is the required amount.

We see therefore that $\$X$ in a year is equivalent to $\$\frac{X}{1+r}$ today. $\frac{X}{1+r}$ is termed the present value of X.

```
> 100/(1+r);
```

$$\frac{100}{1+r} \tag{1}$$

```
> %*(1+r);#  % refers to the last output
```

$$100. \tag{2}$$

Similarly Y dollars today are equivalent to $Y(1+r)$ dollars in a year and the latter is termed the future value of Y. The conversion of dollars of a year from now to dollars of today is done by multiplying it by $\frac{1}{1+r}$, which is termed a *discount factor*. It is usually denoted by d with a sub-index of the time. It is a discount factor for a year from now and will be denoted by d_1. The future value of a dollar in a year can thus be written also as $\frac{1}{d_1}$.

A feature of financial markets therefore is the *opportunity cost* of monies and this is why if one borrows money, one pays for using other peoples' money. Money can be invested and it increases its value. Hence, borrowing \$1000 for a year will require returning \$1000$(1+r)$. In this introduction, we assume a very simplistic model whereby borrowing and lending money is done at the same rate and everybody can borrow and lend at the same risk-free rate. Of course, the return on the investment depends on the duration of the investment. Obviously a dollar invested for a year will yield less than a dollar invested for 2 years. Similarly, borrowing for a year will require less interest payments than borrowing for 2 years.

We again start with a simplistic assumption, which will be relaxed very soon, that the interest charge is r per year regardless of the duration for which money is either borrowed or invested.

This means that if a dollar is invested for a year it will grow to $(1 + r_1)$, and we use r_1 for the interest rate received over a year.

If a dollar is invested for 2 years, it will grow to $(1 + r_2)$ and the relation between r_1 and r_2 is such that $1 + r_2 = (1 + r_1)(1 + r_1)$.

The interest rate r_2 is also referred to as the *simple interest* earned over a period of 2 years.

The expression $(1+r_1)\cdot(1+r_1)$ is referred to as *compound interest.* It can be interpreted as if the dollar was invested first for a year to grow to $(1 + r_1)$, and then this amount is invested again for a year, at the same rate, to grow to $(1 + r_1) \cdot (1 + r_1)$. Thus, at the end of the second year, interest is paid also on the interest earned over the first year, and hence the term compound.

It is not necessarily the case in the market place that the simple interest rate paid over k years, satisfies $(1 + r_1)^k = 1 + r_k$.

However, r_2 must be bigger than r_1.

Assume that the simple rate for one year is $r_1 = 0.02$ and the simple rate for 2 years is $r_2 = 0.018$. Furthermore, assume that one can borrow or lend at the same rate. Hence, \$1000 invested for a year will grow to be \$1020 and \$1000 invested for two years will grow to \$1018.

Time 0:
Borrow \$1000 to be returned in two years
Invest \$1000 for a year

Time 1 (after a year):
Receive $1000 * (1 + 0.02) = $1020
Invest $1020 for a year at the one-year rate in the market
at that time, say $r(1, 2)$
Time 2 (after two years):
Receive $1020 * (1 + r)$
Pay back the loan taken at time 0

```
> 1000*1.018;
```

$$1018.000 \tag{3}$$

that is return $1018 and you keep $\$(2 + 1020 * r(1, 2))$ as seen in the following:

```
> 1020*(1+r(1,2))-1018;
```

$$2 + 1020\, r. \tag{4}$$

Clearly, such situations cannot exist in real markets. Such an investment strategy that produces profit with *no risk* and no *out-of-pocket money* is called *arbitrage*. Note the features of arbitrage strategy: There is no out-of-pocket cost, sometimes referred to as *a self-financed strategy*. No risk is assumed. The position produces profit under any possible circumstances in the future, even though the circumstances that will prevail in the future are currently unknown.

If such a situation exists, investors being rational will exploit it, and as a result will produce demand and supply for money invested and borrowed for different periods. In the above example, all investors would demand to borrow money to be returned in 2 years. Since interest rates can be thought of as the price of money, the interest rate charge for a loan for 2 years will increase due to the demand. Similarly, the interest rate for money over a period of one year will decrease, as there will be an excess supply of money in the market. This arbitrage opportunity thus will never last very long. Hence, the simple interest r_2 will always be greater than r_1 or in general $r_j > r_i$ for $j > i$.

The concept of arbitrage, or the assumption that prices in financial markets do not permit arbitrage, is an essential pricing tool in modern finance. We shall see it in more detail and utilize it to pricing of different securities in more realistic situations in the following lectures.

The example above shows that $r_1 < r_2$ and thus that the discount factors satisfy $d_1 > d_2$. Let's see how the argument above can be done in general and in terms of the discount factors. If $r_1 > r_2$ then it implies that

$$\frac{1}{1+r_2} = d_2 > d_1 = \frac{1}{1+r_1}.$$

One can thus borrow $\$d_2$ to be returned in 2 years which means that \$1 should be paid in 2 years.

Obtaining the $\$d_2$ one would then invest it for a year to receive $d_2(1+r_1) = \frac{d_2}{d_1}$ which is more than a dollar.

Thus, one reaches the end of year one with an amount $1 < \frac{d_2}{d_1}$. At the beginning of the first year, the interest rate that will prevail in the market at the end of year one, for an investment of one year, **is not known**. However, it will be a positive number say, $x > 0$. Thus, investing $\frac{d_2}{d_1}$ at the end of year one for one year will generate $\frac{d_2(1+x)}{d_1}$ which is for sure greater than 1.

Paying back the loan, one would pocket $\frac{d_2(1+x)}{d_1} - 1 > 0$.

We would like to compare the interest charge over a loan of m years to a loan of n years, but we know that $r_n > r_m$ if $n > m$. Hence, we calculate the compound rate per year that is equivalent to a simple rate of n years and to a simple rate of m years, i.e., $(1+r_n)^{(\frac{1}{n})} - 1$ and $(1+r_m)^{(\frac{1}{m})} - 1$, respectively. In fact, this is how interest rates are usually quoted (even though the quoted compounding period is not always a year). That is, if the rate of a loan for k years is reported to be r_k it means that borrowing a dollar for k years requires a return of payment of $(1+r_k)^k$.

Thus, one can define a function $r(t)$ which equals the interest rate paid for an investment or a loan over t years. The simple rate paid over t years will be $(1+r(t))^t - 1$.

The function $r(t)$ is termed the *term structure of interest rates.*

If the function is $r(t) = r$ for every t, like the simplistic assumption we made here, we say that the term structure is *flat* — since graphing it will generate a line parallel to the x-axis.

On the other hand, if we were to graph the discount factor function $d(t)$, with or without the assumption of a flat-term structure, the function $d(t)$ will be a decreasing function. If the assumption of a flat-term structure is adopted, then $d(t) = (1+r)^{(-t)}$ for some value of $r > 0$.

Examples

Let us see how some of the concepts mentioned earlier can be calculated with Maple.

```
> 1000*1.12;
```

$$1120.00 \tag{5}$$

```
> 1/1.12;
```

$$0.8928571429 \tag{6}$$

```
> 1000*(1+r);
```

$$1000 + 1000\,r \tag{7}$$

```
> 1000*(1+r):
```

The symbol # prevents Maple from reading the rest of the line and is used for comments

```
> subs(r=0.03,%);# % means the last output
```

$$1030.00 \tag{8}$$

```
> subs(r=0.10,%%);#%% means the one before last output
```

$$1100.00. \tag{9}$$

Assume the simple 2-year rate is 4%, it will be reported based on an annual compounding as r that solves

$$(1+r)^2 = 1 + 0.04 \textbf{ or } \sqrt{1+0.04} - 1$$

```
> sqrt(1+0.04)-1;
```

$$0.019803903 \tag{10}$$

```
> solve((1+r)^2 = 1+0.04);
```

$$0.01980390272, \ -2.019803903 \tag{11}$$

```
> (1+%[1])^2;# [1] means the first element of the above
output in the sequence 0.1980390272e-1, -2.019803903.
```

$$1.040000001. \tag{12}$$

The following syntax defines a function that calculates the interest rate obtained over 5 years in a market with a flat annual simple rate of r:

```
> r01:=r->(1+r)^5-1;
```

$$r01 := r \mapsto (1+r)^5 - 1 \tag{13}$$

```
> r01(0.02);
```

$$0.104080803 \tag{14}$$

```
> plot(r01(r),r=0..0.20);# plotting a function,
or an expression, is very intuitive
```

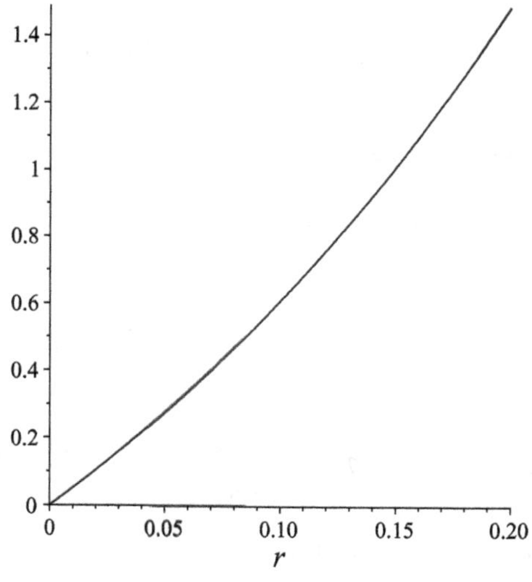

Assuming a market with a flat-term structure where the annual simple rate of 2%, the discount factor function for t years is given by:

```
> d:=t->(1+0.02)^(-t);
```

$$d := t \mapsto 1.02^{-t} \tag{15}$$

```
> d(1);
```

$$0.9803921569 \tag{16}$$

```
> d(2);
```

$$0.9611687812 \tag{17}$$

```
> d(3);
```

$$0.9423223345 \tag{18}$$

```
> plot(d(t),t=0..50);
```

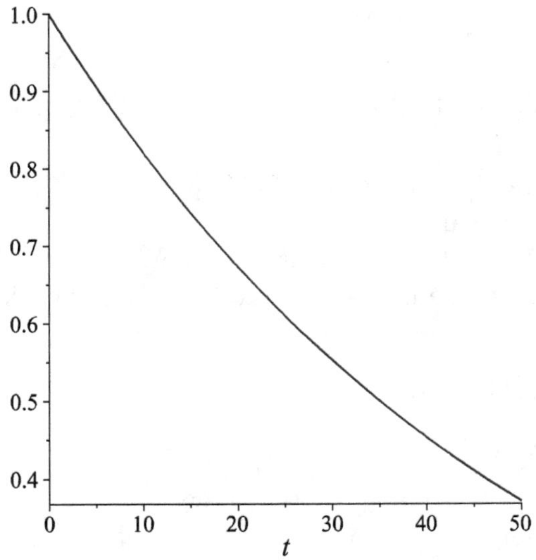

A function of two variables can also be defined. For example, the function that calculates the discount factor function for t years in a market with a flat annual simple rate of r, is defined as follows:

```
> drt:=(t,r)->(1+r)^t;
```

$$drt := (t, r) \mapsto (1 + r)^t. \tag{19}$$

The discount factor for 5 years with a flat rate of 2% is thus

```
> drt(5,0.02);
```

$$1.104080803. \tag{20}$$

Revisiting an Arbitrage Example

Assume that d(1) $= \frac{98}{100}$ but d(2) $= \frac{99}{100}$. This means that the simple rate for one year is

```
> solve((1+r)^(-1)=98/100);
```

$$\frac{1}{49} \tag{21}$$

and the simple rate for 2 years is

```
> solve((1+r)^(-1)=99/100);
```

$$\frac{1}{99}. \tag{22}$$

Thus, investing for a year is more profitable than investing for 2 years...

This implies that borrowing for 2 years is a "good deal" while investing for one year is not.

How can we capitalize on this situation?

Let us borrow an amount that requires paying back \$1 in 2 years, that is

```
> solve(1=x*(1+1/99));
```

$$\frac{99}{100} \tag{23}$$

investing the borrowed amount for a year will generate

```
> 99/100*(1+1/49);
```

$$\frac{99}{98}. \tag{24}$$

Thus, after a year, we can pay back the loan that is due only in a year. This is because $\frac{99}{98} > \frac{99}{100}$

```
> 99/98-99/100;
```

$$\frac{99}{4900}. \tag{25}$$

Note that when we took the 2-year loan we did not know what the one year rate in a year would be. However, this rate must be a positive number. Hence, investing the amount received after the one year, $\frac{99}{98}$, for a year will generate even a larger than $\frac{99}{98}$ at the end of year 2. Thus, we can repay the loan in 2 years, and we will pocket the difference which will be at least $\frac{99}{4900}$.

```
> evalf(99/4900);
```

$$0.02020408163. \tag{26}$$

If instead of borrowing for 2 years

$$\frac{99}{100} \text{ we will borrow } \frac{1000000 \cdot 99}{100}$$

```
> 1000000*99/100;
```

$$990000 \tag{27}$$

we will pocket at least

```
> 990000*99/4900.0;
```

$$20002.04082. \tag{28}$$

Chapter 2

A Basic Model of Bond Markets

Introduction

In the Chapter 1, we revisited the concept of time value of money and its relation to opportunity cost, but over a one period model. We did touch upon multi-period models but only under the assumption that the interest rate from period to period is the same: a phenomena referred to as a flat-term structure of interest rate.

In this chapter, we expand our model to a more realistic situation of a multi-period time and relax our assumption about a flat-term structure. Rather, here we will look into the prices of bonds in the market and infer the term structure of interest rates from these prices. As before, our guideline for the inferences is the satisfaction of the no arbitrage condition. However, in this multi-period model, the formulation of the no arbitrage condition and the consequences of its satisfaction are somewhat different and more structured than our presentation of the one period model. We start with some basic notation and definitions so that we can be in a position to formulate the no arbitrage (**NA**) condition.

Setting the Framework

The *debt market*, as its name implies, is a market in which debts are bought and sold. This market is also referred to as the *bond market.* A bond is a security issued by a particular entity which promises to pay the holder of the bond a fixed amount of money at fixed times in the future, $t_1, t_2, \ldots, t_k$. At each of the payment times except the last one, t_k, the bond pays the same amount of money which we will denote by c. On the last payment date, referred to as the *maturity* of the bond, the bond pays an amount equal to $c + F$. The amount F is referred to as the *principal* or the *face value* of the bond and the payments of the amount c are called *coupon payments.*

The value of c is a certain percentage of the face value F and is called the *coupon rate*. The coupon rate is specified when the bond is issued and remains fixed for the life of the bond. Thus, for example, a bond may pay \$5 every year for the next 3 years and at the end of the 3 years pay \$(100+5). Such a bond has a maturity of 3 years and a face value of \$100 and the annual coupon payments are \$5 each. One immediately recognizes that the cash flow from a bond is like a repayment of a loan that was taken for 3 years at an interest rate of 5%, paid annually. Indeed, buying a bond is giving a loan to the issuer. Such a bond, as in our example, is called a 5% bond since it is like a loan taken at 5%. In most countries though, the payments from a bond are made semiannually: a 5% bond will pay 2.5% of the face value every 6 months.

The coupon rate at which the bond is issued depends, of course, on the interest rate that prevails at the time of issue in the market. In order to induce investors to buy the bond (lend their money), the bond must offer a competitive interest rate. Similarly, after the bond has been issued, it can also be bought and sold in the market (called the *secondary market*). The price in the secondary market will reflect current market conditions with respect to the interest rate prevailing at that time.

Consider the bond in our example that was issued with a coupon rate of 5%. An investor holding the bond for the first 6 months and then selling it in the secondary market, may get more or less than \$100 when it is sold. Buying a bond 6 months after the bond was issued is like giving a loan of \$100 to the issuer for 2.5 years. If at that time the interest rate prevailing in the market for loans over 2.5 years is, for example, 4%, the bond will not be sold for \$100. If the bond did sell for \$100, it would constitute lending at an interest rate higher than the one prevailing in the market. The holder of this bond would not like to pass such a good deal to others. Furthermore, the owner realizes that the bond will attract buyers if it will offer a rate competitive with the current market rate. Hence, the bond will be sold at a price, say P, such that

```
> P=5*(1+0.04)^(-0.5)+5*(1+0.04)^(-1.5)+105
  *(1+0.04)^(-2.5);
```

$$P = 104.8104389. \tag{1}$$

In such an environment, the bond will sell for more than its face value. Such a bond is called a *premium bond.*

Suppose instead that interest rates rise to 8%. The competitive forces in the market will alter the price of the bond in such a way that

```
> P=5*(1+0.08)^(-0.5)+5*(1+0.08)^(-1.5)+105
  *(1+0.08)^(-2.5);
```

$$P = 95.88845520. \tag{2}$$

Thus, the bond will be sold at less than its face value. Such a bond is called a *discount bond.* We thus see that there is an *inverse relationship between the price of a bond and the level of interest rates.* Therefore, implicit in the prices of bonds in the market, is some information about the interest rates in the market. This information can be uncovered using a technique that we will soon introduce.

Moreover, recovering information about interest rates implicit in bond prices is intimately related to the NA condition. This is a condition with which we have already familiarized ourselves in the simplistic model in Chapter 1.

The fuzzy term we just used, "competitive forces in the market", will soon be seen to be the force of investors seeking arbitrage opportunities. Consequently, these investors affect the market so that prevailing prices eliminate such opportunities. Stating it differently, prices in the market satisfy the NA condition. Furthermore, an extension of the way the condition was formulated in Chapter 1 will make it adaptable to a realistic model of the bond market. As well, the discount factors of Chapter 1 will be replaced with a function or the term structure of interest rates in the market.

We limit our focus, almost throughout this course, to national government bonds. These securities are regarded as risk-free securities, since governments do not usually default on their obligations. Bonds, as we see, represent fixed payment amounts which are paid at fixed, deterministic times. For this reason, bonds are also referred to as *fixed income securities*. Thus, if an investor holds a bond to its maturity, the amount of the payments and their timing are certain, provided that the issuer does not default on some payments. Hence, national government bonds are considered non-risky securities.

A bond which is issued by a less creditworthy issuer must offer a higher interest rate, in comparison to a government bond, in order to compensate the investor for taking the risk of the issuer defaulting on the bond. The lower the creditworthiness of the issuer, the higher the interest rate the bond must offer. Indeed, we observe this in the market for corporate bonds (issued by corporations) which offer higher interest rates than government-issued bonds. Agencies exist in the market which engage in rating the creditworthiness of different issuers. The lower the rating, the higher the interest rate they must offer on their bonds. There are other factors that may affect the interest rate at which the bond is issued.

Certain bonds have features that affect the interest rate. For example, some bonds called *callable bonds*, allow the issuer to call the bond back prior to its maturity. The issuer can pay the holder the principal plus a certain amount and buy back the bond at certain times subject to certain conditions. If interest rates decrease, it might be advantageous to the issuer to "call" the bond. If it is advantageous to the issuer, it is disadvantageous to the holder of the bond. The investor holding such a bond would require compensation for this callable feature. The compensation is in terms of a higher interest rate offered on the bond. Bonds with no extra features are sometimes referred to as *straight bonds*.

Studying the interest rate structure is conducted in the market for national government bonds and includes only straight bonds. In this market, the interest rate implicit in the prices of these bonds does not include compensation for risk. It reflects only the economic competitive conditions in the market. For this reason, we limit our attention to the government bond market and to straight bonds. As we proceed, we will discover that there are a few rates in the market and that what we referred to as the "interest rate" in the market is a more complicated structure of interest rates.

Arbitrage in Bond Markets: Introduction

Let us consider a simple case of two bonds both of which mature in a year and pay annual coupons. The bonds were issued in the past, not at the same time but a year a part, with face values of \$100. One bond is a 5% bond with a current price of P1 = \$98 and the other a 6% bond with a current price of P2 = \$100. Let d_1 be the one-year discount factor. Thus, common sense implies that

$$P_1 = 105 \cdot d_1$$
$$P_2 = 106 \cdot d_1$$

and hence that

$$\frac{98}{100} = \frac{P_1}{P_2} = \frac{105}{106}.$$

The two ratios $\frac{98}{100}$ and $\frac{105}{106}$, however, are not equal.

```
> 98/100.0;
```

$$0.9800000000 \tag{3}$$

```
> 105/106.0;
```

$$0.9905660377. \tag{4}$$

The reason for this inconsistency is our implicit assumption that d_1 in $\mathrm{P1} = 105d_1$ has the same value as d_1 in $\mathrm{P2} = 106d_1$. This assumption, however, is very reasonable. Both bonds are government bonds and thus in the same risk category and both pay out in a year. Therefore, the time value of money implicit in each bond must be the same. Hence, solving for d_1 from $98 = 105d_1$ or from $100 = 106d_1$ should result in the same value. If it does not, it means that the interest rate offered by bond 1 is not equal to the one offered by bond 2. Bond 1 offers an interest rate of

```
> 105.0/98.0-1;
```

$$0.071428571 \tag{5}$$

```
> 105/98-1;
```

$$\frac{1}{14} \tag{6}$$

and bond 2 offers an interest rate of

```
> 106.0/100.0-1;
```

$$0.060000000 \tag{7}$$

```
> 106/100-1;
```

$$\frac{3}{50}. \tag{8}$$

Such a situation where there are two different risk-free rates over the same time period cannot exist in the market. This claim can be explained by employing *equilibrium arguments* or *arbitrage arguments.*

The equilibrium argument goes as follows: if the two bonds coexist in the market and everyone can choose to invest in any of the bonds, who would choose to invest in the bond that offers 6% if it is possible to invest in the bond that offers approximately 7%? The answer is no one, and thus this bond will either disappear from the market as nobody will hold it, or the more likely reasonable case is that its price will decrease to the point that both bonds will offer the same interest rates. For example, if the price of bond 2 will decrease to be 98.93333337.

```
> 106/(1+1/14),106/(1+1/14.);
```

$$\frac{1484}{15}, 98.93333337. \tag{9}$$

Having two different interest-free rates in the market that are available to lend or borrow at, allows for opportunities to make money without dipping into one's pocket or taking any risk. Borrowing \$x at 6% will require a repayment of \$x × 1.06 in a year. This can be covered by investing

```
> x*1.06/1.071428571;
```

$$0.9893333337\,x \tag{10}$$

at 7.1428571% for a year which will produce the repayment but will leave a "change" of

```
> x- x*1.06/1.071428571;
```

$$0.0106666663\,x. \tag{11}$$

Thus if $x = 1{,}000{,}000$, the "change" is 10666.66630 of pure arbitrage. No risk was taken as the repayment was offset by the investment. All rates are fixed at the time the transaction is taken and cannot be changed. Furthermore, the transaction was financed not from one's own money, as a loan was taken to facilitate it. It was "self-financed".

Let us now review this *arbitrage argument* from a different angle using the concept of a *short position.* An investor who borrows a bond from a broker and sells it on the open market is said to have a short position in the bond. The investor must eventually return the borrowed bond by buying it back on the open market. Taking a short position in a bond generates positive proceeds. The short seller receives the price of the security being shorted at the time the transaction is initiated. In exchange, the short seller is committed to pay back the value of that security when the position is closed and to make the coupon payments until the position is closed. Consequently, the cash flow from a short position is the negative of that from a long position (buying a bond).

Thus, taking a short position in one unit of the 6% bond is like taking a loan of the price of the bond, \$100, at 6%. To obtain a loan of $\$x$, one will have to short $\frac{x}{100}$ units of the 6% bond. It follows that the arbitrage transaction described above for $x = 1{,}000{,}000$ can be equivalently obtained in the market by the following actions:

Short $\frac{1000000}{100} = 10000$ units of the 6% bond. This will generate proceeds of $\$10000 \cdot 100$. If the short position is kept until the bond matures, it will require a payment of $\$1000000 \cdot 1.06$. Use a portion of the proceeds to buy the 5% bond in order to cover, in a year, the payment of $\$10000 \cdot 106$. This will be generated by having a long position in $\frac{106 \cdot 10000}{105}$ units of the 5% bond, as each unit produces a payment of \$105. Buying $\frac{106 \cdot 10000}{105}$ units of the 5% bond costs

```
> (106*10000/105)*98;(106*10000/105)*98.0;
```

$$\frac{2968000}{3}$$

$$989333.3333 \tag{12}$$

that is approximately \$989,333.333, but the short position generated proceeds of 1,000,000. Hence, an arbitrage profit of

```
> 1000000-(106*10000/105)*98;1000000
  -(106*10000/105)*98.0;
```

$$\frac{32000}{3}$$

$$10666.6667 \tag{13}$$

was made at the purchasing time. In a year, the long position covers the payment needed due to the short positions. Again, no risk was taken and the transaction was financed by the short position, a *self-financed portfolio.*

In reality of course, things are not as simple. There are many bonds in the market with many different maturity times and to find an arbitrage portfolio, a systemic computerized method is required. This will be practiced using the Maple software. However, before this method will be explained, let us consider yet another example of a bond market with two bonds.

Consider a bond market with a zero-coupon bond that matures in a year and a 5% coupon bond that matures in two years. Coupons are paid yearly in this market and the face value of each bond is \$100. The price of the zero-coupon bond is \$90 and of the coupon bond is \$99.

Bond #	Price	Payment in a year	Payment in 2 years
1	90	100	0
2	100	5	105

An arbitrage portfolio must be self-financed and thus it must include at least one short position that generates proceeds at least as the cost of the long position. Furthermore, the cash flow from the total portfolio cannot be negative in any time period. Hence, the payment required due to the short position must be covered by the cash inflow due to the long position.

Shorting one unit of the coupon bond generates proceeds of \$100, which will allow buying $\frac{100}{90}$ units of the zero-coupon bond resulting in a net cash flow of zero. The short position requires a payment of \$5 in a year but the long position pays $\$\frac{100}{90} \cdot 100$ in a year. Hence, the net cash inflow in a year will be $\frac{100}{90} \cdot 100 - 5$

```
> (100/90)*100-5;(100/90)*100-5.;
```

$$\frac{955}{9}$$

$$106.1111111 \tag{14}$$

which is more than the \$105 that is needed to be paid due to the short position in 2 years. An arbitrage portfolio was identified, it requires no financing and no risk is taken, but a profit of **at least** 106.1111111 − 105 will be realized in 2 years. The profit is of **at least** 106.1111111 − 105, since the \$106.1111111 is obtained a year before it is needed, and thus can be invested for a year at the interest rate that will prevail in the market.

In a realistic market with many bonds and many time periods, many combinations of portfolio compositions must be considered before an arbitrage portfolio is identified, or alternately the conclusion of the inexistence of such a portfolio is reached. Hence, a systematic computerized method is needed. It is customary to use positive numbers for long positions and negative numbers for short positions. In this last example, the portfolio is therefore denoted by $(\frac{100}{90}, -1)$, i.e., $\frac{100}{90}$ units of long positions in the zero-coupon bond, bond number 1, and one short position of the coupon bond, bond number 2. The cash inflow at the purchasing time in terms of this notation is

$$\left(-\frac{100}{90}\right) \cdot 90 + (1) \cdot 100$$

i.e., the negative of the number of bonds times the price. While the cash inflow at any future time is the number of bonds times the cash flow from the bonds e.g., after a year the cash flow is

$$\left(\frac{100}{90}\right) 100 - 1 \cdot 5.$$

This last example illustrates the general methodology that will be outlined next. As well, it will be shown that when arbitrage opportunities exist there is an inconsistency in the discount factors. This inconsistency is similar to what was shown in the first example above, but adapted to a realistic bond market with many bonds that mature at different times.

Consider a slightly more realistic market with two bonds both issued now, maturing in 2 years and paying an annual coupon. Each has a face value of \$100. Bond $B1$ is a 5% bond with a price of \$95 and bond $B2$ is an 8% bond with a price of \$97. Clearly if the price of $B2$ is less than or equal to that of $B1$, an arbitrage opportunity exists.

Bond #	Price	Payment in a year	Payment in 2 years
1	95	5	105
2	97	8	108

We would like to determine if the prices above prevent arbitrage opportunities. Let us approach this question from a different angle as we did before, and first try to determine if the discount factors implicit in the price of each bond are consistent with each other. Unlike the first examples, here we are dealing with two periods. We have two discount factors d_1 and d_2 for a dollar obtained in one and two years from now respectively. Furthermore, in this example the discount factors are not as exposed as in the first examples, rather kind of in the shadow. Let us see how we can shed some light on these discount factors.

Bond 1 pays \$5 in a year hence the present value of it is $5 \cdot d_1$. It also pays \$105 in two years and its present value is $105 \cdot d_2$. Hence if the bond costs \$95 it means that the present value of the cash flow \$5 in a year and \$105 in two years, is 95. Therefore, while we cannot determine from this relation the discount factor uniquely, we can identify a relation that they must satisfy, that is:

$$5 \cdot d_1 + 105 \cdot d_2 = 95.$$

Similarly the price of bond 2 implies that

$$8 \cdot d_1 + 108 \cdot d_2 = 97.$$

It might be worth emphasizing here that the discount factors are associated with time and not with bonds. Hence, if bond 1 offers \$5 in a year and bond 2 \$8 in a year, the present value of the \$5 and the \$8 is obtained by applying the same discount factor to each. They are both obtained at the same future time from risk-free bonds.

Furthermore, discount factors are numbers between zero and one, as they encompass the time value of money. Thus the information about d_1 and d_2, which is implicit in the prices of the bonds, will be consistent only if the two equations above have a solution such that $0 < d_1 < 1$, $0 < d_2 < 1$ and also such that $d_1 > d_2$. However, solving these two equations with two unknowns, produces a unique and unacceptable solution, namely $d_1 = -\frac{1}{4}$ and $d_2 = \frac{11}{12}$. (The two equations with two unknowns can be solved using the self-explanatory structure as shown in the following.)

```
> solve({5*d1+105*d2=95,8*d1+108*d2=97});
```

$$\left\{d_1 = -\frac{1}{4}, d_2 = \frac{11}{12}\right\}. \tag{15}$$

Therefore, the above analysis suggests that arbitrage positions exist in this market.

With this in mind let us see if we can find an arbitrage portfolio composed of these two bonds. We start by searching for positions in which either the proceeds of the sale are positive, ensuring that the cash flow in the future is nonnegative, or the proceeds of the sale is zero, ensuring that the future cash flows are nonnegative and that at least in one of the future periods they are positive. The first position we investigate is a position where the proceeds from the sale are \$1, i.e.,

$$-95 * \mathrm{B1} - 97 * \mathrm{B2} = 1$$

and the future cash flows are nonnegative, thus

$$5 \times \text{B1} + 8 \times \text{B2} > = 0,$$

$$105 \times \text{B1} + 108 \times \text{B2} > = 0$$

where B_i is the position (the number of units) in bond i.

In order to find if such a position is feasible, the system of the two inequalities and one equation is solved as follows:

```
> solve({-95*B1-97*B2=1,5*B1+8*B2>=0,105*B1+108*B2>=0});
```

$$\left\{\text{B1} = -\frac{1}{95} - \frac{97\,\text{B2}}{95},\ 7/5 \leq \text{B2}\right\}. \tag{16}$$

We see that there are actually many portfolios that satisfy the above system. As long as $\text{B1} = -\frac{1}{95} - \frac{97\,\text{B2}}{95}$ and $\frac{7}{5} \leq \text{B2}$, the condition is satisfied. For simplicity B2 is set to 2 and thus the obtained portfolio is $\text{B1} = -\frac{1}{95} - \frac{97 \cdot 2}{95} = -\frac{39}{19}$ and $\text{B2} = 2$. This is confirmed as follows.

```
> -1/95-97*2/95;
```

$$-\frac{39}{19}. \tag{17}$$

Utilizing the command below, we determine the cash flow from a portfolio composed of a short position of $\frac{39}{19}$ units of bond 1 and a long position of 2 units of bond 2.

```
> subs(B1=-39/19,B2=2, [CashTime0=-95*B1-97*B2,
CashTime1=5*B1+8*B2,CashTime2=105*B1+108*B2]);
```

$$\left[\text{CashTime0} = 1, \text{CashTime1} = \frac{109}{19}, \text{CashTime2} = \frac{9}{19}\right]. \tag{18}$$

The portfolio produces income, as the proceeds of the sale, of \$1 and also pays $\$\frac{109}{19}$ in the first period and $\$\frac{9}{19}$ in the second period. No liability and no risk is assumed. Note that if an arbitrage portfolio is found, then the arbitrage profit has no limit. One can simply increase the scale of this portfolio by taking a long position of 200 units in bond 2 and $-\frac{3900}{19}$ short position in bond 1. This will produce 100 times the cash flow of the current portfolio (as calculated in the following).

```
> subs(B1=-3900/19,B2=200, [CashTime0=-95*B1-97*B2,
  CashTime1=5*B1+8*B2,CashTime2=105*B1+108*B2]);
```

$$\left[\text{CashTime0} = 100, \text{CashTime1} = \frac{10900}{19}, \text{CashTime2} = \frac{900}{19}\right]. \tag{19}$$

But why stop here? You can make even more money by further increasing the scale.

Markets which allow such arbitrage opportunities are not realistic. If such an opportunity existed, investors would realize this and go for it, affecting prices so that the opportunity would eventually disappear. Hence, our analysis throughout assumes no arbitrage opportunities. Furthermore, if such opportunities exist, the concept of the time value of money is meaningless. If an unlimited amount of money can be generated at zero investment and no risk, then money would be worthless and would consequently render the term 'discount factors' pointless. Our analysis so far exemplifies that, if arbitrage opportunities exist, no discount factors exist. It is also correct that if NA opportunities exist, discount factors exist.

When a bond is purchased between coupon payments, the next coupon is divided between the old owner and the new owner in a prorated fashion. Assume coupon payments are every 6 months and a bond was purchased 2 months before a coupon payment. Thus, the first coupon will be divided such that the old owner will receive $\frac{4}{6}$ of it and the new owner will receive $\frac{2}{6}$. Hence, the new owner, upon purchasing the bond, pays $\frac{4}{6}$ of a coupon to the old owner.

Quoted bond prices (in North America) do not include the payment of the fraction of the first coupon to be paid to the old owner. That is, the quoted price of a coupon bond does not include accrued interest, but only the present value of the future cash flow. A bond price that does not include accrued interest is referred to as a *clean price*, while if the accrued interest is included, it is referred to as a *dirty price*. The latter, in the main, is quoted in European bond markets. Hence, Dirty Price = Clean Price + Accrued Interest.

A price of a bond that is quoted immediately after a coupon payment is clean and dirty, as there is no accrued interest to include. Clean prices change for economic reasons only, while dirty prices change due to the passage of time as well, because the prorated portion changes. Thus, when bond prices are quoted at a time that is not immediately after a coupon payment, clean prices should be used to infer the interest rates that are implicit in bond prices. Note that in the above discussions of arbitrage opportunities clean prices should be used.

Chapter 3

No Arbitrage Condition and the Term Structure, its Estimation and Smoothing

Introduction

In Chapter 2, we investigated the meaning of the discount factors, their relation to the no-arbitrage (NA) condition and valuing future cash flows utilizing the present value concept. Some financial instruments, that also fall into the class of derivative securities, are valued based on risk-free discount factors. The valuation concept of these instruments is induced by the NA condition. These securities are valued either by replication or by applying to their cash flow the discount factors.

The risk-free discount factors are implicit in bond prices, as we saw in Chapter 2. They are consequences of the NA condition. In this chapter, we introduce the reader to some estimation matters, terminology such as *yield*, *yield curve*, *spot curve* and *zero-coupon curve*, and their interrelations.

The Term Structure of Interest Rates and NA

The discount factors, d's, reflect the discounting due to time value of money. Thus, they have implicit in them the interest rate that prevails in the market. For example, if $d_1 = 0.9$ it means that in this market a dollar at time one is worth 0.9 of a dollar today. The difference in value between a dollar today and a dollar received in the future results from the opportunity cost of investing that dollar at the risk-free rate of interest. A dollar today can be invested in a risk-free asset from time zero to time one and will earn a rate of interest which we denote by r_1. Hence, a dollar today will be equal to $1 + r_1$ dollars at time one. Consequently, $\frac{1}{1+r_1}$, if invested at the risk-free rate from time zero to time one, will grow to be one dollar. It thus follows that

$$d_1 = \frac{1}{1+r_1} \tag{1}$$

and we can solve for r_1 in terms of d_1.

```
> solve(d1=1/(1+r1),r1);
```

$$-\frac{d_1 - 1}{d_1}. \tag{2}$$

The rate r_1 is called the *spot rate* spanning the time interval zero to one. It is the rate applied to loans which commence now (at time zero) and which mature at some time in the future, time one in this example. In the same manner, we can calculate the rate r_2, spanning the time interval zero to two, i.e.,

```
>  solve(d2=1/(1+r2),r2);
```

$$-\frac{d_2 - 1}{d_2}. \tag{3}$$

With complete precision of notation, the rates r_1 and r_2 should have a second index. After all, these rates are payable from time zero to times one and two, respectively. For simplicity, however, we omit the index reference to time zero, and thus instead of using r_{01}, we use r_1, with the understanding that if only one index is mentioned, it is the second one, and the first is (implicitly) zero. These rates, as mentioned, are applicable to a loan which commences now (on the spot) and lasts until some future time. Hence, they are termed *spot rates*.

Consider, for simplicity, a bond market with three bonds in which coupons are paid annually, the payment dates of the bonds coincide and the longest maturity is 3 years. The structure of the market is described in the following table/matrix, where time is measured in years, and the current time is a year before the first coupon payment.

Bond #	Price	Payment in year 1	Payment in years 2	Payment in years 3
1	96	105	0	0
2	97	8	108	0
3	89	3	3	103

Our dissection in Chapter 2 suggests that if there are NA opportunities, the system of equations in the following, must have a solution.

```
> solve({96=105*d1,97=8*d1+108*d2,89=3*d1+3*d2+103*d3,
  d1<1,d2<d1,d3<d2,d3>0});
```

$$\left\{d_1 = \frac{32}{35}, d_2 = \frac{3139}{3780}, d_3 = \frac{21109}{25956}\right\} \tag{4}$$

```
> solve({96.0=105*d1,97=8*d1+108*d2,89=3*d1+3*d2+103*d3,
  d1<1,d2<d1,d3<d2,d3>0});
```

$$\{d_1 = 0.9142857143, d_2 = 0.8304232804, d_3 = 0.8132609031\}. \tag{5}$$

In words, the system of equations suggests that the prices of the bonds are consistent with the existence of a set of discount factors in this market. Hence, there are NA opportunities in this market. The simple interest rates for times 1, 2, and 3 can be recovered from the discount factors, as follows.

```
> solve(1/(1+r1)=0.9142857143);
```

$$0.09374999998 \tag{6}$$

```
> solve(1/(1+r2)=.8304232804);
```

$$0.2042051609 \tag{7}$$

```
> solve(1/(1+r3)=.8132609031);
```

$$0.2296176986. \tag{8}$$

Let us see if when the price of the second bond is changed to 119, there are still discount factors that are consistent with the prices of the bonds. To this end, we set the system of equations again with the new price of the second bond and try to solve it.

```
> solve({96.0=105*d1,119=8*d1+108*d2,89=3*d1+3*d2+103*d3,
  d1<1,d2<d1,d3<d2,d3>0});
```

This time the system is inconsistent, which suggests that there are arbitrage opportunities in the market. Consider the portfolio composed of one short position in bond 2 and 3/83 of a long position in bond 3.

Bond #	Position in Bond #	Price	Payment in a year	Payment in 2 years	Payment in 3 years
1	0	$0*96$	$0*105$	0	0
2	-1	$-1*119$	$-1*8$	$-1*108$	0
3	3/83	$(3/83)*89$	$(3/83)*3$	$(3/83)*3$	$(3/83)*103$
Net Cash Flow		$\frac{9610}{83}$ ~115.783	$-\frac{655}{83}$ ~−7.891	$-\frac{8955}{83}$ −107.891	$\frac{309}{83}$ ~3.722

```
> 119-(3/83)* 89;
```

$$\frac{9610}{83} \tag{9}$$

```
> 119-(3/83)* 89.;
```

$$115.7831325 \tag{10}$$

```
> -8+(3/83)*3;
```

$$-\frac{655}{83} \tag{11}$$

```
> -8+(3/83)*3.0;
```

$$-7.891566265 \tag{12}$$

```
> -108+(3/83)*3;
```

$$-\frac{8955}{83} \tag{13}$$

```
> -108+(3/83)*3.0;
```

$$-107.8915663 \tag{14}$$

```
> (3/83)*103;
```

$$\frac{309}{83} \tag{15}$$

```
> (3/83)*103.;
```

$$3.722891566 \tag{16}$$

The proceeds of the transaction at the time it is originated $\left(\frac{9610}{83}\right)$ is exactly enough to cover the liability in year one $\left(-\frac{655}{83}\right)$ and year two $\left(-\frac{8955}{83}\right)$:

```
> 9610/83-655/83-8955/83;
```

$$0. \tag{17}$$

The amount received in year three $\left(\frac{309}{83}\right)$ is pure arbitrage: no out of pocket money was used, no risk was assumed, and yet money was made.

Finding an arbitrage position in a realistic market requires a systematic way (an algorithm) and is beyond the scope of this course. However, an access to an application (routine) that can find arbitrage positions in some complicated cases, is provided. The procedure **NarbitB** determines if the NA condition in a market is satisfied. The input to the procedure is the prices of the bonds and their payoff. The presumption of this procedure is that the time intervals are equal. That is, the time interval between the current time (on which the price of the bonds are given) and the first coupon payment is equal to the time between the first and second coupon payment, etc. The prices of the bonds are represented by an array with its elements being the prices of the bonds. Hence, if there are two outstanding bonds the price of the first being 95 and the second being 95, this will be entered as [95, 95]. The cash flow from each bond is entered in the same manner. If the first bond's cash flow is \$110 followed by \$0, it will be entered as [110, 0] and if the second bond's cash flow is \$0 followed by \$110, it will be entered as [0, 110]. The above example can represent a case where the first bond matures in a year, the second bond in two years and the prices are observed a year before the first bond matures. Both the second bond and the first bond are zero-coupon bonds. The cash flow from the bonds will be entered as the first parameter to the procedure in the form [[110, 0], [0, 110]] and the understanding is that the first price is the price of the first bond and the second is the price of the second bond. To find if the NA is satisfied in this market, you run:

```
> NarbitB([[110,0],[0,110]],[95,95]);
```

The no-arbitrage condition is not satisfied

An arbitrage portfolio is :

$$\textit{Buy}, \frac{1}{110}, \textit{of Bond}, 1$$

$$\textit{Short}, \frac{1}{110}, \textit{of Bond}, 2$$

The cost of this portfolio is zero

This portfolio produces income of, 1, *at time*, 1

This portfolio produces income of, −1, *at time*, 2

The procedure identifies an arbitrage portfolio if it exists, and reports its composition. If an arbitrage portfolio does not exist the procedure states this, and produces further output that will be discussed shortly. The reader may already anticipate the meaning of this output given the discussions above. Note that the arbitrage amount is not known at the time the positions are taken. The arbitrage is actually generated from investing the \$1 cash inflow obtained at time 1 (a year after the initiation of the portfolio) for a year and then using it to pay the cash outflow of \$1 at time 2 (a year after the \$1 was invested). At time 2, the \$1 invested at time 1 for a year will grow to $1+r$, but the r is not known at time zero. Hence, the arbitrage amount is the r obtained at time 2, but the value of r, the one-year spot rate as of time 1, will be known only at time 1.

If a set of discount factors consistent with the price of the bonds exists, and there are NA opportunities, this routine solves for the discount factors. Here is how it is applied to the first case.

```
> NarbitB([[105,0,0],[8,108,0],[3,3,103]],[96,97,89]);
```

The no-arbitrage condition is satisfied.

The discount factor for time, 1, *is given by,* $\frac{32}{35}$

The interest rate spanning the time interval, $[0, 1]$,
is given by, 0.09375

The discount factor for time, 2, *is given by,* $\frac{3139}{3780}$

The interest rate spanning the time interval, $[0, 2]$,
is given by, 0.2042

The discount factor for time, 3, *is given by,* $\frac{21109}{25956}$

The interest rate spanning the time interval, $[0, 3]$,
is given by, 0.2296

The function Vdis([c1,c2,..]), values the cashflow [c1,c2,..]

The rate r_1, for example, applicable to money invested for one year, can be found by solving $\text{Vdis}([1+r_1, 0, 0]) = 1$. The reader may wish to try and solve for some of the r's and compare them to the values reported by **NarbitB**.

```
> solve(Vdis([1+r1, 0, 0]) = 1.0);
```

$$0.09375000000. \tag{18}$$

It is customary to report interest rates for different terms in such a way that they can be compared. Obviously, r_2 is a larger number than r_1, since the former represents the rate earned over the longer period of time $[0, 2]$ for which the first period $[0, 1]$ is a subperiod. If this were not the case, arbitrage opportunities would exist as stipulated in the former lecture.

In order to report the rates in a comparable manner, the rates are reported (usually) on a per annum basis. It is therefore natural to measure the time in units of a year. The spot rate for time n (n years from now) is reported as the annual rate which, if compounded semi-annually, will produce the rate applicable to the period $[0, n]$. Hence, the spot rate applicable to time n is the solution r_n to Eq. (20),

$$d_n = \frac{1}{\left(1+\frac{r_n}{2}\right)^{(2n)}}. \tag{19}$$

The use of the annual rate (and semiannual compounding) gives rise to the term $\frac{r_n}{2}$, and since time is measured in units of a year, the relevant exponent is $2n$. This is where special care should be given to the assumption regarding the length of time intervals $[0, 1]$, $[1, 2]$, and $[2, 3]$ that are used in the input to **NarbitB**.[1] Thus, for example, the spot rate for time one (a year in our example), r_1, is given by the solution to $d_1 = \frac{1}{(1+\frac{r_1}{2})^2}$.

```
> solve({d1=1/(1+r1/2)^2},{r1});
```

$$\tag{20}$$

$$\left\{r_1 = -\frac{2(\sqrt{d_1}-1)}{\sqrt{d_1}}\right\}, \quad \left\{r_1 = -\frac{2(\sqrt{d_1}+1)}{\sqrt{d_1}}\right\}. \tag{21}$$

---

[1]The procedure **NarbitB** assumes that time 1 is the time of the first payment and that the payments are equally spaced between time 0 and the largest maturity. Thus, time 2 is the time of the second payment, and time k is the time of the kth payment. Consequently, the output of **NarbitB**, when reporting a rate spanning the time interval $[0, k]$, pertains to the time interval from the current time to that time of the kth payment, and the reported rate is the simple rate spanning the time interval. It is therefore important to notice the time period entered into **NarbitB** and the way in which the spot rates are reported. Similarly, when **NarbitB** defines a discount factor function for time t, it uses the same units as entered by the user.

If the length of the time intervals $[0, 1]$, $[1, 2]$, etc., used in **NarbitB** is half a year, the spot rate, rs_n, applicable to the time interval $[0, n]$, i.e., n half years, will be reported by **NarbitB** as a simple rate. Thus, when the rate is reported as an annual rate semiannually compounded, the spot rate for n half years, will be the solution $r_{\frac{n}{2}}$ (i.e., $\frac{n}{2}$ years) to the equation

$$1 + rs_n = \left(1 + \frac{\left(r_{\frac{n}{2}}\right)}{2}\right)^n \quad \text{or} \quad r_{\frac{n}{2}} = 2\left(\frac{\ln(1+rs_n)}{n} - 1\right).$$

As we see, there are two solutions to this equation and we choose the positive one, $\frac{2\sqrt{d_1}}{d_1} - 2$. In our example the value of the spot rate is obtained by substituting $d_1 = \frac{1}{1+0.09375}$ in the chosen solution.

```
> subs(d1=1/(1 + 0.09375),-2+2/sqrt(d1));
```

$$0.091650066 \tag{22}$$

In the same manner, r_2 will be given by

```
> solve(d2=1/(1+r2/2)^4,r2);
```

$$\frac{2}{d_2{}^{1/4}} - 2,\ \frac{2I}{d_2{}^{1/4}} - 2,\ -\frac{2}{d_2{}^{1/4}} - 2,\ -\frac{2I}{d_2{}^{1/4}} - 2. \tag{23}$$

We choose again the positive real solution $2d_2^{\left(-\frac{1}{4}\right)} - 2$ and substitute $d_2 = \frac{1}{1+0.2042}$ in it to get the value of r_2 in our example.

```
> subs(d2=1/(1 + 0.2042),-2+2*d2^(-1/4));
```

$$0.095099492. \tag{24}$$

The discount factor for time t is the present value (price) of one dollar obtainable at time t. Hence, the discount factor for time three, for example, will be given by

```
> evalf(Vdis([0,0,1]));1/(1 + 0.2042);
```

$$0.8132609031. \tag{25}$$

We can therefore solve numerically for r_3 by combining the **solve** (or **fsolve** command with the feasible range for r_3) with the value of d_3 given in terms of **Vdis** as follows.

```
> fsolve((Vdis([0,0,1]))=1/(1+r3/2)^(6),r3=0..1);
```

$$0.07010169009 \tag{26}$$

```
> solve({evalf(Vdis([0,0,1]))=1/(1+r3/2)^(6),
r3>=0,r3<=1});
```

$$\{r_3 = 0.07010169007\}. \tag{27}$$

Continuing in this manner, we obtain a schedule, a structure of spot rates for each payment date in the future. This structure is referred to as the *term structure of interest rates* or, in short, the *term structure*. In general, the spot rate r_n spanning the time interval $[0, n]$ based on compounding m times per unit of time, will be the solution to

$$d_n = \frac{1}{\left(1 + \frac{r_n}{m}\right)^{(nm)}}.$$

Thus, if the unit of time is half a year and the rates are reported per annum based on semiannual compounding, a dollar invested from time zero to time three is invested for 1.5 years and will grow to $\left(1 + \frac{r_3}{2}\right)^{2 \cdot 1.5} = \left(1 + \frac{r_3}{2}\right)^3$.

Zero-Coupon, Spot and Yield Curves

The term structure, zero-coupon and spot curves

The term structure is actually a function, which we will denote by $r(t)$, that relates time to the interest rate prevailing in the market. For each t, $r(t)$ is the interest rate per period (a year) paid for a dollar invested for t years, from time zero to time t. **We keep our units of time measured in years and report the interest rate based on semiannual compounding**. Hence, $r(t)$ is the rate such that a dollar invested from time zero to time t will grow to be

$$\left(1 + \frac{r(t)}{2}\right)^{(2t)}$$

at time t. This function is referred to as the *term structure of interest rates*, and for each t the rate $r(t)$ is called a *spot rate*.

These are the rates paid on an investment over a period that starts now (on the spot) and ends at some future time t. The graph of this function is sometimes referred to as the *spot curve* or the *zero-coupon curve*. In what follows, we justify this name followed by a graphical representation of the term structure which will be explored shortly.

Certain bonds pay only one payment at the maturity time of the bond. These bonds are referred to as *zero-coupon bonds*, since they make no coupon payments. Furthermore, zero-coupon bonds are sold at a discount. The interest rate offered by such bonds is implicit in the difference between the face value of the bond and its market price. Namely, if the price of a zero-coupon bond maturing at time t, t years from now, is P and its face value is \$100, the interest it pays is the solution r to the equation

$$P = 100\left(1 + \frac{r}{2}\right)^{(-2t)}. \tag{28}$$

Hence, r will be given by

```
> solve({P=100*(1+r/2)^(-2*t)},{r});
```

$$\left\{ r = 2\,\mathrm{e}^{-\frac{1}{2}\frac{\ln\left(\frac{1}{100}P\right)}{t}} - 2 \right\} \tag{29}$$

where we assume again that t is measured in years and compounding is done semiannually.

The zero-coupon bonds are bonds which repay the principal at some time t and pay nothing at any other time. The zero-coupon bonds, therefore, are the elementary building blocks of coupon bonds as the latter can be interpreted as a portfolio of zero-coupon bonds.

Consider a bond that pays a coupon of $\frac{c}{2}$ at times $t_1, t_2, \ldots, t_{n-1}$ and matures at time t_n where it pays $100 + \frac{c}{2}$. This bond may be replicated by a portfolio of zero-coupon bonds, each with a face value of \$1. A portfolio composed of $\frac{c}{2}$ units of zero-coupon bonds maturing at times $t_1, t_2, \ldots, t_{n-1}$, and $100 + \frac{c}{2}$ of a zero-coupon bond which matures at time t_n, has the same cash flow as the coupon-paying bond. Zero-coupon bonds each with a face value of \$1 is equivalent to $\frac{1}{100}$ of a zero coupon bond with a face value of \$100. Hence, the above argument can be done utilizing zero coupon bonds with \$100 of face value.

If the principle (face value) of a zero-coupon bond maturing at time t is \$1, the price of the bond is the discount factor for time t. Hence, the spot rates extracted from coupon-paying bonds or those extracted from zero-coupon bonds which are the building blocks of the coupon bonds, will be the same. Thus, the term structure of interest rates is sometimes referred to as the *zero-coupon curve*.

Let us consider an example in order to demonstrate this idea. We will start with a market of coupon bonds and estimate the discount factors. Then we will replace the bonds in this market by zero-coupon bonds with face values of \$1. The prices we will assign to these zero-coupon bonds will be the discount factors obtained in the first market. We then re-estimate the discount factors. Of course, the discount factors in these two markets should be the same.

Consider the market specified in **NarbitB**, where executing **NarbitB** confirms that the no-arbitrage condition is satisfied, and the discount factors and the function **Vdis** are solved for.

```
> NarbitB([[105,0,0],[5,105,0],[4,4,104]],[94,97,89]);
```

The no-arbitrage condition is satisfied.

The discount factor for time, 1, *is given by,* $\dfrac{94}{105}$

The interest rate spanning the time interval, $[0, 1]$,

is given by, 0.1170

The discount factor for time, 2, *is given by,* $\dfrac{1943}{2205}$

The interest rate spanning the time interval, $[0, 2]$,

is given by, 0.1348

The discount factor for time, 3, *is given by,* $\dfrac{180577}{229320}$

The interest rate spanning the time interval, $[0, 3]$,

is given by, 0.2699

The function Vdis([c1,c2,..]), values the cashflow [c1,c2,..]

The discount factors are specified above, but of course, the discount factor for time one will be the value of a zero-coupon bond maturing at time one and paying \$1. Hence the discount factors for times one, two, and three are given by

$$Vdis([1, 0, 0]),\ Vdis([0, 1, 0]) \text{ and } Vdis([0, 0, 1]), \text{ respectively.}$$

```
> Vdis([1,0,0]),Vdis([0,1,0]),Vdis([0,0,1]);
```

$$\frac{94}{105}, \frac{1943}{2205}, \frac{180577}{229320}. \tag{30}$$

Let us now re-run **NarbitB** on a market composed of only these three zero-coupon bonds. The prices are specified above and applied to the corresponding zero-coupon bond.

```
> NarbitB([[1,0,0],[0,1,0],[0,0,1]],[94/105, 1943/2205,
  180577/229320]);
```

The no-arbitrage condition is satisfied.

The discount factor for time, 1, *is given by,* $\frac{94}{105}$

The interest rate spanning the time interval, $[0, 1]$, *is given by,* 0.1170

The discount factor for time, 2, *is given by,* $\frac{1943}{2205}$

The interest rate spanning the time interval, $[0, 2]$, *is given by,* 0.1348

The discount factor for time, 3, *is given by,* $\frac{180577}{229320}$

The interest rate spanning the time interval, $[0, 3]$, *is given by,* 0.2699

The function Vdis([c1,c2,..]), values the cashflow [c1,c2,..]

We indeed confirm that the resultant market and discount factors are the same as those in the first market. This should come as no surprise to the reader. The bond market specified by the coupon bonds and the one specified by the zero coupon bonds are in fact the same markets. Two markets are the same if every (risk free) cash flow in these two markets has exactly the same price. That this is the case in our two markets, is evidenced from the fact that the discount factors in these two markets are the same. The price of every (risk free) cash flow in each of these markets, c_1, c_2 and c_3 is the value of the linear function

$$f(c_1, c_2, c_3) = d_1 \cdot c_1 + d_2 \cdot c_2 + d_3 \cdot c_3.$$

Consequently these two markets are equivalent. Hence, the zero-coupon curve, or the discount factor function, is like the DNA of the market.

***Another way of viewing equivalent markets.**
There is another way of viewing equivalent markets. The initial securities defining a market are called primary securities. Consider the market where the primary securities are the coupon bonds. If a primary security is removed from the market (the market is assumed to be complete and not including redundant bonds) and another security (replicated by the primary securities) is added in its place, an equivalent market is obtained. Let us demonstrate this as follows.

The following structure calculates a portfolio of the three primary bonds that replicate the cash flow 0, 1, 0. It also calculates the price of this portfolio.

```
> solve({105*B1+5*B2+4*B3=0,0*B1+105*B2+4*B3=1,0*B1+0*
  B2+104*B3=0,Price=B1*94+B2*97+B3*89});
```

$$\left\{B1 = -\frac{1}{2205}, B2 = \frac{1}{105}, B3 = 0, Price = \frac{1943}{2205}\right\}. \quad (31)$$

Notice that the cash flow 0,1,0 can be generated by a combination of bond 1 and bond 2, specifically a short position in bond 1 and a long position in bond 2. Not surprisingly the price of this portfolio is exactly the value of the second discount factor. If we now replace one of the primary bonds, bond 1 or bond 2, with this new portfolio we will again obtain an equivalent market to our original market. This is demonstrated as follows by solving, utilizing **NarbitB**, for the discount factors in this market and noticing that they are the same as the original discount factors.

```
> NarbitB([[0,1,0],[5,105,0],[4,4,104]],
  [1943/2205,97,89]);
```

The no-arbitrage condition is satisfied.

The discount factor for time, 1, *is given by,* $\frac{94}{105}$

The interest rate spanning the time interval, $[0, 1]$, *is given by,* 0.1170

The discount factor for time, 2, *is given by,* $\frac{1943}{2205}$

The interest rate spanning the time interval, $[0, 2]$, *is given by,* 0.1348

The discount factor for time, 3, *is given by,* $\frac{180577}{229320}$

The interest rate spanning the time interval, $[0, 3]$, *is given by,* 0.2699

The function Vdis([c1,c2,..]), values the cashflow [c1,c2,..]

Yield and spot curves

The financial press reports a measure of a bond's return, which is called a yield. The yield of a bond maturing in n years that pays coupons semiannually, is defined as the rate y that solves the equation

$$\sum_{i=1}^{2n} \left(\frac{c}{2}\right)\left(1+\frac{y}{2}\right)^{(-i)} + FC\left(1+\frac{y}{2}\right)^{(-2n)} = P, \tag{32}$$

where c is the coupon of the bond, FC is its face value, and P is its price. Therefore, the yield of a bond is a rate such that if payments from the bond obtained in i years are discounted to its present value by $\frac{1}{\left(1+\frac{y}{2}\right)^{(2i)}}$, the price of the bond equals its present value. Readers who are already familiar with the concept of *internal rate of return* will immediately recognize that the yield is the same. From Eq. (37), it follows that the yield of a zero-coupon bond, maturing at time t and having a face value of \$1, is the spot rate for time t. Hence, if the market is populated with such zero-coupon bonds only, the concept of a yield would be equivalent to that of a spot rate. Let us calculate the yield for some zero-coupon bonds using the examples above.

Consider the bond with the semiannual cash flow of $(0, 0, 1)$. Since, for this bond, $c = 0$ and $FC = 1$, Eq. (38) reduces to Eq. (37). Hence, we can solve for the yield of this bond by solving the equation:

$$\text{Vdis}([0,0,1]) = \frac{1}{\left(1+\frac{y}{2}\right)^3}.$$

There might be multiple solutions to this equation, and not all solutions must be positive numbers or even real numbers. Let us solve for y numerically (note we use 'fsolve' instead of 'solve')

```
> fsolve(Vdis([0,0,1])=(1+y/2)^(-3));
```

$$0.1658240012. \tag{33}$$

To compare and to confirm that this is the same result as that obtained from **NarbitB**, we can calculate the interest rate which spans the time interval $[0, 1.5]$. This is done as follows.

```
> (1+%/2)^3-1;(1/Vdis([0,0,1.0]))-1;
```

$$0.269929173$$

$$0.269929172. \tag{34}$$

We confirm that the results are those reported by **NarbitB**, albeit 1.5 years is three units of half a year and thus reported as time three in **NarbitB**. The yield of a zero-coupon bond coincides with the spot rate for the length of time corresponding to the maturity of the bond.

A different result is obtained for the case of yields of coupon-paying bonds. We examine now the yield of the bond maturing in a year with a cash flow of $(5, 105, 0)$ and a current price of \$97. To solve for the yield of this bond, Eq. (38) is solved, using values of $\frac{c}{2} = 5$ and $FC = 100$, i.e.,

$$\frac{5}{1+\frac{y}{2}} + \frac{105}{\left(1+\frac{y}{2}\right)^2} = 97$$

```
> fsolve(5/(1+y/2)+105/(1+y/2)^2=97);
```

$$0.1330251780. \tag{35}$$

This time if we solve for the one year spot interest rate, based on this yield, we obtain

```
> (1+%/2)^2-1;(1/Vdis([0,1.0,0]))-1;
```

$$0.137449102$$
$$0.134843026 \tag{36}$$

while, on the other hand, the result from **NarbitB** $((1/\text{Vdis}([0, 1.0, 0])) - 1)$ is 0.1348. This is not due to a roundoff error.

This example serves to demonstrate a few key points. The yields of two bonds which mature at the same time may be different even though their maturity dates coincide. It also highlights that the yield measure suffers from some deficiencies. The price of a bond is the discounted value of its future cash flow. This is a consequence of the NA condition. Hence, the contribution of each future payment to the price of the bond is the present value of that payment.

The price of a sure dollar to be obtained in a future time period is independent of the bond from which it is to be obtained. The bonds, as explained above, can all be constructed from the same basic building blocks: one dollar obtained at time i. These building blocks must therefore also have the same value in the current time period, regardless of the bonds they are used in. The yield concept, however, is a result of using different discount factors for payments obtained from different bonds at the same time.

As was demonstrated by the example, a dollar obtained from the coupon bond with a maturity of one-year (obtaining in one year) was discounted using the yield of the bond, which was different from the one year spot rate. There is no economic rationale for using different discount factors for a dollar which has the same risk characteristics just because it is obtained from a different financial instrument, i.e., a zero-coupon versus a coupon-paying bond. Hence, the calculation of present values using yields (unless it is a zero-coupon bond) is an incorrect procedure.

One should think about the yield to maturity of a bond as some sort of "average" or mixture of returns on the bond. We know that instead of $\frac{1}{(1+\frac{y}{2})^{(2i)}}$ in Eq. (38) we should have used $\frac{1}{(1+\frac{r_i}{2})^{(2i)}}$, where r_i is the spot rate for i years. Solving for the yield as is done in Eq. (38), we are actually constraining the spot rate to be the same for all time periods (referred to as a *flat term structure* of interest rates). The y is really some sort of a "mixture" of the different spot rates r_i.

We demonstrate this below by solving for y, in terms of r_{05} and r_1. Given a bond which matures in one year, pays a coupon of $\frac{c}{2}$, and has a face value of FC, we display the first of the solutions produced (this is the meaning of the "[1]" below).

```
> assume (r05>0,r1>0,c>0,FC>0);
```

```
> simplify(solve((c/2)/(1+r05/2)+(FC+(c/2))/(1+r1/2)^2=
  (c/2)/(1+y/2)+(FC+(c/2))/(1+y/2)^2,y)[1]);
```

$$\begin{aligned}
&-\frac{1}{2}(-c{\sim}r05\,r1{\sim}^2 - 4\,c{\sim}r05\,r1 + 2\,c{\sim}r1^2 + 16\,FC{\sim}r05 \\
&\quad - ((2+r05)(c{\sim}^2r05\,r1{\sim}^2 + 16\,FC{\sim}cr1{\sim}^2 \\
&\quad + 4\,c{\sim}^2r05\,r1{\sim} + 10\,c{\sim}^2r1^2 + 64\,FC{\sim}^2r05 + 64\,FC{\sim}c{\sim}r05 \\
&\quad + 64\,FC{\sim}c{\sim}r1{\sim} + 20\,c{\sim}^2r05 + 40\,c{\sim}^2r1 + 128\,FC{\sim}^2 \\
&\quad + 192\,FC{\sim}c{\sim} + 72\,c{\sim}^2))^{1/2}r1{\sim} + 4\,c{\sim}r05 + 8\,c{\sim}r1{\sim} + 32\,FC{\sim} \\
&\quad - 2\,((2+r05)(c{\sim}^2r05\,r1{\sim}^2 + 16\,FC{\sim}c{\sim}r1{\sim}^2 \\
&\quad + 4\,c{\sim}^2r05\,r1{\sim} + 10\,c{\sim}^2r1{\sim}^2 + 64\,FC{\sim}^2r05 + 64\,FC{\sim}c{\sim}r05 \\
&\quad + 64\,FC{\sim}c{\sim}r1{\sim} + 20\,c{\sim}^2r05 + 40\,c{\sim}^2r1{\sim} + 128\,FC{\sim}^2 \\
&\quad + 192\,FC{\sim}c{\sim} + 72\,c{\sim}^2))^{1/2} + 24\,c{\sim})/(c{\sim}r1{\sim}^2 + 4\,FC{\sim}r05 \\
&\quad + 2\,c{\sim}r05 + 4\,c{\sim}r1{\sim} + 8\,FC{\sim} + 8\,c{\sim})
\end{aligned} \tag{37}$$

The next section elaborates on the term structure of interest rates and on its estimation.

Smoothing of the Term Structure

The term structure is a function $r(t)$ from the time domain to the interest rate domain i.e., the argument of the function is a time and the value of the function is the spot interest rate at that time. A realistic market requires the knowledge of the discount factors and of the spot rates, not only for times one, two, and three, as in our examples, but for every possible t in some interval $[0, T]$. Sometimes the value of $r(t)$ is required even for a time period which extends beyond the maximum maturity, time three in our example. The common practice in the marketplace is to use the knowledge of the spot rate of interest for the discrete points (1, 2, and 3 in our examples) and generate from these an estimation of a discount factor or a spot rate for each t in a certain time interval. This process is referred to as *smoothing*.

In the scope of this chapter, we will give only an overview of these techniques. Since spot rates are recovered from discount factors, and vice versa, the smoothing can be done in terms of either spot rates or discount factors. Our discussion of smoothing will be with respect to discount factors. Equation (22) showed how one determines the discount factor from the spot rate and vice versa.

The general form of smoothing techniques is based on the assumption that the discount factor for time t, $d(t)$ is a function which can be approximated by some structure. Usually the estimation of the discount factor, denoted by d_{es}, is of the form

$$d_{\text{es}}(t) = \sum_{i=0}^{K} \alpha_i f_i(t), \tag{38}$$

where the f_i are certain functions and the α_i, for $i = 0, \ldots, K$ are numerical coefficients. Hence, utilizing (3.5) implicitly assumes that the discount factor function can be written in such a form. The different smoothing techniques are based on choices of the approximating functions f_i, $i = 0, \ldots, K$.

The first step is to choose the set of $K + 1$ functions $f_0, \ldots, f_K$. Next, an optimization problem is solved in order to uncover the values of the α_i, for $i = 0, \ldots, K$, such that the present value of the cash flow from bond i, $\sum_{t=1}^{T_i} d_{\text{es}}(t)a_{\text{it}}$ is as close as possible to P_i, the market price of bond i, where T_i is the maturity of bond i and a_{it} is the payment from bond i at time t.

To this end, one must choose how to measure the distance between the present value, calculated based on d_{es}, and the market price of the bond. Here again, methods differ from one another. Some selection criteria are based on the sum of squared differences and some on the sum of the absolute values of the differences.

The procedure **NarbitB** is also capable of producing the smoothing. It uses the criteria of absolute values for measuring the distance. It is possible to think of, and display, the smoothing process as being done in two phases. In the first phase, the discount factors for the discrete payment dates of the bonds are identified. In the second phase, an optimization problem is solved. It uncovers the values of the α_i, for $i = 0, \ldots, K$, such that the value of the continuous curve $d_{\text{es}}(t)$ is as close as possible to the value of the discount factors at the payment dates. Whenever this is possible, **NarbitB** will demonstrate it with a graph.

Let us now examine an example of smoothing the discount factors. *For simplicity, we assume a market in which coupons are paid annually. Hence in* **NarbitB** *and its output, the time unit is a year.* In order to accomplish this, we need to run the procedure **NarbitB** as before, but with the addition of two parameters. We need to specify the number of approximating functions and the name which will be assigned to our new (smooth) discount factors function. This function is termed the *continuous approximation of the discount factors.*

Suppose we would like to have six approximating functions (i.e., $K = 5$), and we would like to call the continuous approximation **ConApp**. We thus need to run **NarbitB** as demonstrated in the following. The output of the procedure also generates a graph. This is illustrated in the following figure which appears directly following the output. (You can add a zero as a parameter at the end to suppress the graph of the discount factor, i.e., execute 'NarbitB([[105,0,0],[10,110,0],[8,8,108]],[94,97,85],6,ConApp,0);' instead of the following)

```
> NarbitB([[105,0,0],[10,110,0],[8,8,108]],
  [94,97,85],6,ConApp);
```

The no-arbitrage condition is satisfied.

The discount factor for time, 1, *is given by,* $\dfrac{94}{105}$

The interest rate spanning the time interval, $[0,1]$,
is given by, 0.1170

The discount factor for time, 2, *is given by,* $\dfrac{1849}{2310}$

The interest rate spanning the time interval, $[0,2]$,
is given by, 0.2493

The discount factor for time, 3, *is given by,* $\dfrac{82507}{124740}$

The interest rate spanning the time interval, $[0,3]$,
is given by, 0.5119

The function Vdis([c1,c2,..]), values the cashflow [c1,c2,..]

The continuous discount factor is
given by the function, 'ConApp', (.)

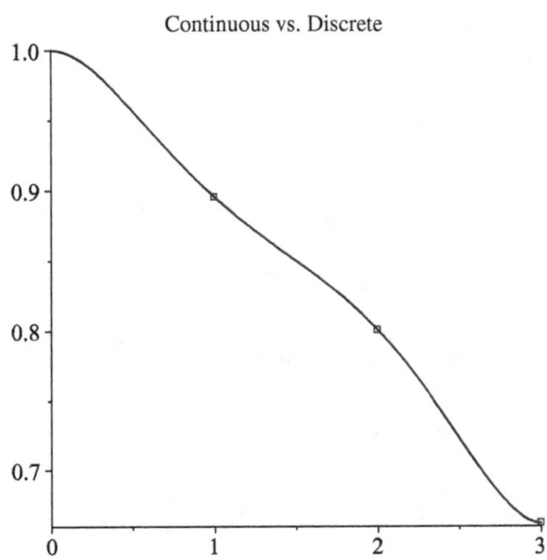

The figure demonstrates the smoothing process. The boxes are the values of the discrete discount factors for the times at which bonds pay coupons, or repay the face value. The continuous graph is the result of our smoothing approximation. The function **ConApp** estimates the discount factor associated with every t in the interval $[0, 3]$ and is used[2] to value the cash flows payable at times other than 1, 2, or 3. Hence, to calculate the present value of \$4 obtainable at time 1.75, we perform the following calculation:

```
> ConApp(1.75)*4;
```

$$3.311229336. \tag{39}$$

[2]By interpolation, it is possible to obtain an estimation for discount factors beyond $t = 3$ as well. To this end, one needs to specify the range over which the function should be extrapolated. This is done when a fifth parameter is added to the input. This added parameter can be either zero for surpassing the graph or one, to produce the graph. The default value of this parameter is one. To produce the extrapolation, a sixth parameter must be added specifying the right end point of the range. However, in this case, the fifth parameter must be specified. Hence, to extrapolate the example in the text for 6.5 years with the graph, one should run

```
> NarbitB([[105,0,0],[10,110,0],[8,8,108]],[94,97,89],
  6,ConApp,1,6.5);
```

The no-arbitrage condition is satisfied.

The discount factor for time, 1, *is given by,* $\frac{94}{105}$

The interest rate spanning the time interval, $[0, 1]$, *is given by,* 0.1170

The discount factor for time, 2, *is given by,* $\frac{1849}{2340}$

The interest rate spanning the time interval, $[0, 2]$, *is given by,* 0.2493

The discount factor for time, 3, *is given by,* $\frac{87127}{124740}$

The interest rate spanning the time interval, $[0, 3]$, *is given by,* 0.4317

Similarly, to value the cash flow \$4 at time 1.75, \$4 at time 2.25, and \$100 at time 2.75, we calculate

```
> ConApp(1.75)*4+ConApp(2.25)*4+ConApp(2.75)*100;
```

$$74.55914878. \tag{40}$$

In this last example, we see that the graph passes through the value of the discrete discount factors obtained directly from the market. In this case above, we manage to fit the estimated discount factor function defined by Eq. (44) to coincide with the discrete factors obtained from the market. This, of course, is not always possible and will depend on the type and number of approximating functions chosen for the approximation. Suppose we attempt to do the same fitting with only three approximation functions. The resultant discount factor function is displayed as follows:

```
> NarbitB([[105,0,0],[10,110,0],[8,8,108]],[94,97,85],
  3,ConApp1);
```

The function Vdis([c1,c2,..]), values the cashflow [c1,c2,..]
The continuous discount factor is given by the function, 'ConApp', (.)

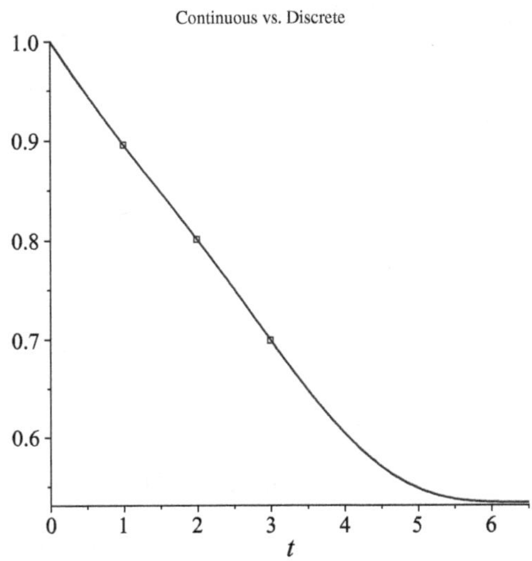

The no-arbitrage condition is satisfied.

The discount factor for time, 1, *is given by,* $\frac{94}{105}$

The interest rate spanning the time interval, $[0, 1]$, *is given by,* 0.1170

The discount factor for time, 2, *is given by,* $\frac{1849}{2310}$

The interest rate spanning the time interval, $[0, 2]$, *is given by,* 0.2493

The discount factor for time, 3, *is given by,* $\frac{82507}{124740}$

The interest rate spanning the time interval, $[0, 3]$, *is given by,* 0.5119

The function Vdis([c1,c2,..]), values the cashflow [c1,c2,..]

The continuous discount factor is given by the function, *'ConApp1',* *(.)*

To produce the extrapolation without a graph, one should run

```
> NarbitB([[105,0,0],[10,110,0],[8,8,108]],[94.5,97,89],
  6,ConApp,0,6.5);
```

The no-arbitrage condition is satisfied.

The discount factor for time, 1, *is given by,* 0.9000000000

The interest rate spanning the time interval, $[0, 1]$, *is given by,* 0.111

The discount factor for time, 2, *is given by,* 0.8000000000

The interest rate spanning the time interval, $[0, 2]$, *is given by,* 0.250

The discount factor for time, 3, *is given by,* 0.6981481481

The interest rate spanning the time interval, $[0, 3]$, *is given by,* 0.432

The function Vdis([c1,c2,..]), values the cashflow [c1,c2,..]

The continuous discount factor is given by the function, *'ConApp',* *(.)* (41)

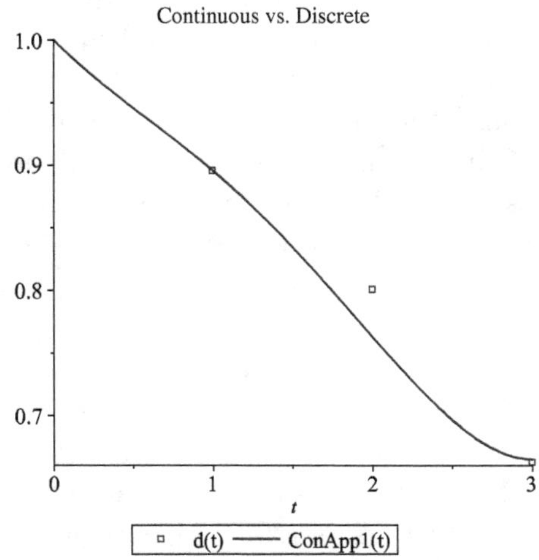

It is now apparent from the above figure that we do not have a perfect fit. The procedure **NarbitB** also defines a variable **SumAbsDiv**. It measures the "goodness-of-fit" in terms of the sum of the absolute deviations of the approximation from the actual observations. Thus, if the value of this variable is zero, the fit is perfect. Each time **NarbitB** is run and a continuous approximation of the term structure is solved for, the variable **SumAbsDiv** is redefined. To check its value, issue the following command:

```
> SumAbsDiv;
```

$$\frac{464839}{111363}. \tag{42}$$

Sometimes a perfect fit is not possible and we have to make do with the best approximation possible. In fact, the situation in real world markets is somewhat more complicated. Realistic markets are incomplete. That is, in realistic markets the number of bonds is smaller than the dates on which there are payments from at least one outstanding bond. Therefore, if the NA condition is satisfied, there will be multiple solutions for the set of discount factors. However, unlike the equity market, trading in the bond market is done via a set of dealers and not in a central market place. Consequently, the quotes of bond prices are with errors. These errors are due to the structure of the market and to non synchronization. Not all the bonds are traded at all times. Hence, the observed prices of the bonds are prices of the last transactions and they may include prices of different times for different bonds. Consequently, even though theoretically there are NA opportunities, the NA is not satisfied by the observed prices. This however means that the set of equations solved in order to determine the discount factors or the term structure, is inconsistent. This is in spite of the fact that there are more equations than variables. Thus, the term structure and/or the discount factor function is estimated based on a second best solution concept (by minimizing absolute deviations). The **NarbitB** procedure is capable of handling such a situation. It will report that the NA is not satisfied and the composition of an arbitrage portfolio. However, when graphing the discount factor, it will not show the discrete solution of the discount factors, as such does not exist. This is demonstrated in the following example.

```
> NarbitB([[105,0,0],[10,110,0],[8,8,108]],[94,10,787],
  5,ConNNA);
```

The no-arbitrage condition is not satisfied

An arbitrage portfolio is:

Short, 1, *of Bond*, 1

$$Buy, \frac{881}{10}, of\ Bond, 2$$

Short, 1, *of Bond*, 3

The cost of this portfolio is zero

This portfolio produces income of, 768, *at time*, 1

This portfolio produces income of, 9683, *at time*, 2

This portfolio produces income of, −108, *at time*, 3

The continuous discount factor is given by the function, *'ConNNA'*, *(.)*

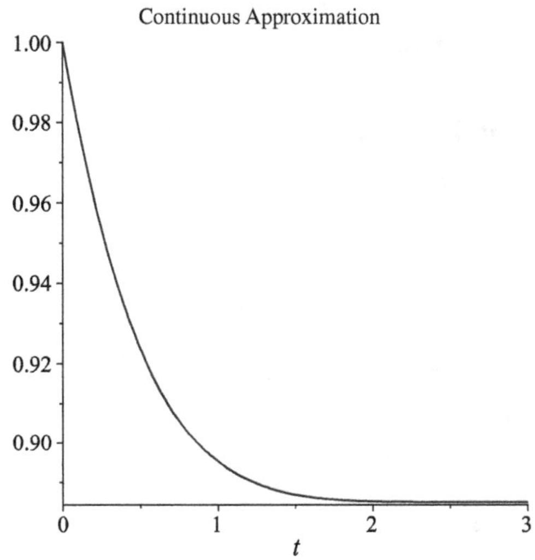

As mentioned before, once we have the continuous approximation of the discount factors, we can generate the continuous approximation of the term structure of interest rates. Let us try an example using only five approximating functions.

```
> NarbitB([[105,0,0],[10,110,0],[8,8,108]],[94,97,85],
  5,ConApp2);
```

The no-arbitrage condition is satisfied.

The discount factor for time, 1, *is given by,* $\dfrac{94}{105}$

The interest rate spanning the time interval, [0, 1],
is given by, 0.1170

The discount factor for time, 2, *is given by,* $\dfrac{1849}{2310}$

The interest rate spanning the time interval, [0, 2],
is given by, 0.2493

The discount factor for time, 3, *is given by,* $\dfrac{82507}{124740}$

The interest rate spanning the time interval, $[0, 3]$,
is given by, 0.5119
The function Vdis([c1,c2,..]), values the cashflow [c1,c2,..]
The continuous discount factor is given by the function,
'ConApp2', (.)

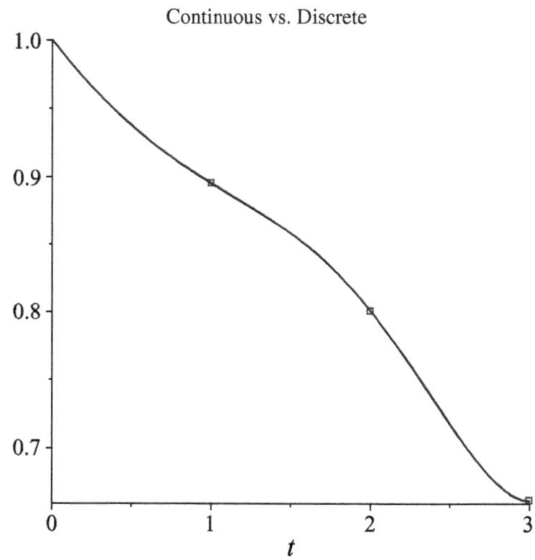


```
> SumAbsDiv;
```

$$0 \tag{43}$$

As we see in this example, the value of **SumAbsDiv** is zero which means that a perfect fit was possible.[3] The relation between the discount factors, $d(t)$ and the zero-coupon curve, $r(t)$, when the letters

[3]In certain cases, multiple solutions exist for the approximation. Hence, running the same procedure with the same parameters may result in a different answer.

reported based on semi-annual compounding is given by

$$d(t) = \left(\frac{1}{1+\frac{r(t)}{2}}\right)^{2\cdot t}.$$

Thus, given the value of $d(t)$, denoted in our calculations by **ConApp2(t)**, it is possible to solve for $r(t)$. The following command solves for $r(t)$ as a function of **ConApp2(t)** and defines the term structure function $r(t)$. Specifically, the spot rate for time t, will be given by the function $r(t)$ defined as follows:

```
> solve(d(t) = (1/(1+(1/2)*r(t)))^(2*t),r(t));
```

$$-\frac{2\left(\mathrm{e}^{\frac{1}{2}\frac{\ln(d(t))}{t}}-1\right)}{\mathrm{e}^{\frac{1}{2}\frac{\ln(d(t))}{t}}} \tag{44}$$

```
> subs(d(t)=ConApp2(t),%):
```

```
> r:=unapply(%,t):
```

```
> simplify(r(t));
```

$$\begin{cases} \mathit{undefined} + \mathit{undefined}\ I & t < 0 \\ -2+2\,\mathrm{e}^{-\frac{1}{2}\frac{-4\ln(2)-7\ln(3)-\ln(5)-\ln(7)-\ln(11)-\ln(23)+\ln(370656\,t^6-569096\,t^5-4900521\,t^4+7474916\,t^3+10467567\,t^2-45304434\,t+309854160)}{t}} & t \leq 3 \\ \mathit{undefined} + \mathit{undefined}\ I & t > 3 \end{cases}$$

```
> r(1);
```

$$-\frac{1}{47}\left(\frac{1}{105}\sqrt{9870}-1\right)\sqrt{9870} \tag{45}$$

```
> r(2):
```

We can now plot this function and see how the spot rate in this market behaves.

```
> plot(r(t),t=0..3,labels=[Time,'Rate'],thickness=2,
  title='A Continuous Approximation of a Term Structure',
  titlefont=[TIMES,BOLD,10]);
```

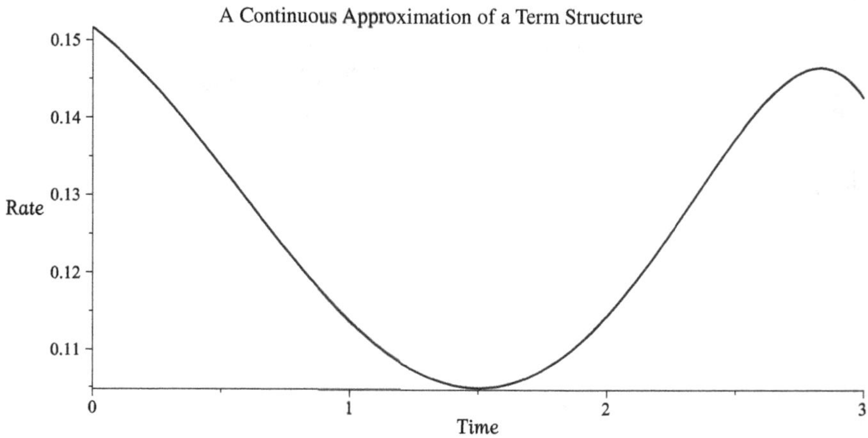

The fact that the rates are reported on an annual basis allows us to compare the rates for different maturities. We see that the rates are decreasing as time increases and then, at about 1.5 years, the rates increase. Different shapes of the term structure are possible. There are a few theories which explain the shape of the term structure of interest rates.

Smoothing and Continuous Compounding

Given the discount factor for time t, $d(t)$, (we will measure time in years henceforth), the continuously compounded rate $r(t)$ is the solution to Eq. (53),

$$d(t) = e^{(-r(t)t)}. \tag{46}$$

Hence, $r(t)$ is given by

$$r(t) = -\frac{\ln(d(t))}{t}. \tag{47}$$

Previously we calculated the discount factor function, **ConApp2**, when the units of time were measured in years. Therefore, the continuous approximation of the term structure based on continuous compounding will be given by $-\frac{\ln(ConApp2(t))}{t}$. Let us define the function Ts to be the continuously compounded term structure in our example.

```
> Ts:=unapply(-ln(ConApp2(t))/t,t);
```

$$Ts := t \to -\frac{1}{t}\left(\ln\left(piecewise\left(0 \le t \textbf{ and } t \le 3, 1 - \frac{193}{1320}t + \frac{105733}{3129840}t^2 + \frac{1868729}{77463540}t^3 - \frac{1633507}{103284720}t^4 - \frac{6467}{3521070}t^5 + \frac{26}{21735}t^6, undefined\right)\right)\right) \quad (48)$$

The graphs of the continuous approximation of the term structure based on semiannual compounding (the upper graph) and based on continuous compounding (the lower graph), are plotted together in the following figure.

```
> plot([r(t),Ts(t)],t=0..3,thickness=2,labels=['Time in
  Years','Rate'],title='Continuous Approximation of the
  Term Structure: Semiannual Compounding vs. Continuous
  Compounding',titlefont=[TIMES,BOLD,8]);
```

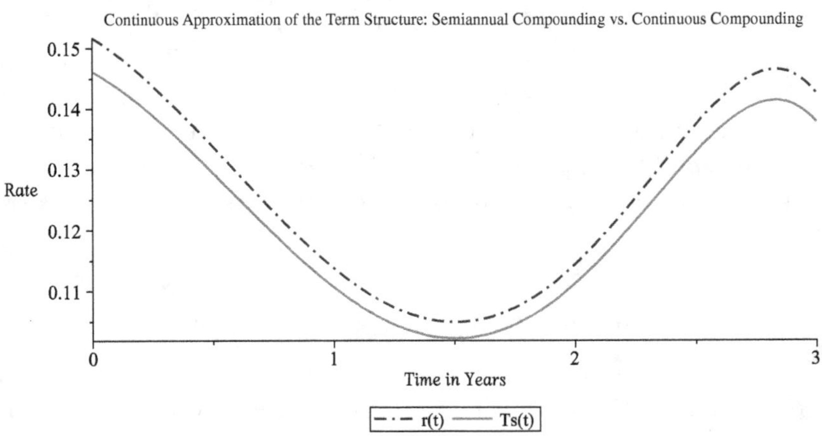

The discount for time t in terms of **Ts** is given by the expression $e^{(-Ts(t)t)}$ and is plotted in the following figure. Note that indeed the discount factor is a decreasing function for which the range is between zero and one, as it should be.

```
> plot(exp(-Ts(t)*t),t=0..3,thickness=2,labels=[ 'Time
  in Years','Rate'],title='The discount factor
  function implied by the term structure Ts.',
  titlefont=[TIMES,BOLD,10]);
```

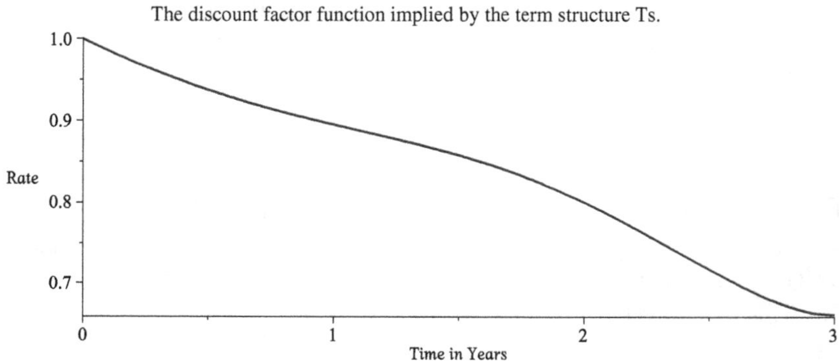

Note that we have not discussed or specified the evolution of the term structure across time. Rather, our discussion has been devoted to the term structure or set of discount factors that prevail in the market at a certain point. It is as if we take a "snapshot" of bond prices in the market at a certain moment, and extract the term structure prevailing in the market at that time. As time passes, the term structure may, and usually does, change.Yet, there are many instruments and types of cash flows that could be valued given only the current discount factor $d(t)$.

Forward Rate: A Classical Approach

Let $r(t)$ be the interest rate which prevails in the market from time zero to time t. For simplicity, we assume that the rates are quoted based on continuous compounding and that time is measured in years. Hence, a dollar invested at time zero for one year will grow into $\mathrm{e}^{r(1)\cdot 1}$ and a dollar invested at time zero for two years will grow into $\mathrm{e}^{r(2)\cdot 2}$.

There is another way to invest money from time zero to time two. The dollar could be invested from time zero to time one, and then invested from time one to time two at the rate that will prevail in the market at that time. At the current time, this rate is unknown, as it is a random variable. Under this investment strategy, a dollar invested from time zero to time one will be worth $e^{r(1)}$ at time one. This amount is then invested for one further time period at the rate prevailing in the market at that time. If the dollar had been invested for two time periods at the prevailing rate of interest covering the interval from time zero to time two, it would have grown to a value of $e^{r(2)\cdot 2}$.

Let us denote by $x_1(1,2)$ the (as yet unknown) interest rate from time one to time two. The subindex 1 of x means that this is the interest rate that will prevail at time one and the $(1,2)$ means that this rate spans the time interval $[1,2]$. Hence, the dollar at time zero amounts to $e^{r(1)}$ at time one, which grows to $e^{r(1)}\ e^{x_1(1,2)}$ at the end of two time periods. The value of $x_1(1,2)$ which solves

$$e^{r(1)}\ e^{x(1,2)} = e^{r(2)\cdot 2} \tag{49}$$

is the *forward rate* from time one to time two, as of time zero. As has been our custom before, we omit the index for zero and use two indexes in order to denote the span of time for which this forward rate is applicable. That is, we use $r(1,2)$ instead of $r_0(1,2)$ in the same manner we use $r(t)$ instead of $r_0(t)$ when the span is $[0,t]$.

The intuitive meaning of the forward rate is that it is a rate implicit in the spot rate which will prevail in the market from time one to time two. If an investor perceives that $r(2)$ is not high enough to induce the investor to pursue a two-period investment horizon, then that investor will prefer to use a rollover strategy. The investor invests for one period, from time zero to time one, and then “rolls over” the investment for another period, from time one to time two. From the definition of a forward rate it is apparent that $r(1,2)$ is the rate that makes our “rollover” strategy equivalent to the “buy and hold” one. The rates prevailing in the market are those which induce an equilibrium: $r(1,2)$ is the value which makes these two strategies equivalent. Hence, these rates convey information about the market’s anticipation of future rates which will prevail from time one to time two.

This discussion was based on an example. One can extract the forward rate as of time zero for any future time period t_1 to t_2 ($t_1 < t_2$). A dollar invested from time zero to time t_1 will grow to be $e^{r(t_1)t_1}$ dollars. If the dollar is invested from time zero to time t_2, it will grow to $e^{r(t_2)t_2}$ and $r(t_1, t_2)$ will be the solution to

$$e^{r(t_1)t_1}\, e^{r(t_1,t_2)(t_2-t_1)} = e^{r(t_2)t_2}. \tag{50}$$

Thus, $r(t_1, t_2)$ denoted by r_{12} below will be given by:

```
> solve({exp(rt1*t1)*exp(r12*(t2-t1))=exp(rt)*t2},{r12});
```

$$\left\{r_{12} = -\frac{\ln(t_2) + rt - rt_1\, t_1}{-t_2 + t_1}\right\} \tag{51}$$

In our example, we defined the continuously compounded term structure of interest rates as the function $\mathbf{Ts}(t)$. It is redefined here again in the following steps:

```
> NarbitB([[105,0,0],[10,110,0],[8,8,108]],[94,97,85],
  5,ConApp2):
```

The no-arbitrage condition is satisfied.

The discount factor for time, 1, *is given by,* $\frac{94}{105}$

The interest rate spanning the time interval, $[0, 1]$, *is given by,* 0.1170

The discount factor for time, 2, *is given by,* $\frac{1849}{2310}$

The interest rate spanning the time interval, $[0, 2]$, *is given by,* 0.2493

$$\textit{The discount factor for time, 3, is given by, } \frac{82507}{124740}$$
$$\textit{The interest rate spanning the time interval, } [0,3],$$
$$\textit{is given by, } 0.5119$$
The function Vdis([c1,c2,..]), values the cashflow [c1,c2,..]
The continuous discount factor is given by the function,
$$'ConApp2',\ (.) \tag{52}$$

The continuously compounded term structure of interest rates is thus the function **Ts**(t) defined as follows.

```
> Ts:=unapply(-ln(ConApp2(t))/t,t);
```

$$Ts := t \to -\frac{1}{t}\left(\ln\left(\mathit{piecewise}\left(0 \le t \textbf{ and } t \le 3, 1 - \frac{193}{1320}t + \frac{105733}{3129840}t^2 + \frac{1868729}{77463540}t^3 - \frac{1633507}{103284720}t^4 - \frac{6467}{3521070}t^5 + \frac{26}{21735}t^6, \mathit{undefined}\right)\right)\right) \tag{53}$$

We can also now define the function **Fr**(t_1, t_2), based on (53) as the forward rate from time t_1 to time t_2.

```
> Fr:=(t1,t2)->(Ts(t2)*t2-Ts(t1)*t1)/(t2-t1);
```

$$Fr := (t_1, t_2) \to \frac{Ts(t_2)t_2 - Ts(t_1)t_1}{t_2 - t_1} \tag{54}$$

The function **Fr** should always have the second argument t_2 greater than the first argument t_1.

Armed with the function so defined, we can plot it together with the term structure and see how the term structure is related to the forward rate. In the following figure, the forward rate (the graph with the lower y-intercept) is graphed together with the term structure (the graph with the higher y-intercept), where the time domain is

0.5–3 and the forward rate is graphed from time 0.5 to any time t in the interval $[0.5, 3]$.

```
> plot([Ts(t),Fr(.5,t)],t=0.5..3,thickness=2,labels=
  [Time,Rate],title='The Forward Rate and the Term
  Structure',titlefont=[TIMES,BOLD,10]);
```

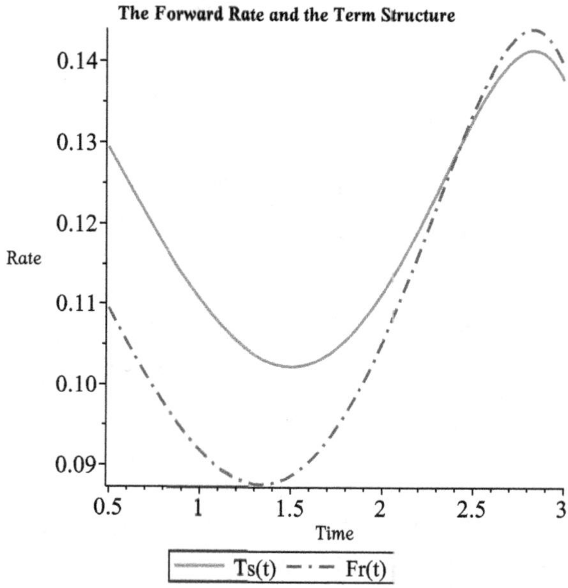

We can also display the forward rate from time t_1 to t_2 where we let t_1 range from 0 to 3 and t_2 from t_1 to 3. This is displayed in the following figure. Note that the graph of the forward rate in the above figure is a slice of the graph in the following figure, for $t_1 = 0.5$.

```
> plot3d(Fr(t1,t2),t1=0..3,t2=t1..3,axes=normal,labels=
  ['Initial Time','End Time',Rate],orientation=[-162,56],
  title='The Forward Rate from Time t1 to t2: 0<t1<3,
  t1<t2<3',axes=framed,titlefont=[TIMES,BOLD,10]);
```

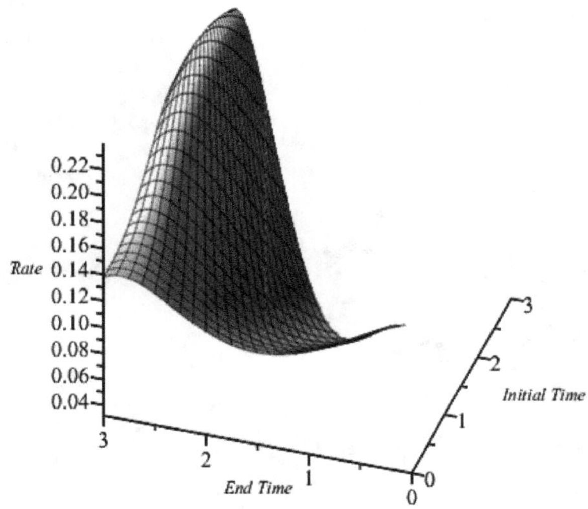
0.22
0.20
0.18
0.16
Rate 0.14
0.12
0.10
0.08
0.06
0.04
3
2
End Time
1
0
0
1
2
3
Initial Time

Chapter 4

Duration and Immunization

Introduction

This chapter is dedicated to the study of the sensitivity of the price of bonds and portfolios of bonds to changes in interest rates. A measure of the sensitivity of bond prices to changes in interest rates, called duration, was first suggested by **Macaulay** in 1938. The field of fixed income securities has evolved tremendously since that time and the academic literature now criticizes this measure. As we proceed with the development and understanding of this measure, we will also gain insight into this critique. And while risk management methods based on durations are also subject to the same critique, empirical observations prove these methods to be quite successful. The literature mentions that pension funds and insurance companies that have used such methods over a few decades rarely missed their goals. Furthermore, we believe that this chapter will significantly help in developing the readers' intuitions about interest rate risk and volatility of bond prices, thereby paving the way to more advanced models that are beyond the scope of this course.

Duration: A Sensitivity Measure of Bonds' Prices to Changes in Interest Rates

Our starting point is the definition of duration and its intuitive motivation. We start by assuming that the term structure is flat, but this assumption can be easily relaxed. That is, the rate spanning one period, the time interval $[0, 1]$, is r, hence a dollar invested for t

periods of time will grow to $(1 + r)^t$. For simplicity, we assume in this section that interest rates are reported based on annual compounding.

Let $c(t)$ be the cash flow (coupon or coupon plus principal at maturity) from a bond at time t, $t = 1, \ldots, n$, where n is the maturity time of the bond. The no-arbitrage (NA) condition implies that the price of the bond P is given by

$$P = \sum_{t=1}^{n} \frac{c(t)}{(1+r)^t}, \tag{1}$$

where interest rates are reported as explained above.

It is customary to use continuous compounding in this development as it leads to a "neater" result. Consequently, the preset value of the cash flow from the bond is written as follows:

$$P = \sum_{t=1}^{n} c(t)e^{-rt}. \tag{2}$$

In this simplistic model, the effect of the change in the interest rate (in r) on the price of the bond can be measured by the derivative of $P = \sum_{t=1}^{n} c(t)e^{-rt}$ with respect to r, and it is given by:

$$\frac{dP}{dr} = -\sum_{t=1}^{n} c(t)e^{-rt}t. \tag{3}$$

Before we continue further, we make our first observation. Since the bond payments are all positive i.e., $c(t) > 0$, $t = 1, \ldots, n$ and so is r, one can easily verify that the expression above is negative. Hence, our first conclusion is that since $\frac{dP}{dr} < 0$, P is a decreasing function of r, i.e., **bond prices increase when interest rates decrease and vice versa**.

This is a direct consequence of the first derivative being negative. A further look confirms that indeed the present value of a positive cash flow decreases as the interest rate increases. The present value of a (positive) future amount at time t, is calculated by multiplying it by the discount factor $\frac{1}{e^{rt}}$ so that as r increases, the discount factor decreases and hence the result.

Traditionally, the sensitivity of bond prices to changes in the interest rate is measured in percentage terms. However, before presenting it in the classical way, we want to highlight the concept behind this traditional presentation. Thinking about the price of the bond as a function of the interest rate (since the present value is a function of r), it is possible to approximate the change in a bond price due to a change in the interest rate. The approximation is based on a first-order Taylor series (see Taylor series) that uses only the first derivative of the approximated function. When the price of the bond P is represented as a function of r i.e., as $P(r)$, where $\frac{\mathrm{d}P(r)}{\mathrm{d}r}$ is its first derivative and a change in r represented by Δr, then $P(r+\Delta r)$ can be linearly approximated by

$$P(r+\Delta r) \approx P(r) + \frac{\mathrm{d}P(r)}{\mathrm{d}r}\Delta r. \tag{4}$$

This approximation can be visualized graphically remembering that $\frac{\mathrm{d}P(r)}{\mathrm{d}r}$ is the slope of the function $P(r)$ at r, which equals the slope of the line tangent to the function P at point r. This visualization is presented as a linear function of r, the rate after the change, when the current rate is r_0, $\left(\frac{\mathrm{d}P(r)}{\mathrm{d}r}\right)_{r=r_0}$ is the value of the derivative at r_0 and $\Delta r = (r - r_0)$. The linear function of r is thus

$$P(r_0) + \left(\frac{\mathrm{d}P(r)}{\mathrm{d}r}\right)_{r=r_0} \cdot \Delta r. \tag{5}$$

Let us look at a few numerical examples. To this end, we defined a function that calculates the price of a bond. The bond has a face value of \$100, pays annually a coupon rate of c (i.e., each coupon payment is $c \cdot 100$) and matures in n years from now (that is, next coupon is paid in 12 months). The function is thus:

$$\sum_{i=1}^{n} \frac{100 \cdot c}{(1+r)^i} + \frac{100}{(1+r)^n}. \tag{6}$$

The parameters of this function are c, r, and n and the function is defined as follows:

```
> BondPriceA:=(c,r,n)->sum(c*100/(1+r)^(i),i=1..n)
  +100/(1+r)^n;
```

$$\mathrm{BondPriceA} := (c, r, n) \mapsto \sum_{i=1}^{n} \frac{100\,c}{(1+r)^i} + \frac{100}{(1+r)^n}. \tag{7}$$

That is, for $n = 2$, a coupon rate of c and interest rate of r, the price is given by

```
> BondPriceA(c,r,2);
```

$$\frac{100\,c}{r+1}+\frac{100\,c}{(r+1)^2}+\frac{100}{(r+1)^2}. \tag{8}$$

The generic formula is

```
> BondPriceA(c,r,n);
```

$$-\frac{100\,c\left(\frac{1}{1+r}\right)^{n+1}(1+r)}{r}+\frac{100\,c}{r}+\frac{100}{(1+r)^n}. \tag{9}$$

Note that Maple presented the expression $\sum_{t=1}^{n}\frac{c(t)}{(1+r)^t}$ in a compact form based on it being a geometric series. For $n = 5$, the result will be

```
> BondPriceA(c,r,5);
```

$$\frac{100\,c}{1+r}+\frac{100\,c}{(1+r)^2}+\frac{100\,c}{(1+r)^3}+\frac{100\,c}{(1+r)^4}+\frac{100\,c}{(1+r)^5}+\frac{100}{(1+r)^5}. \tag{10}$$

Hence, the price of a bond maturing in 5 years with a coupon payment of 5%, when the interest rate is 7%, is calculated as follows:

```
> BondPriceA(0.05,0.07,5);
```

$$91.79960511. \tag{11}$$

The price of the same bond when the interest rate is 5% is thus

```
> BondPriceA(0.05,0.05,5);
```

$$100.0000000. \tag{12}$$

The approximation of Eq. (6) $P(r_0)+\left(\frac{\mathrm{d}P(r)}{\mathrm{d}r}\right)_{r=r_0}\cdot(r_0-r)$ can now be visualized. A large value of r_0 is chosen to make it more pronounced. The chosen parameters are $r_0 = 0.14$, $c = 0.05$, and $n = 5$. For these values, the price of the bond is

```
> BondPriceA(.05,0.14,5);
```

$$69.10227129 \tag{13}$$

and the figure that visualizes this approximation as in (6) is presented as follows:

```
> plot([BondPriceA(.05,r,5),BondPriceA(.05,.14,5)+
  (r-0.14)*subs(r=.14,diff(BondPriceA(.05,r,5),r)),
  [[0.14,0],[0.14,BondPriceA(.05,.14,5)]]],r=0.04...0.30,
  y=0..180,labels=['Interest rate','Bond Price'],
  title='Approximation of the Bond's value',
  thickness=2,titlefont=[TIMES,BOLD,10]);
```

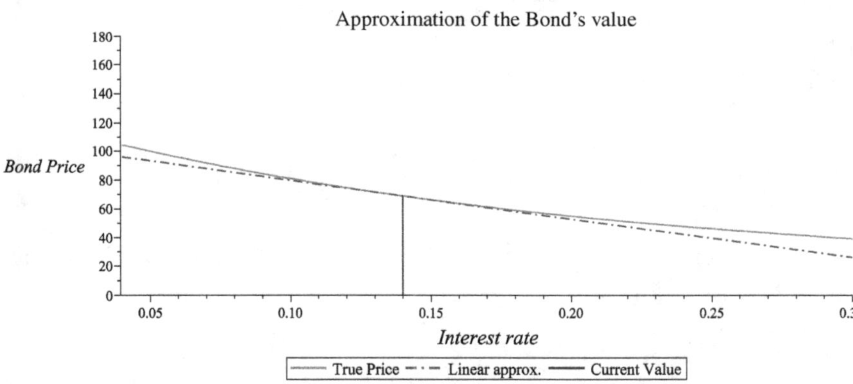

The solid curve is the true value of the bond as a function of the interest rate. The dashed curve is the approximation of the value of the bond after the change in the interest rate. It is the line tangent to the dashed curve at $r = 0.14$, at the intersection of the solid perpendicular line with both curves. Hence, the slope of the dashed curve is the derivative of the solid curve at the point $r = 0.14$. If the interest rate does not change ($r = 0.14$), the approximation and the true value coincide.

Note that the smaller the change in the rate, the better the linear approximation. However, as the change gets bigger, a gap opens between the true value (the solid curve) and the approximation (the dashed curve). This gap is due to the true value not being a linear function of the interest rate.

Let us see how this result can be presented in terms of percentage changes in the bond's price. To this end, we denote $P(r+\Delta r)-P(r)$

by ΔP in Eq. (5), repeated as follows:

$$P(r+\Delta r) \approx P(r) + \left(\frac{\mathrm{d}}{\mathrm{d}r}P(r)\right)\Delta r$$

and write it as

$$\Delta P \approx \left(\frac{\mathrm{d}P(r)}{\mathrm{d}r}\right)\Delta r. \tag{14}$$

Hence, $\frac{\Delta P}{\Delta r} \approx \left(\frac{\mathrm{d}P(r)}{\mathrm{d}r}\right)$ and since $\frac{dP(r)}{\mathrm{d}r} = -\sum_{t=1}^{n} e^{-rt}c(t)\ t$

$$\frac{\Delta P}{\Delta r} \approx -\sum_{t=1}^{n} e^{-rt}c(t)\ t. \tag{15}$$

Dividing (8) by $P = \sum_{t=1}^{n} c(t)e^{-rt}$, we obtain

$$\frac{\frac{\Delta P}{\Delta r}}{P} \approx \frac{-\sum_{t=1}^{n} c(t)e^{-rt}t}{\sum_{t=1}^{n} c(t)e^{-rt}} = -\sum_{t=1}^{n}\left(\frac{c(t)e^{-rt}}{\sum_{t=1}^{n} c(t)e^{-rt}}\right)t. \tag{16}$$

Defining $w(t) = \frac{c(t)e^{-rt}}{\sum_{t=1}^{n} c(t)e^{-rt}} = \frac{c(t)e^{-rt}}{P}$, Eq. (9) can be written as follows:

$$\frac{\Delta P}{P} \approx -\left(\sum_{t=1}^{n} w(t)t\right)\Delta r. \tag{17}$$

Notice that $0 \leq w(t)$, $w(t) \leq 1$, and that $\sum_{t=1}^{n} w(t) = 1$. Hence, $\sum_{t=1}^{n} w(t)t$ can be interpreted as the weighted average of the time of the payment dates of the bond. The weight of time t is the present value of the payment at t, divided by the present value of all the payments, i.e., by the price. Note also that in our notation the current time is time zero so time t is actually the length of the time period from now to t. Consequently, $\sum_{t=1}^{n} w(t)t$, is the weighted average of the length of times to the payment dates.

One may think of a coupon paying bond as maturing gradually, after all it pays coupons along its life so it is not really maturing at the time of the last coupon (and the face value) payment. Hence, $\sum_{t=1}^{n} w(t)t$ is the average 'duration' of the bond and

$$\mathrm{Du} = \sum_{t=1}^{n} w(t)t \tag{18}$$

is defined to be the duration of a bond. Consequently, the approximation in (11) can be written in terms of the bond's duration as

$$\frac{\Delta P}{P} \approx -\text{Du} \cdot \Delta r. \tag{19}$$

In words, *the percentage change in the price of the bond* $\frac{\Delta P}{P}$, *is minus its duration* ($\text{Du} = \sum_{t=1}^{n} w(t)t$) *multiplied by* Δr (the change in interest rate).

Thus, the effect of the change in the interest rate is measured, in this simplistic model, by the duration of the bond. The minus sign indicates that an increase in the interest rate causes a decrease in the price of the bond. Equation (20) can also be written as

$$\Delta P \approx -P\text{Du}\ \Delta r. \tag{20}$$

Thus, a result of a change of Δr in interest rate, the price of the bond is approximated by

$$P + \Delta P \approx P - P\text{Du} \cdot \Delta r = P(1 - \text{Du} \cdot \Delta r). \tag{21}$$

The interpretation of duration as the weighted average of the time of the payment dates of the bond implies that *the duration of a portfolio of bonds is the weighted average of the durations of the bonds in the portfolio.* The weight of the duration of each bond is the price of the bond divided by the price of the portfolio.

To help us in the calculations, we define a function **Dur(c,r,n,F)**, that calculates the duration of a bond where c is the coupon rate (paid annually), r the term structure of the interest rate (assumed to be flat for now), and n the number of years until maturity where the time to the next coupon is 12 months. For simplicity, the function **Dur(c,r,n,F)** calculates the duration assuming that the interest rate is reported as the simple annual rate, coupons are paid annually, and F is the face value of the bond, i.e. it calculates[1]

$$\frac{\left(\sum_{i=1}^{n} Fc(1+r)^{-i}i\right) + F(1+r)^{-n}n}{\left(\sum_{i=1}^{n} Fc(1+r)^{-i}\right) + F(1+r)^{-n}} \tag{22}$$

[1]Defining the duration based on continuous compounding and using it in an environment of discrete compounding, affects the quality of the approximation. For simplicity, we adopted this presentation.

```
> DurA:=(c,r,n,F)->(sum(F*(c)*(1+r)^(-i)*(i),i=1..n)
  +F*(1+r)^(-n)*n)/(sum(F*(c)*(1+r)^(-i),i=1..n)
  +F*(1+r)^(-n));
```

$$DurA := (c, r, n, F) \mapsto \frac{\left(\sum_{i=1}^{n} Fc(r+1)^{-i} i\right) + F(r+1)^{-n} n}{\left(\sum_{i=1}^{n} Fc(r+1)^{-i}\right) + F(r+1)^{-n}}. \tag{23}$$

Thus, the equation for the duration of a bond with a coupon rate of c where the interest rate is r, the time to maturity is 2 years and the face value is F, is given by

```
> DurA(c,r,2,F);
```

$$\frac{\frac{Fc}{r+1} + \frac{2\,Fc}{(r+1)^2} + \frac{2\,F}{(r+1)^2}}{\frac{Fc}{r+1} + \frac{Fc}{(r+1)^2} + \frac{F}{(r+1)^2}} \tag{24}$$

and if the time to maturity is n years it is

```
> DurA(c,r,n,F);
```

$$\frac{-\frac{((n+1)r+1)(1+r)\left(\frac{1}{1+r}\right)^{n+1} Fc}{r^2} + \frac{(1+r)Fc}{r^2} + F(1+r)^{-n} n}{-\frac{(1+r)\left(\frac{1}{1+r}\right)^{n+1} Fc}{r} + \frac{Fc}{r} + F(1+r)^{-n}}. \tag{25}$$

Note again that Maple uses the geometric series formula to simplify the expression in (16).

The duration of a zero-coupon bond that matures in 3 years with a face value of \$100 in a market with a flat-term structure of 7%, will be calculated by executing

```
> DurA(0,.07,3,100);
```

$$3.000000000. \tag{26}$$

Keeping in mind the duration definition and its interpretation, as a weighted average of the times to payments by the bond, it should be clear that the duration of such a bond is 3. The weighted average of one number is the number itself. Since the bond pays only once, the weighted average of the time to the payment of the bond is exactly the time to maturity of the bond.

Let us look at another example. The duration of a 5% coupon bond that matures in $n = 10$, paying semi-annual coupons $r = 7\%$ with a face value of $F = 100$, and the time to the next coupon is 12 months, can be calculated by executing:

```
> DurA(.05,.07,10,100);
```

$$7.935107005. \tag{27}$$

Consider yet another example. A 6% coupon bond, maturing in 5 years in a market in which the interest rate is 7% where the time to the payment of the next coupon is 6 months.

```
> DurA(.06,.07,5,100);
```

$$4.452295541. \tag{28}$$

The result of these calculations should not be that surprising. After all, if the bonds mature in 5 years and the highest weight is given to the maturity time, its duration should be close to 5. The weight of each time is the present value of the payment at that time divided by the present value of the future cash flow (the price of the bond). Hence, the face value of the bond will always tilt the duration measure to be close to the maturity time.

Duration therefore measures the sensitivity of bonds, or portfolio of bonds, to changes in interest rates. It is easy to verify, as mentioned, that *the duration of a portfolio of bonds is a weighted average of the durations of the bonds in the portfolio, where the weight of a bond's duration is the bond's value* ***divided by*** *the portfolio's value.* Interest rate risk is the terminology used to capture the risk one faces as a result of a change in the interest rates and duration is used to manage it. The process of protecting bond portfolios against interest rate risks is dubbed *immunization.*

We conclude this section demonstrating the use of a duration approximation, in order to calculate the percentage change in the value of a bond due to a change in the interest rate. Changes in interest rates are traditionally measured in *basis points* **(bps)**. One basis point is defined to be $\frac{1}{100}$ of 1%. Hence, 1% change equals a change of 100 bps. The function **BondPrice** calculates the price of a bond with a face value of \$100 where c is the coupon rate (paid semiannually), r the term structure of the interest rate (assumed to be flat for now), and n the number of years until maturity where the time to the next coupon is 6 months. That is for $n = 1$, coupon rate of c, when r is the flat-term structure of the interest rate, we have

```
> BondPriceA(c,r,1);
```

$$\frac{100\,c}{r+1} + \frac{100}{r+1}. \tag{29}$$

Thus, the price of a bond with a face value of \$100 that matures in 10 years where $c = 0.1$ and $r = 0.05$ is

```
> BondPriceA(.10,0.05,10);
```

$$138.6086746. \tag{30}$$

Assume now that the interest rate in the market increased by 50 bbps. That is, the new rate is 5.5% and the price of the bond will be

```
> BondPriceA(.10,0.055,10);
```

$$133.9193162. \tag{31}$$

The percentage change in the price of the bond, $\frac{\Delta P}{P}$, was thus

```
> (133.9193162-138.6086746)/138.6086746;
```

$$-0.03383163726. \tag{32}$$

Let us see how the duration will approximate this change. The duration of the bond is

```
> DurA(.10,.05,10,100);
```

$$7.269754832. \tag{33}$$

Hence, by (20), the duration will approximate the percentage change in the bond's price $\frac{\Delta P}{P}$ as $-\mathrm{Du}\Delta r$

```
> -DurA(.10,.05,10,100)*0.005;
```

$$-0.03634877416. \tag{34}$$

Thus, as a result of a 50 bps (0.005) increase in interest rate, the price of the bond by (20) is approximated as

```
> BondPriceA(.10,0.05,10)*(1-0.03634877416);
```

$$133.5704192. \tag{35}$$

In particular, consider a bond portfolio that is composed to meet certain liabilities in the future. The duration of the portfolio, in such cases, is set equal to the duration of the liabilities. Consequently, changes in the values of the portfolio and the liabilities, due to change in interest rates, are approximately equal and hence the liabilities are met under different scenarios of interest rate changes.

Finally, the use of duration defined here to manage the risk of bond portfolios, is not restricted to a flat-term structure world. It is valid also in a world of non-flat term structures, assuming the changes are of a parallel shift type, i.e., the new term structure is the old one plus a constant term. The duration concept can be extended to account for more general changes, but this is beyond the scope of this course.

Immunization

Immunization (in financial terminology) is the process of eliminating (or reducing) interest rate risks from a bond portfolio. Consider an investor who holds a portfolio of bonds in order to meet a certain liability in the future. If the portfolio is not composed of a zero-coupon bond that matures at the time of the liability (with a value equal to the liability value), a risk is assumed. This risk is induced by the uncertainty about the reinvestment rate of the coupons paid by the portfolio prior to the liability time. Perhaps the best way to explain immunization is by using a case as described in the following.

Assume that the current term structure is flat at 11% and that you have a liability of $165.94 to be paid in 4 years from now. Furthermore, assume for simplicity, that in this market the term structure is always flat. Hence, changes in the term structure are always such that the new term structure is flat at another level. The current term structure is flat at 11% and you have \$109.3136605 currently. You make a quick calculation and find out that

```
> 109.3136605*(1+0.11)^4;
```

$$165.9458334. \tag{36}$$

Thus, you actually have a present value of \$165.945 that is equal to the present value of your liability. In order to ensure your ability to fulfill your obligation, you are looking into an investment strategy that could guarantee meeting your liability. Being conservative, you do not want to assume any default risk and hence you are only looking in the government bond market.

You take a look at the bond market and find out that there is a bond that pays an **annual** coupon of \$13.52 and matures in 5 years. A coupon was just paid by the bond so the next coupon payment is in a year. As it should be in a market where the NA condition is satisfied, such a bond should have the following price (as a function of r):

```
> sum(13.52*(1+r)^(-i),i=1..5)+100*(1+r)^(-5);
```

$$\frac{13.52000000}{1.+r} + \frac{13.52000000}{(1.+r)^2} + \frac{13.52000000}{(1.+r)^3} + \frac{13.52000000}{(1.+r)^4} + \frac{13.52000000}{(1.+r)^5} + \frac{100}{(1+r)^5} \tag{37}$$

and thus if the interest rate is 11%, the price of the bond is

```
> subs(r=0.11,sum(13.52*(1+r)^(-i),i=1..5)
  +100*(1+r)^(-5));
```

$$109.3136605. \tag{38}$$

You are considering buying this bond now and selling it in 4 years to pay your liability. You are just about to buy it when your broker hears that you are going to buy it in order to be able to pay your liability in 4 years. In this case, the broker says perhaps you should reconsider, since by buying this bond you may assume a risk you do not want. After all, you are not sure what price you will be able to get for the bond in 4 years. Furthermore, you assume a risk of re-investing, since when the coupons are paid, you are not sure what the interest rate in the market will be at that time.

You thus perform the following analysis: You calculate the value of the bond at time 4 as a function of the interest rate. That is, the future value of every payment obtained before time 4 is calculated as of time 4, and the present value of every payment obtained after time 4, is also calculated as of time 4. This generates the following expression for the value of the cash flow from the bond at time 4.

```
> sum(13.52*(1+r)^(i),i=-1..3)+100*(1+r)^(-1);
```

$$27.04000000 + \frac{13.52000000}{1. + r} + 13.52000000\, r + 13.52000000\, (1. + r)^2 + 13.52000000\, (1. + r)^3 + \frac{100}{1 + r}. \quad (39)$$

Then you calculate the value of the cash flow as of time 4 for different scenarios of interest rates. Specifically, the value of the cash flow is calculated for values of r of $0.05, 0.06, \ldots, 0.15$. This is done by defining the above expression as a function of r and substituting the different values of r in the function:

```
> ValueAt4:=unapply(%,r);
```

$$\text{ValueAt4} := r \to 27.04000000 + \frac{13.52000000}{1. + r} + 13.52000000\, r + 13.52000000\, (1. + r)^2 + 13.52000000\, (1. + r)^3 + \frac{100}{1 + r}. \quad (40)$$

```
> seq(ValueAt4(r/100),r=5..15);
```

166.3871757, 166.2391479, 166.1214873, 166.0337454,
165.9754931, 165.9463200, 165.9458334, 165.9736574,
166.0294324, 166.1128142, 166.2234735. (41)

Observing the sequence of values, you see that you will be able to meet the liability in all these scenarios. In fact, the minimal value of the bond at time 4 across these scenarios is the value of the liability, so even in the worst case the liability will be met. To be fully convinced, the function **ValueAt4** is graphed and indeed it is verified that the minimal value of the bond is the value of the liability.

```
> plot(ValueAt4(r),r=0.05..0.15);
```

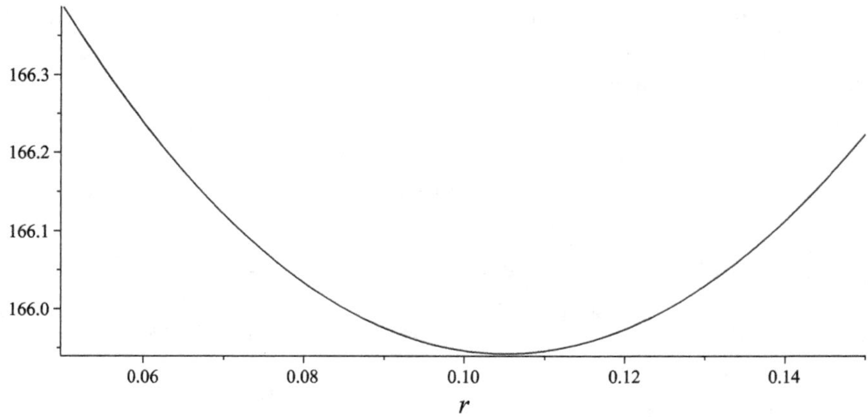

You are puzzled by the result and since duration is a measure of interest rate risks, you try to calculate the duration of this bond. Taking advantage of the function Dur$A$ defined above, you calculate the bond's duration

```
> DurA(0.1352,0.11,5);
```

$$3.990816117 \tag{42}$$

and realize that it is approximately 4. The liability in the above case has a duration of 4 (as it is a cash flow like that of a zero-coupon bond) which equals the duration of the bond's cash inflow (the asset). Hence, both the asset and the liability have the same sensitivity to changes in interest rates. However, the cash flow from the bond is positive (cash inflow) and the cash flow (cash outflow) from the liability is negative. Thus, a change in interest rates affects the asset and liability values in opposing ways so that they offset each other. Consequently, the liability is always met. Hence, the general conclusion from this case is that eliminating interest rate risks requires the duration of liabilities to equal the duration of assets. Immunization is not a static strategy. As time passes bonds mature, coupons are being paid and the term structure changes. Hence, the duration of the liabilities and the assets change. Consequently, immunization requires periodically reshuffling the portfolio in order to readjust durations to be equal to that of liabilities.

Chapter 5

Portfolio Choice Under Uncertainty: The Mean–Variance Framework

Introduction

The development of intuition and a deep understanding of risk is as important as being able to analyze situations in a rigorous manner. The rate of return of a risky security, e.g., a stock, is a random variable and it is customary to use its variance as the security's risk measure. This practice does suffer from caveats on which we will elaborate later. A portfolio's rate of return is therefore a linear combination of random variables.

In order to facilitate development of our model and clarify concepts, a model of a market in which the risk is captured by a simplistic assumption is presented. Consider a market consisting of two risky securities and one risk-free security over a period of time, where the securities' prices at the beginning of the time are given. The prices of the risky securities at the end of the period are not known. It is assumed that at the end of the period the market can be in one of three states and that the prices of the risky securities are a function of this state. The securities' prices at the beginning of the period are specified in the first column, column 0, followed by the prices in each possible states of nature, 1, 2, and 3, at the end of the period.

A Simple Market				
0	1	2	3	Security
\$60	\$80	\$60	\$50	S1
\$105	\$90	\$110	\$120	S2
\$100	\$110	\$110	\$110	SF (Bond)

Note that for now we have not specified the probability of each of the three states. Rather, we want to examine a property of this market and its reflection when the risk is measured by the variance of the securities.

Consider a portfolio composed of short positions of 20 units in security 1 and security 2 and a long position of 33 units in security 3. Recall that a short position is a symmetric image of a long position and that the cash flow from a short position is the negative of the cash flow from a long position. In a short position, the investor borrows the stock from the broker, sells it in the market and when the position is closed, purchases the stock in the market to return it to the broker. Hence, a short position of 20 units in security 1 will produce a cash inflow of $60 \cdot 20$ at the beginning of the period and a cash outflow (denoted with a negative sign) of $20 \cdot 80$, $20 \cdot 60$, and $20 \cdot 50$ at the end of the period in states 1, 2, and 3, respectively. This is a simplistic view of a short position that omits some details of realistic markets, but it suffices for us.

The cash inflow (outflow if it is negative) at the beginning of the period is therefore

$$+20 \cdot 60 + 20 \cdot 105 - 33 \cdot 100 = 0$$

```
> +20*60+20*105-33*100;
```

$$0. \tag{1}$$

On the other hand, the value of this portfolio at the end of the period is 230 in each of the possible states as stipulated in the following:

$$-20 \cdot 80 - 20 \cdot 90 + 33 \cdot 110 = 230$$

```
> -20*80-20*90+33*110;
```

$$230 \tag{2}$$

$$-20 \cdot 60 - 20 \cdot 110 + 33 \cdot 110 = 230$$

```
> -20*60-20*110+33*110;
```

$$230 \tag{3}$$

$$-20 \cdot 50 - 20 \cdot 120 + 33 \cdot 110 = 230$$

```
> -20*50-20*120+33*110;
```

$$230. \tag{4}$$

Obviously there is something wrong here as an arbitrage portfolio exists in this market. It is not conceivable that in financial markets one can purchase a portfolio that requires no use of out-of-pocket money and yet produces a positive cash flow in the next time period. Our aim is not to investigate how this portfolio was found, but rather the demonstration of the reflection of this phenomenon when risk is measured by the variance. To this end, we will assume that each of the states is equally likely and instead of looking at the payoff of each of the securities, we transfer our analysis to deal with the rate of return on each of the securities.

Risk and Return in an Uncertain Environment: A First Look

Since the following analysis will be conducted mostly in terms of rate returns as opposed to payoffs, let us convert the data of the simple market as follows, to be presented in a return form.

A Simple Market				
0	1	2	3	Security
\$60	\$80	\$60	\$50	S1
\$105	\$90	\$110	\$120	S2
\$100	\$110	\$110	\$110	SF (Bond)

The rate of return on security 1 varies depending on the state of the market at the end of the period. In states 1, 2, and 3, it will be

$$\frac{80-60}{60} = \frac{4}{3} - 1, \quad \frac{60-60}{60} = 1 - 1 = 0,$$
$$\frac{50-60}{60} = \frac{5}{6} - 1 = -\frac{1}{6}, \text{ respectively.}$$

We can define an array for each security that will hold the value of the security in each state, e,g., for security 1 that array will be named RSs1 and is defined as follows:

```
> Rs1:=[80,60,50];
```

$$\text{Rs1} := [80, 60, 50]. \tag{5}$$

The rate of return in each state can be calculated in one step by applying to each element the function $\frac{x}{60} - 1$ as demonstrated in the following:

```
   Note the syntax of the map command to operate on each
element of an array, list, vector or a matrix.
```

```
> Rs1:=map(x->x/60-1,Rs1);
```

$$\text{Rs1} := \left[\frac{1}{3}, 0, -\frac{1}{6}\right]. \tag{6}$$

We can do the same for each security and combine the above two steps as demonstrated in the following, where Rs2 is the array of the rate of return on security 2 and Rs1 is the array of the rate of return on security 1.

```
> Rs2:=map(x->x/105-1,[90,110,120]);
```

$$\text{Rs2} := \left[-\frac{1}{7}, \frac{1}{21}, \frac{1}{7}\right]. \tag{7}$$

Note that since the bond is not risky, **its rate of return is the same for each state of the market** at the end of the period.

```
> Rs3:=map(x->x/100-1,[110,110,110]);
```

$$\text{Rs3} := \left[\frac{1}{10}, \frac{1}{10}, \frac{1}{10}\right]. \tag{8}$$

Can we have a combination of assets 1 and 2 that will create a risk-free portfolio? Since we converted the data to returns, we have also normalized the portfolio composition problem. Rather than having the variables denoting the dollar amount to be invested in each asset, the variables now denote the fraction of the portfolio which is invested in each asset. Alternatively, one can interpret it as the absolute dollar amount invested in each asset where the total portfolio is \$1.

Consider a portfolio of a combination of assets 1 and 2 where α is the percentage invested in asset 1, hence $1 - \alpha$ is the percentage invested in asset 2. The rate of return of such a portfolio will be the weighted average of the rate of return on the securities in the portfolio for each state at the end of the period. We define in the following an array that holds the rate of return of the portfolio in each state at the end of the period. Of course, it is a function of alpha.

```
> Rs1cRs2:=map(x->alpha*x,Rs1)+map(x->(1-alpha)*x, Rs2);
```

$$\text{Rs1cRs2} := \left[-\frac{1}{7}+\frac{10\,\alpha}{21}, \frac{1}{21}-\frac{\alpha}{21}, \frac{1}{7}-\frac{13\,\alpha}{42}\right]. \tag{9}$$

The first element of the array- the rate of return in state 1 is

```
> Rs1cRs2[1];
```

$$-\frac{1}{7}+\frac{10\,\alpha}{21}. \tag{10}$$

Let us solve for α for which the rate of return on the portfolio **is the same in each of the possible states**, i.e., an α that **makes the portfolio risk free**.

```
> solve({Rs1cRs2[1]=Rs1cRs2[2],Rs1cRs2[2]=Rs1cRs2[3]});
```

$$\left\{\alpha=\frac{4}{11}\right\} \tag{11}$$

substituting $\alpha = \frac{4}{11}$ in the array will display the rate of return of the portfolio in each state for this value of alpha

```
> subs(alpha = 4/11,Rs1cRs2);
```

$$\left[\frac{1}{33}, \frac{1}{33}, \frac{1}{33}\right]. \tag{12}$$

The above portfolio, composed of a combination of Rs1 Rs2 as outlined, produces a risk-free rate of return of $\frac{1}{33}$, while the bond offers a risk-free rate return of $\frac{1}{10}$. We already saw in Chapters 1–4 that the existence of two different risk-free rates produces arbitrage opportunities and thus they cannot coexist in the market. Can you the reader form such an arbitrage portfolio?

Note that α stands for the percentage of the value of the portfolio that is invested in security 1. Hence, if for example $\alpha = -2$, it means that a short position in asset 1 was taking place. The absolute dollar amount was exactly twice the investment dedicated to the portfolio. Thus, if the investor had \$100 to be invested, it means that \$200 worth of asset 1 was in a short position. In that case, $1 - \alpha = 3$ which means that indeed \$100 of the investor's money (equity) is invested in this portfolio, but the investor is financing an additional

\$200 to invest in another asset by shorting asset 1. Essentially the investor took a loan at a risky rate, the rate of return of security 1, in order to facilitate an investment of \$300 in another asset. The investor could have chosen to invest −2 in the bond, in the risk-free rate. Shorting the risk-free rate is equivalent to taking a loan at the risk-free rate, while shorting a risky security can be interpreted as a risky loan.

In order to demonstrate how the existence of arbitrage is being reflected in a mean–variance framework, the possible states at the end of the period are assumed to be equally likely. In the mean–variance framework, the mean is the expected value of the rate of return and the variance, or its square root (the standard deviation), measures the risk. A risk-free security is characterized by a variance, or standard deviation, of zero. The higher the standard deviation the higher the risk, and common sense implies that the higher the risk the higher the expected value. The investor must be compensated for taking the risk and the compensation is in terms of higher expected rates of return. Consequently, there is a trade off between the expected value and the standard deviation. This tradeoff will be quantified as we proceed, but for now let us refresh the definitions of expected values and variances in a simplistic environment and introduce the mean–variance framework.

Expected Value, Variance, and the Mean–Variance Framework

Let us refresh the definitions of expected value and variance for the case of a discrete random variable, where Y denotes a random variable with possible realizations of y_i $i = 1, \ldots, n$. The expected value, denoted by E, is calculated as

$$E(Y) = \sum_{i=1}^{n} y_i \, Pr_i \tag{13}$$

where Pr_i is the probability of y_i. The expected rate of return is therefore a weighted average of the possible rates of return. To simplify the matter, let us assume that the states at the end of period are equally likely, that is $Pr_i = \frac{1}{3}$, for $i = 1, 2, 3$. Thus the expected rate of return of security 1, Es1, is calculated as follows:

```
> Es1:=sum(Rs1[i]*1/3,i=1..3);
```

$$\text{Es1} := \frac{1}{18}. \tag{14}$$

Similarly the expected value of security 2 and 3 can be calculated as follows:

```
> Es2:=sum(Rs2[i]*1/3,i=1..3);
```

$$\text{Es2} := \frac{1}{63} \tag{15}$$

```
> Es3:=sum(Rs3[i]*1/3,i=1..3);
```

$$\text{Es3} := \frac{1}{10}. \tag{16}$$

Three useful properties of the expected value are easy to verify:

(i) The expected value of a deterministic constant c satisfies $E(c) = c$, (interpret c as a random variable that takes the value c with probability 1 and utilize (1)), as demonstrated in the case of the bond.

(ii) The expected value of a random variable that is generated by multiplying another random variable by a constant, for example $c \cdot Y$ when c is constant, satisfies $E(cY) = cE(Y)$, since for example for $c = \frac{1}{2}$

$$E\left(\frac{Y}{2}\right) = \sum_{i=1}^{n} \frac{y_i}{2} Pr_i = 2\sum_{i=1}^{n} \frac{y_i}{2} Pr_i = \frac{1}{2}\, E(Y). \tag{17}$$

Consider the rate of return of security 1 multiplied say by 1/2

```
> Rs1;Rs1/2;
```

$$\left[\frac{1}{3}, 0, -\frac{1}{6}\right]$$

$$\left[\frac{1}{6}, 0, -\frac{1}{12}\right]. \tag{18}$$

Its expected value is

```
> sum((1/2)*Rs2[i]*1/3,i=1..3);Es2/2
```

$$\frac{1}{126}$$

$$\frac{1}{126} \tag{19}$$

which indeed is $\frac{1}{2}$Es2, and

(iii) The expected value of a linear combination of random variables is the same combination of their expected value, that is

$$E(aY + bV) = aE(Y) + bE(V) \tag{20}$$

as demonstrated by the linear combination of security 1 and 2:

```
> (4/11)*Es1+(1-4/11)*Es2;
```

$$\frac{1}{33} \tag{21}$$

```
> subs(alpha = 4/11,Rs1cRs2);
```

$$\left[\frac{1}{33}, \frac{1}{33}, \frac{1}{33}\right] \tag{22}$$

```
> sum(%[i]/3,i=1..3);
```

$$\frac{1}{33}. \tag{23}$$

The Variance of Y is defined by

$$\text{Var}(Y) = E((Y - E(Y))^2). \tag{24}$$

In words, the variance is the weighted average (by the probabilities) of the squared deviations of the possible realizations from the expected value. Hence, the variances of securities 1, 2 and 3 (Vs1, Vs2 and Vs3) are calculated as follows:

```
> Vs1:=sum((Rs1[i]-Es1)^2,i=1..3)/3;
```

$$\text{Vs1} := \frac{7}{162} \tag{25}$$

```
> Vs2:=sum((Rs2[i]-Es2)^2,i=1..3)/3;
```

$$\mathrm{Vs2} := \frac{8}{567} \tag{26}$$

```
> Vs3:=sum((Rs3[i]-Es3)^2,i=1..3)/3;
```

$$\mathrm{Vs3} := 0. \tag{27}$$

It is easy to show that, as demonstrated by the variance of security 3

$$\mathrm{Var}(c) = 0 \tag{28}$$

which means a risk-free security has a variance of zero.

The variance is a measure of dispersion. It measures the variability of the possible realization around the mean. We adopted it here as a measure of risk, but under what conditions is this a sensible measure? What are the parameters of the distribution? We shall come back to some of these questions later. Meanwhile, let us assume that the measure of the risk is the standard deviation, the square root of the variance, σ, and that together with μ (the expected value of the rate of return), characterize the random rate of return of the security. Obviously, if the rate of return is assumed to follow the Normal distribution, the density function of the rate of return is identified by these two parameters (μ and σ).

Let us generate the array SDEX $= [[\sigma_1, \mu_1], [\sigma_2, \mu_2], [\sigma_3, \mu_3]]$ where σ_i and μ_i, $i = 1, \ldots, 3$, are the standard deviations and the expected values of the rate of return of security i, respectively.

```
> SDEX:=[[sqrt(Vs1),Es1],[sqrt(Vs2),Es2],
  [sqrt(Vs3),Es3]];
```

(29)

$$\mathrm{SDEX} := \left[\left[\frac{\sqrt{14}}{18}, \frac{1}{18}\right], \left[\frac{2\sqrt{14}}{63}, \frac{1}{63}\right], \left[0, \frac{1}{10}\right]\right]. \tag{30}$$

We now plot the points (σ_i, μ_i) $i = 1, \ldots, 3$ in the (σ, μ) plane, where σ is the x-axis and μ the y-axis.

```
> plot(SDEX,x=0..0.3,y=0..0.11,style=point,symbol=
  solidcircle,thickness=1,labelfont=[SYMBOL],
  labels=[s,m]);
```

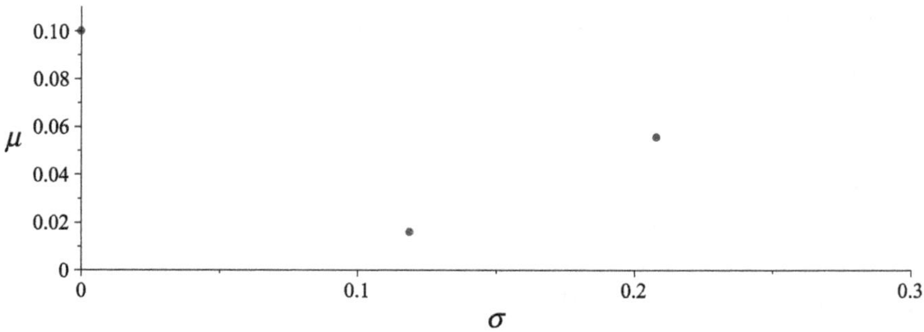

Each of the solid squares above corresponds to a security. In our model, a security or a portfolio is represented by the two characteristics, its expected rate of return and its standard deviation. Hence, each portfolio in this model is represented by a coordinate of a point in the two dimensional space (σ, μ). Two portfolios with different compositions, having the same value of μ and σ, are equivalent portfolios in this model.

There is however something that does not look right in the above graph. If the risk is measured by the variance (standard deviation), why do we have a non-risky portfolio with an expected rate of return which is larger than the two risky portfolios? Why would an investor hold a risky asset if it cannot offer a higher rate of return than that of the risk-free asset? Furthermore, as we saw, in this example a combination of the two risky securities generates a risk-free portfolio with a rate of return that is lower than the (primary) risk-free rate. Indeed this phenomenon is the reflection of the existence of arbitrage opportunities.

In competitive markets, investors holding a risky asset must be compensated for the risk they bear, otherwise they would have no incentive to prefer it to the risk-free rate. This compensation is in the form of a higher expected rate of return. Risky assets and a risk-free asset can coexist in the market only if it is possible to have risky assets with a rate of return higher than that of the risk-free asset. In other words, there is a trade off between risk and rate of return.

The Feasible Set with Two Assets: A Specific Case

Portfolios are combinations of securities that exist in the market. Thus, the investigation of portfolios in the mean–variance framework requires the calculations of the expected value and the standard deviation of combinations of securities. It is customary to investigate portfolios in this setting by considering the portfolio's percentage invested in each security. Hence, a portfolio of N securities is represented by the array $(x_1, x_2, \ldots, x_N)$ where x_i is the percentage invested in security i and $\sum_{i=1}^{N} x_i = 1$. As before, negative x_i stands for a short position and positive x_i a long position.

Consider the case of a combination of the two risky securities Rs1 and Rs2, i.e., $x_1\,\mathrm{Rs1} + x_2\,\mathrm{Rs2}$ where $N = 2$ and $x_1 + x_2 = 1$. The portfolio's expected value, by (2) and (3) satisfies

$$\begin{aligned} E(x_1\,\mathrm{Rs1} + x_2\,\mathrm{Rs2}) &= x_1\,E(\mathrm{Rs1}) + x_2\,E(\mathrm{Rs2}) \\ &= x_1\,E(\mathrm{Rs1}) + (1 - x_1)E(\mathrm{Rs2}). \qquad (31) \end{aligned}$$

The expected value of the portfolio as a function of x_1 (used as x in the following calculation) is

```
> Exp:=x->x*Es1+(1-x)*Es2;
```

$$\mathrm{Exp} := x \mapsto x\mathrm{Es1} + (1 - x)\mathrm{Es2}. \qquad (32)$$

Note: Make sure to execute the assignments that are defined in the file before this point.

Hence, the expected value of a portfolio that is equally invested in both securities is

```
> Exp(1/2);
```

$$\frac{1}{28} \qquad (33)$$

```
> Es1/2+Es2/2;
```

$$\frac{1}{28}. \qquad (34)$$

The portfolio's variance by (4) is

$$\begin{aligned} &\mathrm{Var}(x_1\,\mathrm{Rs1} + x_2\,\mathrm{Rs2}) \\ &\quad = E([(x_1\,\mathrm{Rs1} + x_2\,\mathrm{Rs2}) - E(x_1\,\mathrm{Rs1} + x_2\,\mathrm{Rs2})]^2) \\ &\mathrm{Var}(x_1\,\mathrm{Rs1} + (1 - x_1)\mathrm{Rs2}) \\ &\quad = E([(x_1\,\mathrm{Rs1} + (1 - x_1)\mathrm{Rs2}) - E(x_1\,\mathrm{Rs1} + (1 - x_1)\mathrm{Rs2})]^2) \end{aligned}$$

The value of $E(x_1\,\mathrm{Rs1} + (1 - x_1)\mathrm{Rs2})$ by (6) is $x_1\,E(\mathrm{Rs1}) + (1 - x_1)E(\mathrm{Rs2})$ which equals

```
> x*Es1+(1-x)*Es2;
```

$$\frac{5\,x}{126}+\frac{1}{63} \tag{35}$$

can be calculated by the function *Exp* as

```
> Exp(x);
```

$$\frac{5\,x}{126}+\frac{1}{63}. \tag{36}$$

The value of $(x_1\,\text{Rs1}+(1-x_1)\text{Rs2})$ depends on the state of the market, so it can be represented, as before, by an array with three components. Since Rs1 and Rs2 are as follows

```
> Rs1;
```

$$\left[\frac{1}{3},0,-\frac{1}{6}\right] \tag{37}$$

```
> Rs2;
```

$$\left[-\frac{1}{7},\frac{1}{21},\frac{1}{7}\right] \tag{38}$$

the first component of $(x_1\,\text{Rs1}+(1-x_1)\text{Rs2})$ is

```
> x*Rs1[1]+(1-x)*Rs2[1];
```

$$\frac{10\,x}{21}-\frac{1}{7} \tag{39}$$

and thus the array is

```
> [x*Rs1[1]+(1-x)*Rs2[1],x*Rs1[2]+(1-x)*Rs2[2],x*Rs1[3]
  +(1-x)*Rs2[3]];
```

$$\left[\frac{10\,x}{21}-\frac{1}{7},\frac{1}{21}-\frac{x}{21},-\frac{13\,x}{42}+\frac{1}{7}\right] \tag{40}$$

```
> #map(y->y*x,Rs1)+map(y->(1-x)*y,Rs2);# or in a
  compact way
```

$$\left[\frac{10\,x}{21}-\frac{1}{7},\frac{1}{21}-\frac{x}{21},-\frac{13\,x}{42}+\frac{1}{7}\right]. \tag{41}$$

The squared deviation, in terms of x, of the value in state one from the expected value is $\left(\frac{10\,x}{21}-\frac{1}{7}-\left(\frac{5\,x}{126}+\frac{1}{63}\right)\right)^2$. Thus the variance, the weighted average by the probabilities, of the squared deviations, across the three states of the market, is

```
> sum((1/3)*(%[i]-Exp(x))^2,i=1..3);
```

$$\frac{\left(\frac{55\,x}{126}-\frac{10}{63}\right)^2}{3}+\frac{\left(\frac{2}{63}-\frac{11\,x}{126}\right)^2}{3}+\frac{\left(-\frac{22\,x}{63}+\frac{8}{63}\right)^2}{3}. \tag{42}$$

The standard deviation, as a function of x will be

```
> sd:=x->sqrt((1/3)*(55*x*(1/126)-10/63)^2+(1/3)*
  (2/63-11*x*(1/126))^2+(1/3)*(-22*x*(1/63)+8/63)^2);
```

$$\mathrm{sd} := x \mapsto \sqrt{\frac{\left(\frac{55\,x}{126}-\frac{10}{63}\right)^2}{3}+\frac{\left(\frac{2}{63}-\frac{11\,x}{126}\right)^2}{3}+\frac{\left(-\frac{22\,x}{63}+\frac{8}{63}\right)^2}{3}}. \tag{43}$$

Thus, the coordinate (sd(1), Exp(1))

```
> sd(1),Exp(1);
```

$$\frac{\sqrt{14}}{18}, \frac{1}{18} \tag{44}$$

corresponds to Rs1 and (sd(0), Exp(0)) to Rs2

```
> sd(0),Exp(0);
```

$$\frac{2\sqrt{14}}{63}, \frac{1}{63}. \tag{45}$$

Varying the proportion invested in asset 1 from 0 to 1, while at the same time the proportion in asset 2 varies from 1 to 0, generates the different feasible portfolios without using short positions. When the proportion invested in asset 1 is negative, portfolios requiring short positions in asset 1 are also considered. When the proportion invested in asset 1 is larger than 1, portfolios requiring short positions in asset 2 are also considered. For example, the portfolios generated by the proportions of 1, 3/4, 2/4, 1/4, 0, that are invested in asset 1, are represented by the coordinates in the following array. E.g., the first element of the array is the coordinate of the first security (σ_1, μ_1), the second (σ_2, μ_2) of a portfolio generated by investing $3/4$ in security 1 and $1/4$ in security 2, etc. Since none of the proportions invested in asset 1 is negative or larger than one, no short position was used.

```
> [[sd(0),Exp(0)],[sd(3/4),Exp(3/4)],[sd(2/3),Exp(2/3)],
  [sd(1/3),Exp(1/3)],[sd(1),Exp(1)]];
```

$$\left[\left[\frac{2\sqrt{14}}{63}, \frac{1}{63}\right], \left[\frac{17\sqrt{14}}{504}, \frac{23}{504}\right], \left[\frac{5\sqrt{14}}{189}, \frac{8}{189}\right], \left[\frac{\sqrt{14}}{378}, \frac{11}{378}\right], \left[\frac{\sqrt{14}}{18}, \frac{1}{18}\right]\right] \tag{46}$$

```
> [seq([sd(i/4),Exp(i/3)],i=0..4)]; # A short
  way of generating the above
```

$$\left[\left[\frac{2\sqrt{14}}{63}, \frac{1}{63}\right], \left[\frac{5\sqrt{14}}{504}, \frac{11}{378}\right], \left[\frac{\sqrt{14}}{84}, \frac{8}{189}\right], \left[\frac{17\sqrt{14}}{504}, \frac{1}{18}\right], \left[\frac{\sqrt{14}}{18}, \frac{13}{189}\right]\right] \tag{47}$$

We now plot, as before, the points (σ_i, μ_i) $i = 0, \ldots, 4$ in the (σ, μ) plane, where σ is the x-axis and μ the y-axis.

```
> plot([seq([sd(i/4),Exp(i/4)],i=0..4)],x=0..0.3,
  style=point,symbol=solidcircle,thickness=1,
  labelfont=[SYMBOL],labels=[s,m]);
```

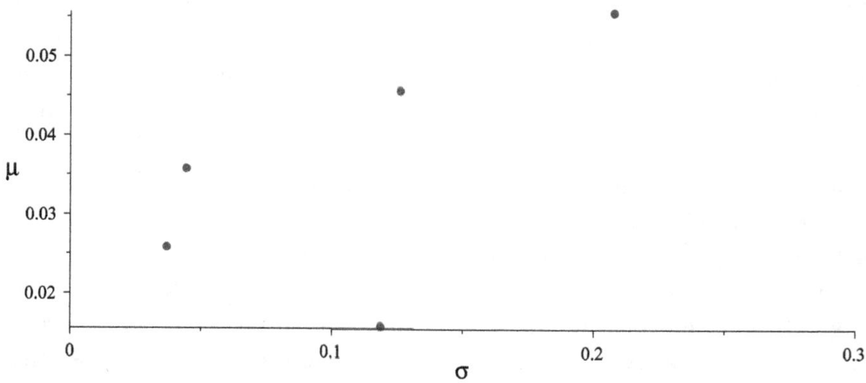


```
> CorRs1Rs2:=plot([seq([sd(i/4),Exp(i/4)],i=0..4)],
  style=point,symbol=solidcircle,thickness=1,
  labelfont=[SYMBOL],labels=[s,m]):# Keep the
  graph in the object CorRs1Rs2
```

One can think about these possible combinations as a path that connects (sd(0), Exp(0) to (sd(1), Exp(1)). Varying x from 0 to 1 generates the path that connects the two portfolios as demonstrated in the following figure.

```
> plot([sd(x),Exp(x),x=0..1],thickness=4,labels=[s,m],
  labelfont=[SYMBOL],thickness=3);
```

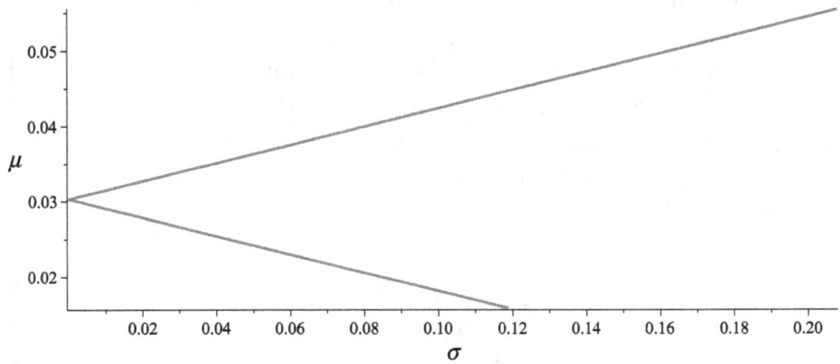


```
> PathRs1Rs2:=plot([sd(x),Exp(x),x=0..1],thickness=4,
  labels=[s,m],labelfont=[SYMBOL],thickness=3): # Keep
  the graph in the object PathRs1Rs2

> plots[display](PathRs1Rs2,CorRs1Rs2);# imposing
  one graph on the other
```

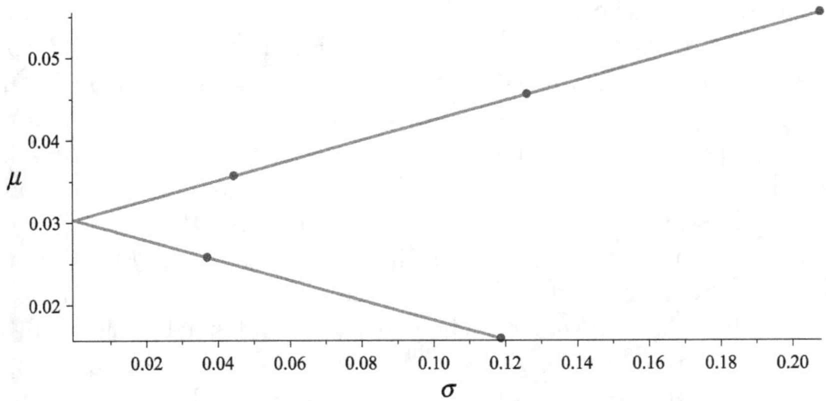

The two end points of the piecewise linear graphs correspond to the portfolios of only Rs1 and only Rs2, where Rs1 is the upper end point since Es1 = 1/18 is greater than Es2 = 1/63 as confirmed in the following:

```
> Es1,Es2;
```

$$\frac{1}{18}, \frac{1}{63}. \tag{48}$$

As anticipated, there is a portfolio that is composed of combination of the two risky securities Rs1 and Rs2 that generate a risk-free asset. This is reflected in the graph by the fact that there is a point with a coordinate of $\sigma = 0$ on the path from Rs1 to Rs2, i.e., the graph touches the μ axis. To find the μ coordinate of this point, the portfolio that corresponds to this point must be identified. This is done by solving for the portfolio that has a standard deviation, a variance, of 0. Hence, the following equation must be solved.

```
> solve(sd(x)=0);
```

$$\frac{4}{11}. \tag{49}$$

Note the that the solution provided is the combination solved for before.

Therefore, the portfolio is (4/11, 7/11) and its expected value, the μ coordinate of the point with a coordinate of $\sigma = 0$, is thus

```
> Exp(4/11);
```

$$\frac{1}{33}. \tag{50}$$

The segment of the piecewise linear line that connects Rs1 to the risk-free asset, is the lower part of the piecewise linear line. It corresponds to portfolios in which the proportion invested in Rs1 is in the range $0, \ldots, 4/11$. This segment is not efficient, as every portfolio on the lower part of the piecewise linear line has a portfolio that dominates it. For every portfolio in this segment with a certain risk level (standard deviation), a portfolio with a higher expected rate of return exists. The dominating portfolios are those in which the proportion invested in Rs1 is in the range $4/11, \ldots, 1$, which is termed the *efficient frontier*. The concept of efficient frontier will be revisited in a general environment. Given the above explanations, the feasible sets can be plotted in two parts imposed on one another: the non-efficient part — the thicker line in the following figure, and the efficient part — the thinner line in the following figure.

```
> plot([sd(x),Exp(x),x=4/11..1],thickness=1,labels=[s,m],
  labelfont=[SYMBOL],thickness=3):PathRs1Rs2:=
  plot([sd(x),Exp(x),x=0..4/11],thickness=4,labels=
  [s,m],labelfont=[SYMBOL],thickness=6):plots
  [display](%,%%);
```

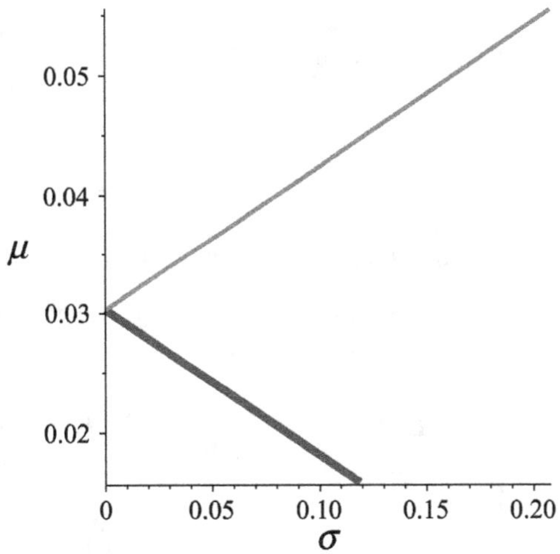

The Feasible Set with Two Assets: The Generic Case

In order to investigate the generic case of the feasible set with two assets, there is a need to review properties of the variance–standard deviation and the covariance.

A helpful property of the variance is related to a random variable that is generated by multiplying another random variable by a constant, for example, $c \cdot Y$ for a constant c. It is easy to verify that

$$\begin{aligned} \mathrm{Var}(cY) &= E((cY - E(cY))^2) = E((cY - cE(Y))^2) \\ &= c^2 E((Y - E(Y))^2) = c^2 \mathrm{Var}(Y). \end{aligned} \tag{51}$$

***Note*: Make sure to execute the assignments that are defined in the file before this point.**

Hence, for example, the variance of 2 Rs1 is

```
> sum((2*Rs2[i]-2*Es2)^2,i=1..3)/3;
```

$$\frac{32}{567} \tag{52}$$

which equals

```
> (2^2)*Vs2;
```

$$\frac{32}{567}. \tag{53}$$

The standard deviation of Y, denoted by σ_Y, is $\sqrt{\mathrm{Var}(Y)}$ and from (5) it follows that

$$\sigma_{cY} = c\sigma_Y. \tag{54}$$

A Useful Variance Property

Using algebraic operations and the expected value properties, it is easy to show that

$$\begin{aligned}\mathrm{Var}(Y) &= E((Y - E(Y))^2) = E(Y^2 - 2YE(Y) + E(Y)^2) \\ &= E(Y^2) - E(Y)^2.\end{aligned}$$

Consider the random variable $(\mathrm{Rs2})^2$, denoted by Rs22 that is

```
> Rs22:=map(x->x^2,Rs2);
```

$$\mathrm{Rs22} := \left[\frac{1}{49}, \frac{1}{441}, \frac{1}{49}\right] \tag{55}$$

its expected value is

```
> Es22:=sum(Rs22[i],i=1..3)/3;
```

$$\mathrm{Es22} := \frac{19}{1323}. \tag{56}$$

Thus $E(Y^2) - E(Y)^2$ when Y is Rs2 equals

```
> Es22-Es2^2;
```

$$\frac{8}{567} \tag{57}$$

```
> Vs2;
```

$$\frac{8}{567}. \tag{58}$$

The portfolio's variance, by definition, is

$$\mathrm{Var}(x_1\,\mathrm{Rs1} + x_2\,\mathrm{Rs2})$$
$$= E([(x_1\,\mathrm{Rs1} + x_2\,\mathrm{Rs2}) - E(x_1\,\mathrm{Rs1} + x_2\,\mathrm{Rs2})]^2)$$

since $E(x_1\,\mathrm{Rs1} + x_2\,\mathrm{Rs2}) = E(x_1\mathrm{Rs1}) + E(x_2\mathrm{Rs2}) = x_1 E(\mathrm{Rs1}) + x_2\,E(\mathrm{Rs2})$

$$\mathrm{Var}(x_1\,\mathrm{Rs1} + x_2\,\mathrm{Rs2})$$
$$= E([(x_1\,\mathrm{Rs1} - E(x_2\,\mathrm{Rs2})) + (x_2\,\mathrm{Rs1} - E(x_2\,\mathrm{Rs2}))]^2). \tag{59}$$

Thinking about $(x_1\mathrm{Rs} - E(x_2\,\mathrm{Rs2}))$ as a, about $(x_2\,\mathrm{Rs2} - E(x_2\,\mathrm{Rs2}))$ as b and applying the formula for $(a+b)^2$ together with the expected value properties result in

$$\mathrm{Var}(x_1\,\mathrm{Rs1} + x_2\,\mathrm{Rs2}) = x_1^2\mathrm{Var}(\mathrm{Rs1}) + x_2^2\mathrm{Var}(\mathrm{Rs2}) + 2x_1x_2E((\mathrm{Rs1} - E(\mathrm{Rs1}) \cdot (\mathrm{Rs2} - E(\mathrm{Rs2})). \tag{60}$$

A consequence of Eq. (8) is that $\mathrm{Var}(x_1\,\mathrm{Rs1}) = x_1^2\mathrm{Var}(\mathrm{Rs1})$ and that the standard deviation of $\mathrm{Var}(x_1\,\mathrm{Rs1})$ is $+\sqrt{x_1^2} \cdot \sqrt{\mathrm{Var}(\mathrm{Rs1})}$.

The expression $E((\mathrm{Rs1} - E(\mathrm{Rs1}) \cdot (\mathrm{Rs2} - E(\mathrm{Rs2}))$ is the covariance between the two random variables Rs1 and Rs2, denoted by $\mathrm{Cov}(\mathrm{Rs1}, \mathrm{Rs2})$ or by $\sigma_{\mathrm{Rs1},\mathrm{Rs2}}$. It is apparent from the definition that the covariance is symmetric in Rs1 and Rs2, i.e.,

$$\mathrm{Cov}(\mathrm{Rs1}, \mathrm{Rs2}) = \mathrm{Cov}(\mathrm{Rs2}, \mathrm{Rs1}).$$

Covariance, as the name implies, is related to the co-movements of two random variables and indeed is defined almost like a variance.

The variance of Rs1 is defined as $E((\mathrm{Rs1} - E(\mathrm{Rs1}) \cdot (\mathrm{Rs1} - E(\mathrm{Rs1}))$. Replacing Rs1 in one of the terms of the product with Rs2 yields the definition of covariance. If on average when $\mathrm{Rs1} > E(\mathrm{Rs1})$ also $\mathrm{Rs2} > E(\mathrm{Rs2})$, or when $\mathrm{Rs1} < E(\mathrm{Rs1})$ also $\mathrm{Rs2} < E(\mathrm{Rs2})$, the covariance is positive, otherwise it is negative. Hence, a positive covariance means that if when one variable on average is above (below) its expected value so is the other, i.e., the variables are moving in tandem. A negative covariance means that the two random variables are moving in opposite directions, i.e., when Rs1 $> E(\text{Rs1})$, Rs2 $< E(\text{Rs2})$ or vice versa.

Let us first look at how the covariance is calculated in this scenario. To this end, we specify the possible values of $\text{Rs1} - E(\text{Rs1})$, and $\text{Rs2} - E(\text{Rs2})$ followed by the the possible realizations of $(\text{Rs1} - E(\text{Rs1})) \cdot (\text{Rs2} - E(\text{Rs2}))$

```
> Rs1_E:=map(x->x-Es1,Rs1);
```

$$\text{Rs1\_}E := \left[\frac{5}{18}, -\frac{1}{18}, -\frac{2}{9}\right] \tag{61}$$

```
> Rs2_E:=map(x->x-Es2,Rs2);
```

$$\text{Rs2\_}E := \left[-\frac{10}{63}, \frac{2}{63}, \frac{8}{63}\right] \tag{62}$$

```
> Rs1_E[1]*Rs2_E[1],Rs1_E[2]*Rs2_E[2],Rs1_E[3]*Rs2_E[3];
```

$$-\frac{25}{567}, -\frac{1}{567}, -\frac{16}{567}. \tag{63}$$

Hence, the covariance will be the weighed average, by the probabilities of the states, of the above sequence. Therefore, it is calculated as

```
> Cov:=sum(Rs1_E[i]*Rs2_E[i]/3,i=1..3);
```

$$\text{Cov} := -\frac{2}{81}. \tag{64}$$

A Useful Covariance Property and Generalization of the Variance Formula for N Securities

Using algebraic operations and expected value properties, it is easy to show that the covariance between Rs1 and Rs2 $E((\text{Rs1} - E(\text{Rs1})(\text{Rs2} - E(\text{Rs2}))$, can be written also as

$$E(\text{Rs1} \cdot \text{Rs2}) - E(\text{Rs1}) \cdot E(\text{Rs2}).$$

As well the covariance between $x * \text{Rs1}$ **and** $(1 - x) * \text{Rs2}$ is given by

$$\text{Cov}(x \cdot \text{Rs1}, (1 - x) \cdot \text{Rs2}) = x \cdot (1 - x) \cdot \text{Cov}(\text{Rs1}, \text{Rs2})$$

In the case of 3 assets, it is easy to show that the variance, $\mathrm{Var}(x_1\,\mathrm{Rs1} + x_2\,\mathrm{Rs2} + x_3\,\mathrm{Rs3})$ equals

$$x_1^2\mathrm{Var}(\mathrm{Rs1}) + x_2^2\mathrm{Var}(\mathrm{Rs2}) + x_3^2\mathrm{Var}(\mathrm{Rs3}) + 2x_1x_2\mathrm{Cov}(\mathrm{Rs1},\mathrm{Rs2})$$
$$+ 2x_1x_3\mathrm{Cov}(\mathrm{Rs1},\mathrm{Rs3}) + 2x_1x_2\mathrm{Cov}(\mathrm{Rs1},\mathrm{Rs2})$$
$$+ 2x_3x_2\mathrm{Cov}(\mathrm{Rs3},\mathrm{Rs2}).$$

Thus, in words, the covariance part is composed of all the different couples out of the 3 securities, and since $\mathrm{Cov}(\mathrm{Rsi},\mathrm{Rsj}) = \mathrm{Cov}(\mathrm{Rsj},\mathrm{Rsi})$ the general expression is $2\,\mathrm{Cov}(\mathrm{Rsi},\mathrm{Rsj})$ for all i and i, $i \neq j$. The generalization to N securities is obvious and can be written in a compact way when the notation σ_{ij} replaces $\mathrm{Cov}(\mathrm{Rsi},\mathrm{Rsj})$ and σ_{ii} replaces $\mathrm{Var}(\mathrm{Rs2})$, as

$$\mathrm{Var}\left(\sum_{i=1}^{N} x_i\,\mathrm{Rsi}\right) = \sum_{j=1}^{N}\left(\sum_{i=1}^{N} x_ix_j\sigma_{ij}\right)$$
$$= \sum_{i=1}^{N} x_i^2\sigma_{ii} + \sum_{j=1}^{N}\left(\sum_{i=1,\ i\neq j}^{N} x_ix_j\sigma_{ij}\right).$$

Consequently, the variance of the portfolio $(x, 1-x)$, as a function x, is

```
> Var:=x->x^2*Vs1+(1-x)^2*Vs2+2*x*(1-x)*Cov;
```
(65)

$$\mathrm{Var} := x \mapsto x^2\mathrm{Vs1} + (1-x)^2\mathrm{Vs2} + 2\,x(1-x)\mathrm{Cov}. \tag{66}$$

Hence, the variance of a portfolio that is equally invested in both securities is

```
> Var(1/2);
```

$$\frac{1}{504}. \tag{67}$$

Note that the function Var calculates the variance using the covariance applying Eq. (60). The function sd, defined above, calculates the variance from its definition applying Eq. (24). Both obviously must generate the same results. For example the variance of a portfolio invested 50% in Rs1 and 50% in Rs2 using the sd function is calculated as

```
> sd(1/2)^2;
```

$$\frac{1}{504} \tag{68}$$

and is confirmed to coincide with the variance calculated by Eq. (60).

As solved for and visualized in the figure earlier, there exists a combination of Rs1 and Rs2 that produces a risk-free asset. The feasibility of combining two risky assets to produce a risk-free asset is quite rare. It requires a combination of the assets that causes the movements of the assets to exactly offset each other, so as to generate an asset producing a constant rate of return. The co-movements of the rate of return of two assets, as explained above, is measured by the covariance. However, the covariance only conveys if the assets are moving in the same or opposite direction, e.g., when one moves up the other moves down, etc. The correlation coefficient, denoted by ρ, also conveys the degree of co-movements. It is defined as

$$\rho_{\mathrm{Rs1,Rs2}} = \frac{\mathrm{Cov(Rs1, Rs2)}}{\sigma_{\mathrm{Rs1}}\sigma_{\mathrm{Rs2}}}. \tag{69}$$

Since for every two assets ρ satisfies

$$-1 \leq \rho \leq 1 \tag{70}$$

then the degree of co-movements is conveyed by ρ. When $\rho = 1$ ($\rho = -1$), a perfect positive (negative) correlation, or more precisely a linear relation exists between the two assets. Thus when $\rho = -1$, the assets are perfectly negatively correlated. Hence, it is possible to combine the two assets, using only long positions to generate a risk-free asset. When $\rho = 1$, it is also possible to generate a risk-free asset, but a short position must be used, since if the two long positions are perfectly positively correlated with one another, a short position in one of the assets is perfectly negatively correlated with the other asset. The value $\rho_{\mathrm{Rs1,Rs2}}$ in our example is indeed confirmed below to be -1

```
> Cov/(sqrt(Vs1)*sqrt(Vs2))
```

$$-1 \tag{71}$$

which explains why it was possible to generate a risk-free portfolio. The shape of the path of feasible portfolios from Rs1 to Rs2 depends on ρ. From (69), it follows that

$$\rho_{\text{Rs1,Rs2}}\,\sigma_{\text{Rs1}}\,\sigma_{\text{Rs2}} = \text{Cov}(\text{Rs1}, \text{Rs2}).$$

Hence utilizing (69), the covariance can be eliminated from the variance expression, Eq. (60), and can be written in terms of $\rho_{\text{Rs1,Rs2}}$ as

$$\begin{aligned}\text{Var}(x_1\,\text{Rs1} + (1 - x_1)\text{Rs2}) &= x_1^2\text{Var}(\text{Rs1}) + (1 - x_1)^2\text{Var}(\text{Rs2}) \\ &\quad + 2x_1(1 - x_1)\rho_{\text{Rs1,Rs2}}\,\sigma_{\text{Rs1}}\,\sigma_{\text{Rs2}}.\end{aligned} \tag{72}$$

Note that when short sales are not used, i.e., when both x_1 and $1 - x_1$ are positive, a consequence of a negative covariance (which is equivalent to a negative rho), is

$$\text{Var}(x_1\,\text{Rs1} + (1 - x_1)\text{Rs2}) < x_1^2\text{Var}(\text{Rs1}) + (1 - x_1)^2\text{Var}(\text{Rs2}).$$

The risk for the case $\rho < 0$ is thus reduced relative to the cases of $\rho = 0$ or $\rho > 0$, which is a result of one asset offsetting the volatility of the other as they move in opposite directions.

The relation between the standard deviation of the portfolio and the standard deviations of the assets in the portfolio, is worth highlighting for three cases. When $\rho = 1$

$$\begin{aligned}\text{Var}(x_1\,\text{Rs1} + (1 - x_1)\text{Rs2}) &= x_1^2\text{Var}(\text{Rs1}) + (1 - x_1)^2\text{Var}(\text{Rs2}) \\ &\quad + 2x_1(1 - x_1)\sigma_{\text{Rs1}}\,\sigma_{\text{Rs2}} \\ &= (x_1\,\sigma_{\text{Rs1}} + (1 - x_1)\sigma_{\text{Rs2}})^2\end{aligned}$$

and thus the standard deviation of the portfolio $x_1\,\text{Rs1} + (1 - x_1)\text{Rs2}$ is

$$x_1\,\sigma_{\text{Rs1}} + (1 - x_1)\sigma_{\text{Rs2}}.$$

Following a similar argument when $\rho = -1$, the standard deviation of the portfolio $x_1\,\text{Rs1} + (1 - x_1)\text{Rs2}$ is

$$x_1\,\sigma_{\text{Rs1}} - (1 - x_1)\sigma_{\text{Rs2}}.$$

Finally, when $\rho = 0$ the standard deviation of the portfolio $x_1\,\mathrm{Rs1} + (1 - x_1)\mathrm{Rs2}$ is simply

$$\sqrt{x_1\,\sigma_{\mathrm{Rs1}}{}^2 + (1 - x_1)\sigma_{\mathrm{Rs2}}{}^2}.$$

Keeping the expected values and variances of the two securities as is, and varying the value of ρ from -1 to 1, it is possible to visualize the possible paths of feasible portfolios that can be generated. This can be done by Maple utilizing animation in which the graph of the feasible portfolios is animated based on the value of ρ. To this end, $\mathrm{Var}(x_1\mathrm{Rs1} + (1 - x_1\mathrm{Rs2})$ should be redefined as in (72), i.e., to be a function of ρ and x as follows:

```
> VarRho:=(x,rho)->x^2*Vs1+(1-x)^2*Vs2+2*x*(1-x)*
  rho*sqrt(Vs1)*sqrt(Vs2);
```

$$\mathrm{VarRho} := (x, \rho) \mapsto x^2\mathrm{Vs1} + (1 - x)^2\mathrm{Vs2} + 2\,x(1 - x)\rho\,\sqrt{\mathrm{Vs1}}\sqrt{\mathrm{Vs2}}. \tag{73}$$

Before the animation, the path for $\rho = -1$ is presented below followed by its imposition on the path $\rho = 1$. Both paths are visualized when short sales are not allowed, i.e., when $0 \leq x \leq 1$. If short sales are allowed, x could take any value.

```
> plot([sqrt(VarRho(x,-1)),Exp(x),x=0..1],labels=[s,m],
  labelfont=[SYMBOL],thickness=3);
```

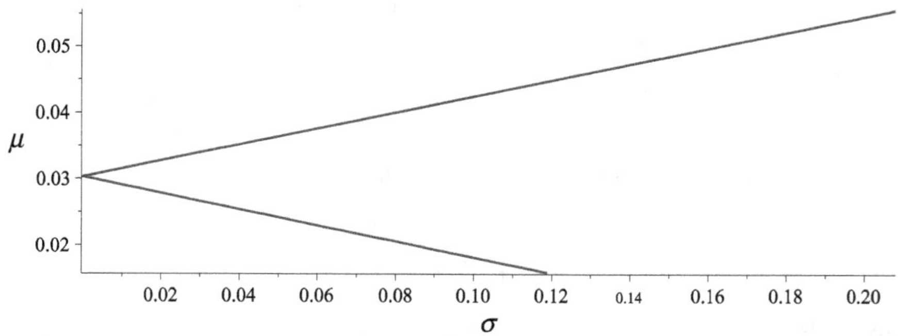


```
> plot([sqrt(VarRho(x,1)),Exp(x),x=0..1],labels=[s,m],
  labelfont=[SYMBOL],thickness=3):plots[display](%,%%);
```

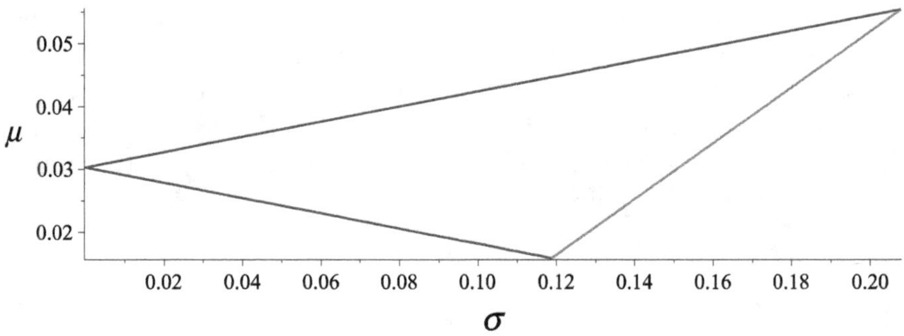

The graph for $\rho = 1$ is a line connecting the coordinates of Rs1 and Rs2. The graph for $\rho = -1$ is piecewise linear, connecting the coordinates of Rs1 and Rs2 passing by a point on the μ axis, i.e., a point representing a risk-free asset. The path for $\rho = 0$, as well as for any $-1 < \rho < 1$, is somewhere between that for $\rho = 1$ and $\rho = -1$ but does not touch the μ axis. Observing the above graphs and the following animation, one can see the animation generates graphs that are bounded by the triangle created from the graphs for $\rho = 1$ and $\rho = -1$.

```
> plots[animate]([sqrt(VarRho(x,rho)),Exp(x),x=0..1],
  rho=-1..1,labels=[s,m],labelfont=[SYMBOL],thickness=3):
  plots[display](%%,%);
```

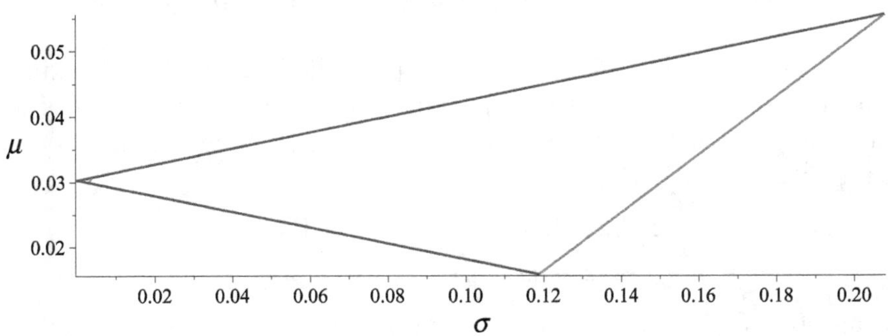

For the case of $\rho = -1$, the minimum variance portfolio is the risk-free portfolio. However, for different values of ρ, the minimum variance portfolio is a risky portfolio. We already mentioned that for $\rho = -1$ the lower part of the feasible set is not efficient. Observing the animation, it is clear that it is a generic property. A portfolio on the part of the path below the minimum variance, is dominated by another feasible portfolio that offers a higher rate of return with the same risk (value of σ). The schematic graph in the following demonstrates this property, e.g., the portfolio corresponding to the lower intersection of the vertical line at $\sigma = 1$ with the path connecting the risky portfolios, the non-solid box, being dominated by the upper intersection, the solid box.

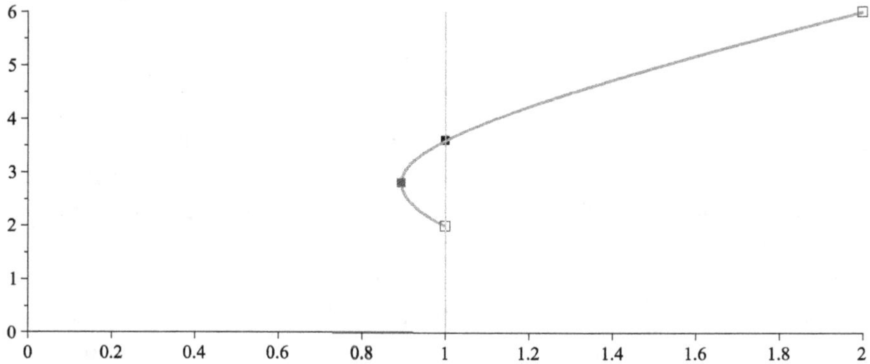

The minimum variance portfolio is identified by minimizing the expression of the variance, (72), with respect to x, i.e.,

$$\begin{aligned}&\text{Min}_x x^2\text{Var(Rs1)} + (1-x)^2\text{Var(Rs2)}\\&\quad + 2x(1-x)\rho_{\text{Rs1,Rs2}}\,\sigma_{\text{Rs1}}\,\sigma_{\text{Rs2}},\end{aligned} \tag{74}$$

where x is constrained to satisfy $0 \leq x \leq 1$ if short sales are not allowed.

In general, the minimum variance portfolio is identified by taking the derivative of (74) with respect to x and finding the value of x at which it vanishes. Hence, the minimum variance is obtained for x that solved Eq. (75).

$$\begin{aligned}&2x\,\text{Var(Rs1)} - 2(1-x)\text{Var(Rs2)}\\&\quad + (2-4x)\rho_{\text{Rs1,Rs2}}\,\sigma_{\text{Rs1}}\,\sigma_{\text{Rs2}} = 0.\end{aligned} \tag{75}$$

Equation (75) can be solved by hand or using Maple, as exemplified in the following. For simplicity σ_{Rs1} is replaced by $\sigma 1$ and σ_{Rs2} by $\sigma 2$ and Var by σ^2.

```
> solve({2*x*sigma1^2-2*(1-x)*sigma2^2+(2-4*x)*rho*
  sigma1*sigma2=0},{x});
```

$$\left\{x = \frac{\sigma 2(\rho\,\sigma 1 - \sigma 2)}{2\,\rho\,\sigma 1\,\sigma 2 - \sigma 1^2 - \sigma 2^2}\right\} \tag{76}$$

The solutions of the special cases $\rho = 0, 1$ and -1 are presented below.

```
> solve({subs(rho=0,2*x*sigma1^2-2*(1-x)*sigma2^2
  +(2-4*x)*rho*sigma1*sigma2=0)},{x});# rho=0.
```

$$\left\{x = \frac{\sigma 2^2}{\sigma 1^2 + \sigma 2^2}\right\} \tag{77}$$

```
> solve({subs(rho=1,2*x*sigma1^2-2*(1-x)*sigma2^2
  +(2-4*x)*rho*sigma1*sigma2=0)},{x});#rho=1
```

$$\left\{x = -\frac{\sigma 2}{\sigma 1 - \sigma 2}\right\} \tag{78}$$

```
> solve({subs(rho=-1,2*x*sigma1^2-2*(1-x)*sigma2^2
  +(2-4*x)*rho*sigma1*sigma2=0)},{x});#rho=-1
```

$$\left\{x = \frac{\sigma 2}{\sigma 1 + \sigma 2}\right\}. \tag{79}$$

In our example, the value of ρ is -1. Hence,based on the above solution for x, the proportion invested in Rs1, in the minimum variance portfolio (which in this case is a risk-free asset), is $\frac{\sigma 2}{\sigma 1+\sigma 2}$. Thus, the proportion value as anticipated is

```
> sqrt(Vs2)/(sqrt(Vs1)+sqrt(Vs2));
```

$$\frac{4}{11}. \tag{80}$$

Substituting the obtained value in the standard deviation function confirms that indeed the minimum variance, which is a non-risky portfolio, is the solution.

```
> sd(4/11);
```

$$0. \tag{81}$$

When short sales are allowed, the feasible set of portfolios composed of two risky portfolios extends beyond the two original portfolios. Consider the two risky securities Rs1 and Rs2 with expected values of 1/18 and 1/63, respectively. Assume that a short position is taken in security 2, the security with the lower expected rate of return. As a result, the long position in security 1, with the higher expected rate of return, can increase to be above 1. The expected value of a portfolio composed of a long position of 1 in security 1 (and 0 in security 2), is 1/18, the expected value of security 1. If a short position, say of 1/2, is taken in security 2, a long position of 1.5 can be taken in security 1. This will increase the portfolio's expected rate of return. The 1/2 short position in security 2 causes a decrease of $(1/2) * 1/63$ in the expected value of the portfolio, but the 1/2 increase in the long position of security 1 increases the expected value of the portfolio by $(1/2) * 1/18$. Consequently, the net change in the expected value of the portfolio is an increase of $(1/2)(1/18 - 1/63)$. Thus, by increasing the long position and the absolute value of the short position, the expected value of the portfolio increases with no bounds. The catch, of course, is that the risk of the portfolio also increases with no bounds.

To demonstrate this case, we present the following animation of portfolios with short positions for different values of rho. If the short position would have been taken in security 2, in the one with the higher expected value, obviously the results would have been a decrease in the expected value of the portfolio. This is demonstrated below by the animation with respect to rho. It is apparent again that the extension past the minimum variance is not efficient regardless of the value of rho and whether or not short positions are used.

```
> plot([sqrt(VarRho(x,-1)),Exp(x),x=-1..2],labels=[s,m],
  labelfont=[SYMBOL],thickness=3):

> plot([sqrt(VarRho(x,1)),Exp(x),x=-1..2],labels=[s,m],
  labelfont=[SYMBOL],thickness=3):

> plots[animate]([sqrt(VarRho(x,rho)),Exp(x),x=-1..2],
  rho=-1..1,labels=[s,m],labelfont=[SYMBOL],thickness=3):
  plots[display](%,%%,%%%);
```

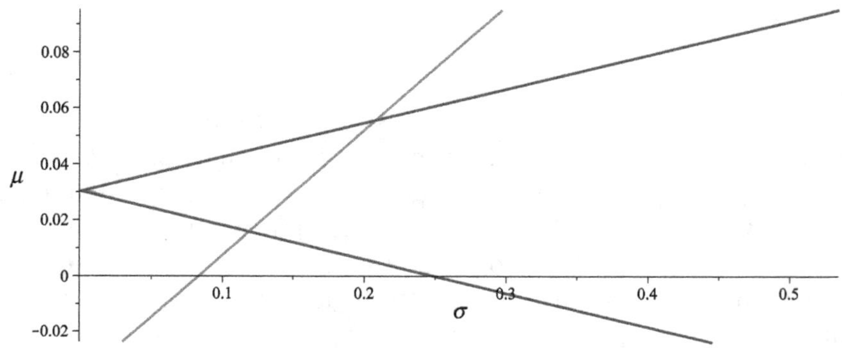

This section ends with the investigation of the feasible portfolios that can be composed from a risk-free asset and a risky asset. The variance of a risk-free asset is zero by (5) and thus so is its standard deviation. Assume that the risk-free rate of return is 0.1 and that the expected rate of return on the risky asset is 0.14 and its standard deviation is 0.05. Thus, the representation of the risk-free asset in the $\sigma - \mu$ space is $(0, 0.1)$ and of the risky asset is $(0.05, 0.14)$ as displayed in the following:

```
> plot([[0,0.1],[0.05,0.14]],style=point,symbol=
  solidcircle,thickness=3,labelfont=[SYMBOL],
  labels=[s,m]);
```

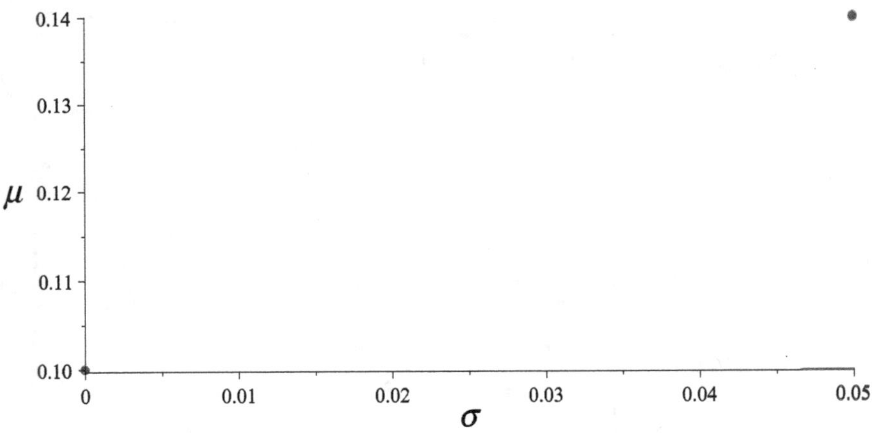

The covariance between a risky asset Rs and a risk-free asset Rf is defined to be

$$E((\text{Rs} - E(\text{Rs})(\text{Rf} - E(\text{Rf})).$$

However, $E(\text{Rf}) = \text{Rf}$ and hence $(\text{Rf} - E(\text{Rf}) = 0$, consequently

$$\begin{aligned} E((\text{Rs} - E(\text{Rs})(\text{Rf} - E(\text{Rf})) &= E((\text{Rs} - E(\text{Rs}) \cdot 0) \\ &= \text{Cov}(\text{Rs}, \text{Rf}) = 0 \end{aligned}$$

and thus $\rho_{\text{Rs},\text{Rf}} = 0$. It follows that

$$\begin{aligned} \text{Var}(x \cdot \text{Rs} + (1 - x) \cdot \text{Rf}) &= x^2 \text{Var}(\text{Rs}) + (1 - x)^2 \text{Var}(\text{Rf}) \\ &\quad + 2\,\text{Cov}(\text{Rs}, \text{Rf}) = x^2 \text{Var}(\text{Rs}) + 0 + 0 \end{aligned}$$

and thus the standard deviation of the portfolio is $x \cdot \sigma_{\mathrm{Rs}}$ or in our case $x \cdot 0.05$ which can be written as

$$x \cdot 0.05 + (1 - x) \cdot 0$$

The expected value of the portfolio $(x \cdot \mathrm{Rs} + (1 - x)\mathrm{Rf})$ is

$$\begin{aligned} E(x \cdot \mathrm{Rs} + (1 - x) \cdot \mathrm{Rf}) &= xE(\mathrm{Rs}) + (1 - x) \cdot E(\mathrm{Rf}) \\ &= x \cdot E(\mathrm{Rs}) + (1 - x) \cdot \mathrm{Rf}. \end{aligned}$$

Thus, the coordinate, as a function of x, of the asset $(x \cdot \mathrm{Rs} + (1 - x) \cdot \mathrm{Rf})$ is $x \cdot (0.05, 0.15) + (1 - x) \cdot (0, 0.10)$ and can be plotted for x between 0 and 1 as follows.

```
> plot([(1-x)*0+x*0.05,(1-x)*0.1+x*C.14,x=0..1],
  thickness=3,labelfont=[SYMBOL],labels=[s,m]);
```

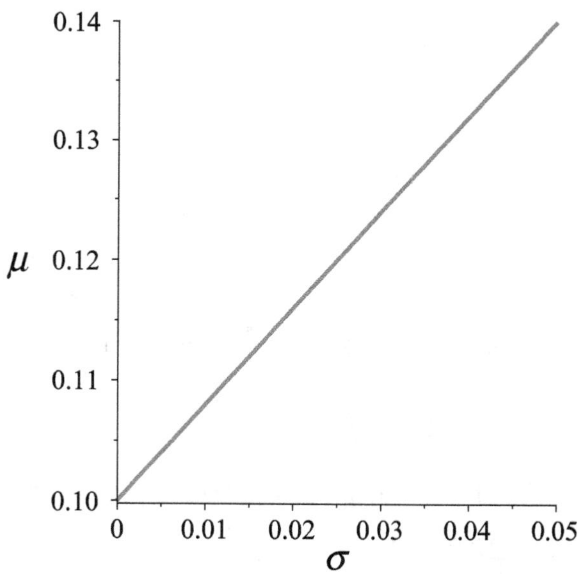

Imposing one graph on the other shows that the feasible set in this case is the linear function (line) connecting the coordinate of the risk-free asset with the risky asset.

```
> plots[display](%,%%);
```

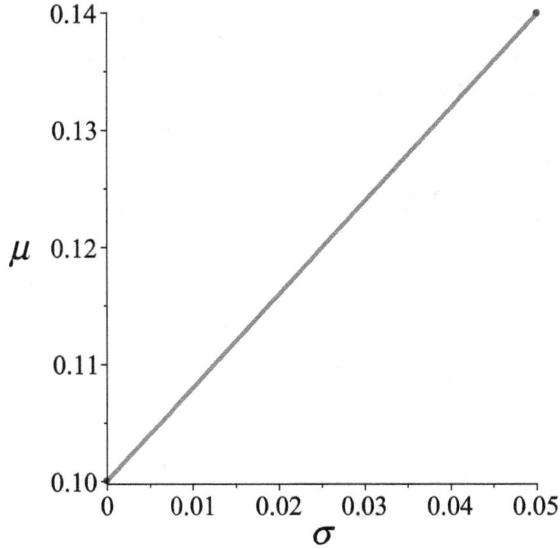

Appendix: Estimation of Expected Values Variances, Covariances and Regressions

The CAPM is a one period model and hence when implementing it, one has to choose "the period". Given the period, the estimation is done from a sample of the rate of returns of the securities over a few of these periods. It is common to choose a period of a month and have a sample of the rates of return of the securities over the last $N = 60$ months. Thus, if there are S securities in the market, a sample of $N \cdot S$ observations is gathered,

$$r_{ij} \quad \text{for } i = 1, \ldots, S \quad \text{and} \quad j = 1, \ldots, N$$

where r_{ij} is the observed rate of return of security i in period (month) j.

The expected value of the rate of return of a security is estimated by the arithmetic average of its rate of return over a few periods. That is, if the sample is over N periods, the expected rate of return is estimated as

$$E_i = \sum_{j=1}^{N} \frac{r_{ij}}{N}, \quad i = 1, \ldots, S.$$

The variance is actually an expected value of the squared deviation of the rate of return from its expected value. Hence, it is estimated by the arithmetic average of the realized deviations as stipulated in the following:

$$V_i = \sum_{j=1}^{N} \frac{(r_{ij} - E_i)^2}{N} \quad i = 1, \ldots, S.$$

which after some algebraic manipulations can be presented as

$$V_i = \sum_{j=1}^{N} \frac{r_{ij}^2}{N} - E_i^2 = \sum_{j=1}^{N} \frac{r_{ij}^2}{N} - \left(\sum_{j=1}^{N} \frac{r_{ij}}{N}\right)^2 \quad i = 1, \ldots, S.$$

The covariance between security n and security k is defined in terms of an expected value. It is the expected value of the product of security n's rate of return minus its expected value and security k's rate of return minus its expected value.

That is, given two securities Rs1 and Rs2, the expression $E((\mathrm{Rs1} - E(\mathrm{Rs1}) \cdot (\mathrm{Rs2} - E(\mathrm{Rs2}))$ is the covariance between the two random variables Rs1 and Rs2, denoted by $\mathrm{Cov}(\mathrm{Rs1}, \mathrm{Rs2})$ or by $\sigma_{\mathrm{Rs1},\mathrm{Rs2}}$. Thus, it is estimated as the arithmetic average of these products over the periods sampled. Hence, it is estimated as

$$\mathrm{Cov}_{nk} = \sum_{j=1}^{N} \frac{(r_{nj} - E_n)(r_{kj} - E_k)}{N}$$

which after some algebraic manipulations can be presented as

$$\mathrm{Cov}_{nk} = \sum_{j=1}^{N} \frac{r_{nj} \cdot r_{kj}}{N} - \sum_{j=1}^{N} \frac{r_{nj}}{N} \cdot \sum_{i=1}^{N} \frac{r_{kj}}{N}.$$

It is apparent from the definition that the covariance is symmetric in Rs1 and Rs2, i.e.,

$$\mathrm{Cov}(\mathrm{Rs1}, \mathrm{Rs2}) = \mathrm{Cov}(\mathrm{Rs2}, \mathrm{Rs2}).$$

The correlation coefficient between security n and security k, is estimated based on its definition as the ratio of the covariance between the two securities divided by the product of the standard deviations of the two securities. That is as

$$\rho = \frac{\mathrm{Cov}_{nk}}{V_n^{\frac{1}{2}} V_k^{\frac{1}{2}}}.$$

Estimation with Maple

The observations of the rate of return on a security will be simulated using a random number generator from the normal distribution $N(\mu, \sigma)$. In order to generate an array of n observations from $N(0,1)$, use the following command:

stats[random, normald](n), and 10 observations from $N(0,1)$ will be generated as follows:

```
> [stats[random,normald[0,1]](10)];
```

$$[-0.8074455437, 0.5638425484, 0.7668276240, -0.9578304704, 0.09625284163, -0.5899328337, 0.8199273967, 1.522884874, -0.2965618588, -0.7531006391] \tag{A.1}$$

To generate an array of 10 observations, from say a $N(20, 15)$, use the command as follows.

```
> In1:=[stats[random,normald[20,15]](10)];
```

$$\text{In1} := [24.72680952, 9.93250554, 14.06306695, 25.35590124, 20.06842407, 16.10899199, 32.28045686, 9.36013214, 17.71664992, 19.78911289]. \tag{A.2}$$

An array of 10 observations from $N(10, 5^2)$ is defined as follows:

```
> In2:=[stats[random,normald[10,5]](10)];
```

$$\text{In2} := [6.921002606, 6.280124455, 13.92127843, 22.27499950, 14.16931442, 5.253832848, 6.128621242, 10.85862833, 2.321821035, 15.43729742]. \tag{A.3}$$

We can find the estimation for the expected value and standard deviation of In1 and In2, EIn1,VIn1 and EIn2, VIn2 respectively and the covariance by definition or utilizing the Maple commands mean, variance, and covariance. Both options are demonstrated as follows:

```
> EIn1:=sum(In1[i],i=1..10)/10; # Expected value by
  definition of In1
```

$$EIn1 := 18.94020511 \tag{A.4}$$

```
> VIn1:=sum((In1[i]-EIn1)^2,i=1..10)/10; # Variance by
  definition In1
```

$$VIn1 := 46.08175678 \tag{A.5}$$

```
> stats[describe,mean](In1);#Expected value using
  Maple command of In1
```

$$18.94020511 \tag{A.6}$$

```
> stats[describe,variance](In1);#Variance using
  Maple command of In1
```

$$46.08175678. \tag{A.7}$$

You can replace the 'variance' above with the 'standarddeviation' to get an estimation of σ e.g.,

```
> SdIn1:=stats[describe,standarddeviation](In1);
  Maple standard deviation In1
```

$$SdIn1 := 6.788354497 \tag{A.8}$$

```
> EIn2:=sum(In2[i],i=1..10)/10;# Expected value by
  definition of In2
```

$$EIn2 := 10.35669203 \tag{A.9}$$

```
> VIn2:=sum((In2[i]-EIn2)^2,i=1..10)/10;# Variance by
  definition In2
```

$$VIn2 := 33.22501810 \tag{A.10}$$

The estimation of the covariance using the Maple command is given by

```
> CovIn12:=stats[describe,covariance](In1,In2);
```

$$\text{CovIn12} := 4.759949235. \tag{A.11}$$

The estimation of the covariance by definition is

```
> sum((In1[i]-EIn1)*(In2[i]-EIn2),i=1..10)/10;
```

$$4.759949235. \tag{A.12}$$

The standard deviation of In1 and In2 is calculated as follows:

```
> SdIn1:=stats[describe,standarddeviation](In1);
```

$$\text{SdIn1} := 6.788354497 \tag{A.13}$$

```
> SdIn2:=stats[describe,standarddeviation](In2);
```

$$\text{SdIn2} := 5.764114685. \tag{A.14}$$

The correlation coefficient by definition is thus given by

```
> CovIn12/(SdIn2*SdIn1);
```

$$0.1216480619. \tag{A.15}$$

This can also be done directly by stats[describe,linearcorrelation]

```
> rhoIn12:=stats[describe,linearcorrelation](In1,In2);
```

$$\text{rhoIn12} := 0.1216480619. \tag{A.16}$$

Regression with Maple

Few models studied henceforth require running regressions. There are a few ways of running a regression with Maple since essentially it is a second-best solution of a system of linear equations utilizing a quadratic optimization problem. One of these methods (for a single independent variable) is explained as follows.

This method requires the observations on the dependent and independent variables to be given in the form of an array (a list). As well, most of the models covered here assume that securities' rates of return follow a normal distribution, thus the observations will be simulated utilizing a normal random number of generators. Generating 10 observations from the normal distribution with an expected value of 3 and a standard deviation of 2 (naming the generated array (list) S1) is done as follows:

```
> #S1:=[stats[random,normald[3,2]](10)];
```

$$S1 := [5.551352068, 3.952372179, -2.240108430, 4.709441589, 0.821996392, 4.433085519, 2.940071276, 5.661711286, 0.407309762, 2.059339194] \quad (A.17)$$

```
> S1:=[5.551352068, 3.952372179, -2.240108430,
  4.709441589, 0.821996392, 4.433085519, 2.940071276,
  5.661711286, 0.407309762, 2.059339194];
```

$$S1 := [5.551352068, 3.952372179, -2.240108430, 4.709441589, 0.821996392, 4.433085519, 2.940071276, 5.661711286, 0.407309762, 2.059339194]. \quad (A.18)$$

Another array of observations named 'In', on an index or another security in the market that follows the normal distribution with expected value of 15 and standard deviation of 5 is generated as follows:

```
> #In:=[stats[random,normald[15,5]](10)];
```

$$In := [11.43868459, 14.56410496, 21.41126504, 6.581396570, 16.63273662, 15.40899091, 16.06378235, 11.36026565, 18.42788685, 13.11985972]. \quad (A.19)$$

```
> In:=[11.43868459, 14.56410496, 21.41126504,
  6.581396570, 16.63273662, 15.40899091, 16.06378235,
  11.36026565, 18.42788685, 13.11985972];
```

$$\text{In} := [11.43868459, 14.56410496, 21.41126504, 6.581396570, 16.63273662, 15.40899091, 16.06378235, 11.36026565, 18.42788685, 13.11985972]. \tag{A.20}$$

Assume that S1 is the dependent variable and In is the independent variable i.e., a regression of the form is contemplated:

$$\text{S1} = \alpha + \beta\,\text{In}$$

The coefficient in this regression α and β are estimated by executing the command

stats[fit,leastsquare[[Independent,Dependent]]]([In,S1]), e.g.,

```
> stats[fit,leastsquare[[Index,Security1]]]([In,S1]);
```

$$\text{Security1} = -0.5048458926\,\text{Index} + 10.15037554. \tag{A.21}$$

Thus in the regression $\text{S1} = \alpha + \beta\,\text{In}$, β is estimated as -0.5048458926 and α as 10.15037554.

Note that Index and Security1 are only names that are used to display the results of the regression. The actual observations are in the array In and S1. **As well, the order of In and S1 is significant. Reversing the order will solve for the regression** $\text{In} = \alpha + \beta\,\text{S1}$. **You cannot use the names of the variables that hold the data as names in the procedure**, i.e., you cannot run the procedure as follows:

```
> #stats[fit,leastsquare[[In,S1]]]([In,S1]);
```

In certain instances, the residuals of the regression will be needed. Thus, the prediction of the regression for S1 is calculated and subtracted from the actual observations on S1. The predicted S1 is $\alpha + \beta\,\mathrm{In}$.

The value of $\beta \cdot \mathrm{In}$ can be simply calculated as

```
> -0.5048458926*In;
```

$$[-5.774772932, -7.352628568, -10.80938921, -3.322591026, -8.396968765, -7.779165770, -8.109734539, -5.735183452, -9.303242986, -6.623507291]. \tag{A.22}$$

Now there is a need to add 10.15037554 to each element in the array. This can be done by

```
> PredS1:=map(x->x+10.15037554,%);
```

$$\mathrm{PredS1} := [4.375602608, 2.797746972, -0.65901367, 6.827784514, 1.753406775, 2.371209770, 2.040641001, 4.415192088, 0.847132554, 3.526868249]. \tag{A.23}$$

The residuals of the regression are therefore the array

```
> Res:=S1-PredS1;
```

$$\mathrm{Res} := [1.175749460, 1.154625207, -1.581094760, -2.118342925, -0.931410383, 2.061875749, 0.899430275, 1.246519198, -0.439822792, -1.467529055] \tag{A.24}$$

```
> Res;
```

$$[1.175749460, 1.154625207, -1.581094760, -2.118342925, -0.931410383, 2.061875749, 0.899430275, 1.246519198, -0.439822792, -1.467529055] \tag{A.25}$$

Note: The result of the calculation is shown in the following. These are properties of the regression and are satisfied for every regression.

```
> sum(Res[i]*In[i],i=1..10);
```

$$-1.38\,10^{-6} \tag{A.26}$$

```
> sum(Res[i],i=1..10);
```

$$-2.6\,10^{-8}. \tag{A.27}$$

Hence, the estimated covariance between the residuals and the index is zero, as it is

```
> sum(Res[i]*In[i],i=1..10)/10-(sum(Res[i],i=1..10)/10)*
  sum(In[i],i=1..10)/10;
```

$$-1.002976670\,10^{-7}. \tag{A.28}$$

Chapter 6

The Feasible Set: A General Formulation

Introduction

In the case of a market with only two risky assets, finding the feasible set is simple, as it involves only the span of the possible combinations of the two assets. Once the expected value of the portfolio is given, the portfolio composition is determined and consequently its variance is also determined. In the general case however, where N risky assets exist, there are many possibilities of generating a portfolio with a given expected value, and thus, an optimization problem must be solved to identify the one with the minimal variance and, consequently, the efficient frontier.

Our investigation starts with a market in which a risk-free asset does not exist, and short sales are allowed. There are "dual" ways of formulating this optimization problem. In one approach, the standard deviation of the portfolio is minimized, subject to the constraint that the expected value of the portfolio equals a given value. In the other approach, the expected value of the portfolio is maximized, subject to the constraint that the standard deviation of the portfolio does not exceed a given value. We will formulate the optimization problem using the first approach. It is possible to show, formally, that the shape of the efficient frontier even in the general case of N assets is concave, as in the case of two assets.

The Efficient Frontier Without a Risk-Free Asset

Building the efficient frontier amounts to finding the portfolio with the minimum standard deviation for each given expected rate of return. The portfolio that minimizes the standard deviation also minimizes the variance. Since it is easier to formulate the problem in terms of the variance, this approach is commonly used. Minimizing the variance requires the ability to calculate the variance of each portfolio.

The generalization of the variance formula for a portfolio $(x_1, x_2, \ldots, x_N)$ composed of N securities is given as

$$\sum_{j=1}^{N}\left(\sum_{i=1}^{N} x_i x_j \sigma_{ij}\right) = \sum_{i=1}^{N} x_i^2 \sigma_{ii} + \sum_{j=1}^{N}\left(\sum_{i=1, i\neq j}^{N} x_i x_j \sigma_{ij}\right) \tag{1}$$

where x_i is the proportion invested in security i, $i = 1, \ldots N$, σ_{ij} is the covariance between i and j is σ_{ii} is the variance of security i, and x_i is the proportion invested in security i.

σ_{ij} is not just a notation for the variance of security i but an actual property of the covariance. Hence, the variance of a portfolio $(x_1, x_2, \ldots, x_N)$ can be thought of as the sum of the covariance between each two securities, including between each security and itself, i.e., between security 1 and security 1, security 1 and security 2, security 1 and security 3, etc., which is the meaning of the double summation $\sum_{j=1}^{N}(\sum_{i=1}^{N} x_i x_j \sigma_{ij})$. For $N = 2$, the expression $\sum_{j=1}^{N}(\sum_{i=1}^{N} x_i x_j \sigma_{ij})$ equals $x_1 x_1 \sigma_{11} + x_1 x_2 \sigma_{12} + x_2 x_1 \sigma_{21} + x_2 \sigma_{12}$ since $\sigma_1 = \sigma_{21}$ and $\sigma_{ii} = \sigma_i^2$.

The variance of a portfolio composed of two securities, as stipulated before, is $\sum_{j=1}^{2}(\sum_{i=1}^{2} x_i x_j \sigma_{i,j}) = x_1\sigma_1^2 + x_2\sigma_2^2 + 2x_1x_2\sigma_{12}$, which now is apparent to be a specific case of the generalized formula for the variance for $N > 2$.

While we will show more formally the significance of the covariance in our analysis, the following explanation sheds some light on the covariance's role in determining the risk of a diversified portfolio composed of a "large" number of securities. The covariance is more important than the variance; in fact, the contribution of the variance of each single security to the overall risk of a "large" portfolio is kind of negligible.

The variance of a portfolio composed of N securities, where σ_{ij} is the covariance between i and j and x_i the fraction invested in security i is $\frac{1}{N}$, is given by Eq. (1) as follows:

$$\sum_{j=1}^{N}\left(\sum_{i=1}^{N}\frac{\sigma_{i,j}}{N^2}\right)=\sum_{i=1}^{N}\frac{\sigma_{i,i}}{N^2}+\sum_{j=1}^{N}\left(\sum_{i=1,i\neq j}^{N}\frac{\sigma_{i,j}}{N\,N}\right).$$

This can be written as

$$\sum_{i=1}^{N}\frac{\sigma_{i,i}}{N^2}+\frac{(N-1)\left(\sum_{j=1}^{N}\left(\sum_{i=1,i\neq j}^{N}\frac{\sigma_{i,j}}{N(N-1)}\right)\right)}{N}.$$

Let us denote by σ_N the average of the N variances and by σ_{NN} the average of the N covariances. Hence, we get that the variance of the portfolio is $\frac{\sigma_N}{N}+\frac{(N-1)\sigma_{NN}}{N}$ which, when N approaches infinity, approaches σ_{NN}.

This enforces the idea that the significant part of the risk is induced by the covariance, provided the portfolio is diversified. Of course, our example is for a very naive diversification. We invested an equal amount in each of the securities. Nevertheless, as we will progress with our model, we will indeed confirm that investors will be rewarded for taking a risk, but only the risk that could not be diversified away. This is the risk that is contributed to the portfolio by the covariances. We will make this statement much more precise as we will add more structure to the model.

It is therefore clear that the knowledge of the covariance between each of the two securities in the market is required to calculate the variances of all the portfolios in the market. Of course, the expected rate of return of each security in the market is also needed to determine the expected value of all portfolios in the market. Given an expected value, the set of portfolios with this specified expected rate of return must be formulated, and of this set, the portfolio with the minimum variance must be identified. This last step is not needed in the case of only two risky assets, as given an expected rate of return, there is only one portfolio with the specified expected rate of return.

Assume that for the covariance between each of the two securities, the expected rate of return and the variance of the rate of return of each security in the market are estimated. Thus, we have an estimate for the following:

μ_i is the expected value of security i, $i = 1, \ldots N$,
$\sigma_i^2 = \sigma_{ii}$ is the variance of security i, for $i = 1, \ldots N$ and
σ_{ij} is the covariance between security i and j, $i = 1, \ldots N$, $j = 1, \ldots, N_i \neq j$.

Given a certain expected rate of return, say e, all portfolios with such an expected rate of return are those that satisfy $\sum_{j=1}^{N} x_i \mu_i = e$ and $\sum_{j=1}^{N} x_i = 1$. Of these portfolios, the one with the minimum variance should be identified. Thus, the optimization problem to be solved for each given e is given as

$$\text{Minimize}_{(x_1, x_2, \ldots, x_N)} \sum_{i=1}^{N} x_i^2 \sigma_{i,i} + \sum_{j=1}^{N} \left(\sum_{i=1, i \neq j}^{N} x_i x_j \sigma_{i,j} \right)$$

$$\text{such that} \sum_{j=1}^{N} x_i \mu_i = e$$

$$\sum_{j=1}^{N} x_i = 1. \tag{2}$$

The type of optimization in (2) can be solved analytically and the solution can be presented as a function of e. That is, given an estimate of the covariances variances and expected values of all securities in the market, the portfolio with the minimum variance can be expressed in terms of the given expected value e. Consequently, the minimum standard deviation as a function of e can be constructed. The inverse of this function, i.e., the standard deviation as a function of e, is the required efficient frontier. If short sales are not allowed, the constraints $x_i \geq 0$, for $i = 1, \ldots N$, are added to the optimization in (2). However, in that case, a parametric solution (as a function of e) is not feasible and there is a need to solve the optimization for each value of e. Occasionally, other constraints are required, e.g., the holding of certain securities might be bounded or the holding of securities from a specific section cannot constitute more than a certain percent of the portfolio. Portfolio managers may desire to add different constraints given the time and investment environment. To illustrate the process of building the efficient frontier, let us examine a market with three securities only.

An Example

Assume a market with three risky securities. The expected values of the rate of return of the securities are 10/100, 12/100 and 18/100. The estimate of all the covariances (including variances) in the market is usually given in the form of a table (a matrix) called the variance–covariance (VarCov) matrix. If there are three securities in the market, such a matrix will have three rows and three columns — a 3×3 matrix. The solution implemented below is dependent on the VarCov matrix having the properties of a VarCov matrix. Since $\sigma_{ij} = \sigma_{ji}$, the elements above and below the diagonal are the same, e.g., the cell in row 2 column 1 has the same value as the cell in column 1 row 2. The diagonal elements are the variances. Assume that the variances of the rate of return of securities 1, 2 and 3, respectively, are $\frac{4}{100}$, $\frac{9}{100}$ and $\frac{16}{100}$. To make sure that the covariances are specified in a manner that adhere to the properties of the VarCov matrix, they will be set based on the assumed correlation coefficients ρ_{12}, ρ_{13} and ρ_{23}.

Of course, in reality, the variances and covariances are estimated from historical data as was explained, and thus, the VarCov matrix will satisfy the required properties. For each of the two securities, i and j, $\rho_{ij} = \frac{\sigma_{ij}}{\sigma_i \sigma_j}$; thus, it is clear that $\rho_{ij} = \rho_{ji}$ and $\sigma_{ij} = \rho_{ij}\sigma_i\sigma_j$. Setting $\rho_{12} = \frac{1}{2}$, $\rho_{13} = \frac{4}{75}$ and $\rho_{23} = \frac{9}{100}$ implies that the covariance between security 1 and 2 is given by

```
> (1/2)*sqrt(4/100)*sqrt(9/100);# 1 and 2
```

$$\frac{3}{100} \tag{3}$$

```
>
```

the covariance between security 1 and 3 is given by

```
> (2/3)*sqrt(4/100)*sqrt(16/100);# 1 and 3
```

$$\frac{4}{75} \tag{4}$$

and the covariance between security 2 and 3 is given by

```
> (3/4)*sqrt(16/100)*sqrt(9/100);# 2 and 3
```

$$\frac{9}{100}. \tag{5}$$

Hence, the optimization problem to be solved is as follows:

$$\begin{aligned} \text{Minimize}_{(x_1,x_2,x_3)} \quad & \frac{x_i^2}{25} + \frac{x_2{}^2 9}{100} + \frac{x_3{}^2 4}{25} \\ & + 2x_1x_2\frac{3}{100} + 2x_1x_3\frac{4}{75} + 2x_2x_3\frac{9}{100} \\ \text{such that} \quad & \frac{x_1 10}{100} + \frac{x_2 12}{100} + \frac{x_3 18}{100} = e \\ & x_1 + x_2 + x_3 = 1. \end{aligned}$$

The VarCov matrix is defined by

```
> Sigma:=Matrix(3,3,[[4/100,3/100,4/75],[3/100,9/100,
  9/100],[4/75,9/100,16/100]]);
```

$$\sum := \begin{bmatrix} \frac{1}{25} & \frac{3}{100} & \frac{4}{75} \\ \frac{3}{100} & \frac{9}{100} & \frac{9}{100} \\ \frac{4}{75} & \frac{9}{100} & \frac{4}{25} \end{bmatrix}. \tag{6}$$

The input of the expected values of each security and the fact that there are constraints on $\sum_{j=1}^{N} \mu.\ x_i$ and $\sum_{j=1}^{N} x_i$ is represented by a matrix with two columns, where the number of rows equals the number of securities in the market. In the first column, the expected rate of return of each security is listed, i.e., the ith element in the first column is the expected rate of return of security i, etc., representing the constraint $\sum_{j=1}^{N} \mu \cdot x_i = e$. The second column is a column of 1's representing the constraint $\sum_{j=1}^{N} x_i = 1$. In our example, this is the matrix A defined below:

```
> A:=Matrix(3,2,[[10/100,1],[12/100,1],[18/100,1]]);
```

$$A := \begin{bmatrix} \frac{1}{10} & 1 \\ \frac{3}{25} & 1 \\ \frac{9}{50} & 1 \end{bmatrix}. \tag{7}$$

The right-hand side of the first and second constraints in the optimization (2) are e and 1. That is, the optimization will solve for the minimal variance portfolio as a function of e, where $\sum_{j=1}^{N} x_i$ is constrained to be equal to 1 and $\sum_{j=1}^{N} \mu \cdot x_i = e$. These two elements, e and 1, are represented by the vector defined below.

```
> b:=Vector(2,1,[e,1]);
```

$$b := \begin{bmatrix} e \\ 1 \end{bmatrix}. \tag{8}$$

With these inputs, the portfolio $(x_1, x_2, \ldots, x_N)$ of the minimal variance as a function of the given expected rate of return e can be solved. The solution method is based on the Lagrangian method. Maple can calculate the solutions x_1, x_2 and x_3 in our case, in a parametric form as a function of e by the following expression.

Note that in Sigma the element in cell ij σ_{ij} is the covariance between i and j; hence, the ii elements (the ones in the diagonal) are the variances σ_{ii} and the ij elements equal the ji elements as $\sigma_{ij} = \sigma_{ji}$. Also, since $-1 \le \rho = \frac{\sigma_{ij}}{\sigma_i \sigma_i} \le 1$ $\sigma_i \sigma_i \le \sigma_{ij} \le \sigma_i \sigma_i$ and we finally observe that the variance of a portfolio $x_1, \ldots, x_n$ is $\sum_{i=1}^{n} \sum_{j=1}^{n} x_i x_j \sigma_{ij}$. This expression must be non-negative. Hence, Sigma, the Variance–Covariance matrix, must satisfy these properties. If a Sigma matrix that does not confirm to these properties is specified, the solutions below will not work appropriately. If the Sigma matrix is built based on the estimated quantities from a sample, it will always satisfy these properties.

```
> with(LinearAlgebra):x:=MatrixInverse(Sigma).A.Matrix
  Inverse(Transpose(A).MatrixInverse(Sigma).A).b;
```

$$x := \begin{bmatrix} -\frac{25}{3}e + \frac{23}{14} \\ -\frac{50}{9}e + \frac{17}{21} \\ \frac{125}{9}e - \frac{61}{42} \end{bmatrix}. \tag{9}$$

Under certain circumstances, this parametric solution will not work and there will be a need to solve the problem numerically as explained henceforth. This will be the case, for example, if it is possible to generate a risk-free asset from a portfolio of risky assets, a very rare case in reality.

That is, the position in security 1which is the first element of the above vector is

```
> x[1];
```

$$-\frac{25\,e}{3} + \frac{23}{14} \tag{10}$$

and the position in security 2 is

```
> x[2];
```

$$-\frac{50\,e}{9} + \frac{17}{21}. \tag{11}$$

It is possible to check that the constraint $\sum_{j=1}^{N} x_i = 1$ is satisfied by summing up the components of the vector x done below:

```
> add((x[i]), i=1..3);
```

$$1. \tag{12}$$

The minimal variance $\sum_{j=1}^{N}(\sum_{i=1}^{N} x_i x_j \sigma_{ij})$, as a function of the given expected rate of return e, is calculated by Maple as shown below.

```
> MinVar:=simplify(add(add(x[j]*Sigma[i,j]*x[i],j=1..3),
  i=1..3));
```

$$\text{MinVar} := \frac{350}{27}e^2 - \frac{19}{9}e + \frac{62}{525} \tag{13}$$

```
> MinVar:=simplify(Transpose(x).Sigma.x);# a short way
  of calculating it
```

$$\text{MinVar} := \frac{350}{27}e^2 - \frac{19}{9}e + \frac{62}{525} \tag{14}$$

and the minimal standard deviation is given as

```
> sqrt(MinVar);
```

$$\frac{1}{315}\sqrt{1286250\,e^2 - 209475\,e + 11718.} \tag{15}$$

The minimum variance must be a convex quadratic function, and thus, if the coefficient of e^2 is not positive, something is wrong. The minimum standard deviation for an expected rate of return of $e = 0.3$ can now be calculated by

```
> evalf(subs(e=0.03,sqrt(eval(MinVar))));
```

$$0.2577374079. \tag{16}$$

The standard deviation as a function of e is plotted as follows:

```
> plot(sqrt(MinVar),e=0.0..0.9,labels=[m,s],labelfont
  =[SYMBOL]);
```

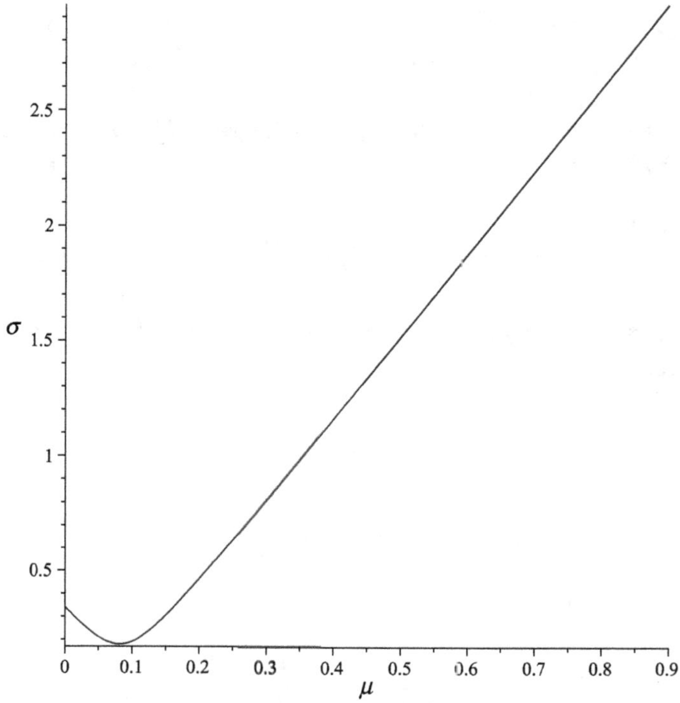

The expected rate of return as a function of the standard deviation is the inverse of the above function. It is solved for the following case:

```
> Sol_e:=solve({sqrt(MinVar)=sd},{e});
```

$$Sol\_e := \left\{e = \frac{57}{700} + \frac{3}{700}\sqrt{-135 + 4200\,sd^2}\right\}, \left\{e = \frac{57}{700} - \frac{3}{700}\sqrt{-135 + 4200\,sd^2}\right\}. \quad (17)$$

Observing the two solutions of e as a function of sd, it is clear that the efficient frontier function is the solution with the larger e. The first (larger) solution can be chosen using the following command: (or can just be copied and pasted)

```
> rhs(op(Sol_e[1]));
```

$$\frac{57}{700} + \frac{3}{700}\sqrt{-135 + 4200\,sd^2}. \quad (18)$$

Furthermore, since the minimal value of the expression in the square root is zero, it follows that the minimal sd is the one for which this expression vanishes. This expression can be copied and pasted or it can be chosen using the following maple command:

```
> op(2,op(2,%));
```

$$\sqrt{4200\, sd^2 - 135} \tag{19}$$

```
> solve(%=0);
```

$$\frac{3\sqrt{70}}{140}, -\frac{3\sqrt{70}}{140}. \tag{20}$$

Thus, the minimal standard deviation is the positive solution. The expected rate of return that corresponds to it is obtained by substituting this value in $\frac{3\sqrt{70}}{140}$, which of course should result in $\frac{57}{700}$.

```
> subs(sd=3*sqrt(70)*(1/140),rhs(op(Sol_e[1])));
```

$$\frac{57}{700}. \tag{21}$$

That is, the minimal variance portfolio has the (μ, σ) coordinate of

```
> [3*sqrt(70)*(1/140),57/700];
```

$$\left[\frac{3\sqrt{70}}{140}, \frac{57}{700}\right] \tag{22}$$

from which the efficient part of the frontier, the upper graph below, starts. The lower graph, which does not include the minimal variance portfolio, is the non-efficient part of the frontier as visualized in the following graph:

```
> plot([rhs(op(Sol_e[1])),rhs(op(Sol_e[2]))],sd=0..0.90,
  thickness=3,labels=[s,m],labelfont=[SYMBOL]);
```

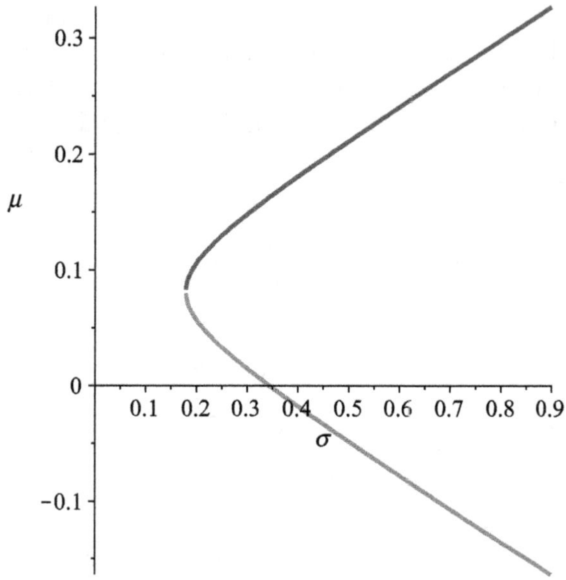

The coordinates of the risky securities are listed in the array

$$\left[\left[\frac{2}{10}, \frac{10}{100}\right], \left[\frac{3}{10}, \frac{12}{100}\right], \left[\frac{4}{10}, \frac{18}{10}\right]\right].$$

Note that security 2 with the coordinate $[\frac{3}{10}, \frac{12}{100}]$ is not on the efficient frontier. Indeed, the portfolio on the efficient frontier that corresponds to a standard deviation of 3/10 has an expected rate of return larger than 12/100 as verified in the following:

```
> evalf(subs(sd=3/10,rhs(op(Sol_e[1]))));
```

$$0.1482362454. \tag{23}$$

The risky securities and the minimum variance portfolio (the solid box) can be visualized in relation to the efficient frontier shown as follows:

```
> plots[display](plot([[3*sqrt(70)*(1/140),57/700]],
  style=point,symbol=solidbox,thickness=8,colour=black),
  plot([[2/10,10/100],[3/10,12/100],[4/10,18/100],
  [3*sqrt(70)*(1/140),57/700]],style=point,symbol=box,
  thickness=8), plot([rhs(op(Sol_e[1])),
```

```
rhs(op(Sol_e[2]))],sd=0..0.90,thickness=1,labels=
[s,m],labelfont=[SYMBOL]));
```

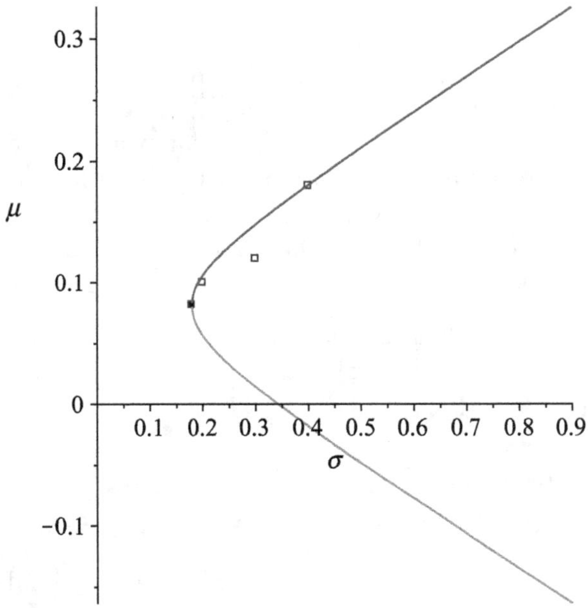

Solving Numerically for the Efficient Frontier

When short sales are not allowed, the optimization in (2) cannot be solved analytically in a parametric form, but must be solved numerically. This is presented below. First, the numerical solution of the optimization in (2), when short sales are allowed, is presented and compared to the parametric solution. It is followed by the numerical solution when short sales are not allowed.

Since x was assigned to the solution of the parametric form, the variables z are used for the numerical solution. That is $z[i]$ is the percentage invested in security i; hence, the variance of the portfolio is given as

```
> Sigma:=Matrix(3,3,[[4/100,3/100,4/75],[3/100,9/100,
  9/100],[4/75,9/100,16/100]]):add(add(z[i]*z[j]
  *Sigma[i,j],i=1..3),j=1..3);
```

$$\frac{1}{25}z_1^2 + \frac{3}{50}z_2 z_1 + \frac{8}{75}z_3 z_1 + \frac{9}{100}z_2^2 + \frac{9}{50}z_3 z_2 + \frac{4}{25}z_3^2 \qquad (24)$$

and the expected value of the portfolio is

```
> 0.1*z[1]+0.12*z[2]+0.18*z[3];
```

$$0.1\, z_1 + 0.12\, z_2 + 0.18\, z_3. \qquad (25)$$

The syntax for the optimization is self-explanatory. The first element is the function to be minimized followed by the constraints that are written between the two brackets '{' and '}'. The minimum variance for a given expected value of 0.03 when short sales are allowed is solved as follows:

```
> Optimization:-Minimize(add(add(z[i]*z[j]*Sigma[i,j],i
  =1..3),j=1..3), {z[1]+z[2]+z[3]=1,0.1*z[1]+0.12*z[2]
  +0.18*z[3]=0.03});
```

$$[0.0664285714285710, [z_1 = 1.39285714285714,$$
$$z_2 = 0.642857142857142, z_3 = -1.03571428571429]]. \qquad (26)$$

The first element in the output is the minimal variance, 0.0643188020587941, and the second element is the value of z's that minimize the variance, i.e.,

$$z_1 = 1.39730694354315, \;\; z_2 = 0.636924075275793,$$
$$z_3 = -1.03423101881895.$$

The parametric solution of the portfolio composition that corresponds to $e = 0.3$ is displayed below.

```
> seq(subs(e=0.03,x[i]),i=1..3);
```

$$1.392857143, \;\; 0.6428571428, \;\; -1.035714285. \qquad (27)$$

When short sales are not allowed, the non-negativity constraints are added between '{' and '}'.

```
> Optimization:-Minimize(add(add(z[i]*z[j]*Sigma[i,j],i
  =1..3),j=1..3), {z[1]+z[2]+z[3]=1,0.1*z[1]+0.12*z[2]
  +0.18*z[3]=0.03,z[1]>=0,z[2]>=0,z[3]>=0});
```

```
Error, (in Optimization:-OPSolve) no feasible solution
   found
```

The output above suggests that without short sales it is not feasible to obtain an expected value of 0.03. This is because, without short sales it is not possible to generate a portfolio with an expected value that is smaller than the minimum expected value among the given securities. Hence, the minimization for an expected rate of 0.11 is solved as follows:

```
> Optimization:-Minimize(add(add(z[i]*z[j]*Sigma[i,j],i
  =1..3),j=1..3), {z[1]+z[2]+z[3]=1,0.1*z[1]+0.12*z[2]
  +0.18*z[3]=0.11,z[1]>=0,z[2]>=0,z[3]>=0});
```

$$[0.0427248677248677, [z_1 = 0.726190476190476, z_2 = 0.198412698412699, z_3 = 0.753968253968249]] \tag{28}$$

```
> %[1];
```

$$0.0427248677248677. \tag{29}$$

This time, a feasible solution is obtained. Note that when short sales are not allowed, the expected values of the rates of return of feasible portfolios are between the minimum expected value and the maximum expected value of market securities, i.e., in our example in the range of 0.10–0.18. Let us solve for the minimum variance for a portfolio with an expected value of 0.10 (the minimum expected value).

```
> Optimization:-Minimize(add(add(z[i]*z[j]*Sigma[i,j],i
  =1..3),j=1..3), z[1]+z[2]+z[3]=1,0.1*z[1]+0.12*z[2]
  +0.18*z[3]=0.10,z[1]>=0,z[2]>=0,z[3]>=0);
```

$$[0.0400000000000000, [z_1 = 1.00000000000000, z_2 = -6.66133814775094\,10^{-16}, z_3 = 0.]] \tag{30}$$

The solution for $z[2]$ is essentially 0. Hence, the optimal portfolio as expected is composed of security 1 only, i.e., $z[1] = 1$.

The generation of a sequence of coordinates of portfolios on the efficient frontier, when short sales are not allowed, is solved for below. It is followed by the plot of the approximate efficient frontier, based on these discrete coordinates.

```
> sqrt(Optimization:-Minimize((add(add(z[i]*z[j]
  *Sigma[i,j],i=1..3),j=1..3)), {z[1]+z[2]+z[3]=1,
  0.1*z[1]+0.12*z[2]+0.18*z[3]=10/100,z[1]>=0,z[2]>=0,
  z[3]>=0})[1]);
```

$$0.2000000000 \tag{31}$$

```
> [sqrt(Optimization:-Minimize((add(add(z[i]*z[j]
  *Sigma[i,j],i=1..3),j=1..3)),{z[1]+z[2]+z[3]=1,
  0.1*z[1]+0.12*z[2]+0.18*z[3]=10/100,z[1]>=0,z[2]>=0,
  z[3]>=0})[1]),10/100];
```

$$\left[0.2000000000, \frac{1}{10}\right] \tag{32}$$

```
> [seq([sqrt(Optimization:-Minimize((add(add(z[i]*z[j]
  *Sigma[i,j],i=1..3),j=1..3)),{z[1]+z[2]+z[3]=1,
  0.1*z[1]+0.12*z[2]+0.18*z[3]=i/100,z[1]>=0,z[2]>=0,
  z[3]>=0})[1]),i/100],i=10..18)];
```

$$\left[\left[0.2000000000, \frac{1}{10}\right], \left[0.2066999461, \frac{11}{100}\right], \left[0.2267786838, \frac{3}{25}\right], \left[0.2504493316, \frac{13}{100}\right], \left[0.2767919013, \frac{7}{50}\right], \left[0.3051638904, \frac{3}{20}\right], \left[0.3354101966, \frac{4}{25}\right], \left[0.3671398462, \frac{17}{100}\right], \left[0.4000000000, \frac{9}{50}\right]\right] \tag{33}$$

```
> plot(%,labels=[s,m],labelfont=[SYMBOL]);
```

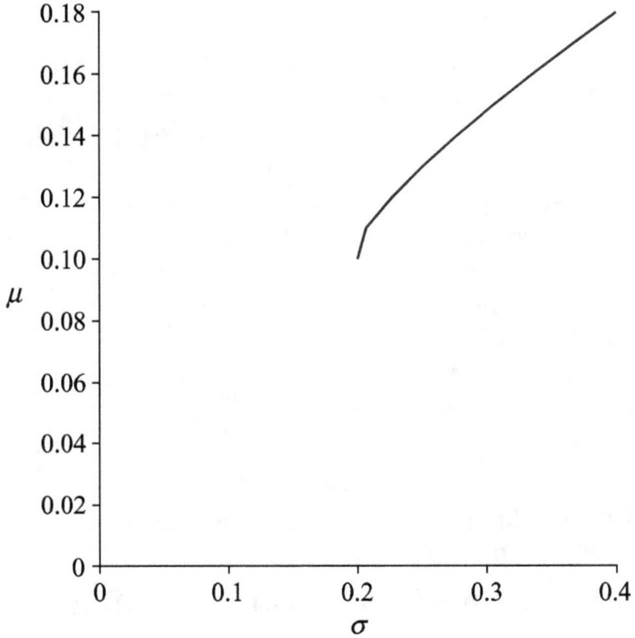

As mentioned above, the efficient frontier can be built by finding the maximum expected value for a sequence of given standard deviations. It is exemplified below for a standard deviation of $\sqrt{0.04}$.

```
> seq(Optimization:-Maximize(0.1*z[1]+0.12*z[2]+0.18
  *z[3],{z[1]+z[2]+z[3]=1, sqrt(add(add(z[i]*z[j]
  *Sigma[i,j],i=1..3),j=1..3))=i/10}),i=2..4);
```

$$
\begin{aligned}
&[0.106048125628446968, [z_1 = 0.759122762115202,\\
&\quad z_2 = 0.220367556705613, z_3 = 0.0205096811791843]],\\
&\quad [0.148236245434799546, [z_1 = 0.407555097568119,\\
&\quad z_2 = -0.0140108873374846, z_3 = 0.606455789769366]],\\
&\quad [0.180742544796485466, [z_1 = 0.136669269553348,\\
&\quad z_2 = -0.194601439345890, z_3 = 1.05793216979254]]. \qquad (34)
\end{aligned}
$$

The Efficient Frontier with a Risk-Free Asset

The existence of a risk-free asset in the market changes the shape of the efficient frontier. Any portfolio on the efficient frontier (without a risk-free asset) when combined with the risk-free asset introduces a new set of portfolios. These new portfolios are the ones that lie on the line connecting the coordinate of the risk-free assets with the portfolio on the efficient frontier. The part of the efficient frontier (without a risk-free asset) that lies underneath the line is no longer efficient. Consider the equation of the efficient frontier (without a risk-free asset) solved for before, i.e.,

$$e = \frac{57}{700} + \frac{3\sqrt{4200\,sd^2 - 135}}{700}$$

and a portfolio on it with a standard deviation of 0.2. The expected rate of return of this portfolio is found by substituting sd = 0.2 in the expression for the efficient frontier.

```
> subs(sd=0.2,57/700+3*sqrt(4200*sd^2-135)*(1/700));
```

$$0.1060481256. \tag{35}$$

Hence, the coordinate of this portfolio is $[0.2, 0.1060481256]$.

Assume that the risk-free rate in this market is 0.06. Thus, the line connecting the risk-free asset and the portfolio [0.2, 0.1060481256] on the efficient frontier has a slope of

```
> (0.1060481256-0.06)/0.2;
```

$$0.2302406280 \tag{36}$$

and a μ intercept of 0.06. Hence, the equation of this line is

```
> 0.06+0.2302406280*sd;
```

$$0.06 + 0.2302406280\,\mathrm{sd}. \tag{37}$$

Consider the graph of the efficient frontier together with the line connecting the risk-free asset and the portfolio represented by the point [0.2, 0.1060481256] on the efficient frontier. This line represents all the portfolios that can be generated by combining the risk-free asset with the portfolios [0.2, 0.1060481256] on the efficient frontier.

Recall that the coordinate of the minimum standard deviation portfolio was

```
> evalf([3*sqrt(70)*(1/140),57/700]);
```

$$[0.1792842914, 0.08142857143] \tag{38}$$

and observe the figure below of the efficient frontier with the above line, as well as the minimum standard deviation portfolio, the risk-free asset and the portfolios $[0.25, 0.1298210991]$ and $[0.2, 0.1060481256]$. These four portfolios are marked by solid circles in the figure below.

```
> plot([[3*sqrt(70)*(1/140),57/700],[0,0.06],
  [0.2,.1060481256],[0.25,.1298210991]],style=point,
  symbol=solidcircle,thickness=8,colour=black):
```

```
> plot([0.06+0.2302406280*sd,57/700+3*sqrt(4200*sd^2-135)
  *(1/700)],sd=0..0.90,thickness=3,labels=[s,m],
  labelfont=[SYMBOL]):plots[display](%,%%);
```

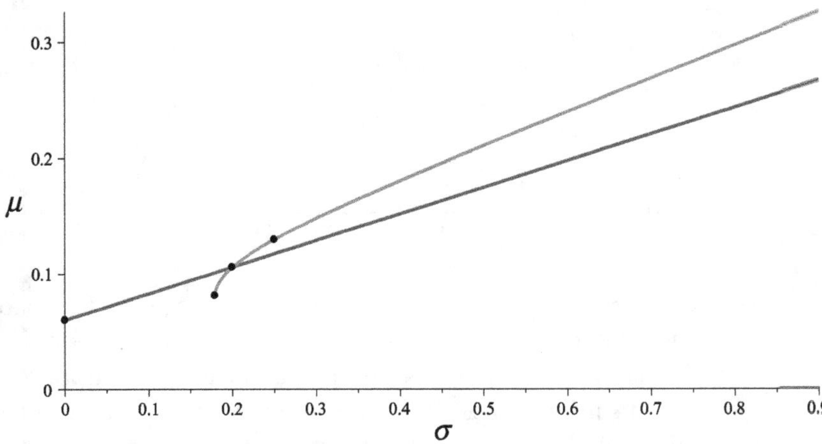

The risk-free asset is obviously the point on the μ axis, the minimum variance portfolio is the point on the efficient frontier with the minimum standard deviation and minimum expected rate of return. It is clear that the portion on the efficient frontier between the minimum standard deviation portfolio and the point chosen on the efficient frontier (the intersection of the line and the efficient frontier) is no longer efficient. It is dominated by portfolios on the line connecting the risk-free asset and the intersection of the line and the efficient frontier. However, this portion of the line is also not efficient. Better portfolios can be generated by combining the risk-free asset and a portfolio with a higher expected rate of return on the efficient frontier, e.g., with the portfolio that has a standard deviation of 0.25 demonstrated below.

```
> plot([[3*sqrt(70)*(1/140),57/700],[0,0.06],
  [0.2,.1060481256],[0.25,.1298210991]],style=point,
  symbol=solidcircle,thickness=8,colour=black):

> plot([0.06+((.1298210991-0.06)/0.25)*sd,57/700
  +3*sqrt(4200*sd^2-135)*(1/700)],sd=0..0.90,
  thickness=3,labels=[s,m],labelfont=[SYMBOL]):
  plots[display](%,%%);
```

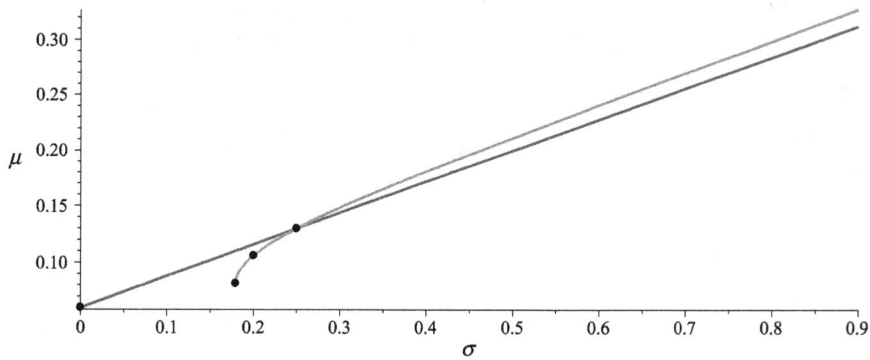

By the same argument, a better and more efficient set of portfolios can be generated by combining the risk-free asset with a point on the efficient frontier with a higher standard deviation. It is apparent that the efficient frontier, when a risk-free asset exists, will be formed by a line combining the risk-free asset with a point on the frontier such that the line is above the frontier. This point is the one that maximizes the slope of the line connecting the risk-free asset to a point on the efficient frontier. Given the shape of the efficient frontier (concave) without a risk-free asset, the slope will be maximized for a line with a μ intercept of the risk-free rate that tangents to the efficient frontier (without a risk-free asset). This is demonstrated by the animation shown below.

```
> plots[display](%,plots[animate](0.06+v*((57/700
  +3*sqrt(4200*sd^2-135)*(1/700)-0.06)/sd),v=0..1,
  sd=57/700..0.7));
```

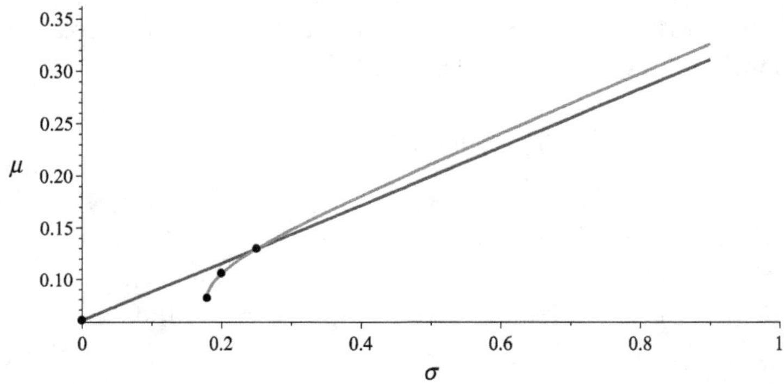

Consider our example where the VarCov matrix is given by

```
> Sigma:=Matrix(3,3,[[4/100,3/100,4/75],[3/100,9/100,
  9/100],[4/75,9/100,16/100]]);
```

$$\Sigma := \begin{bmatrix} \frac{1}{25} & \frac{3}{100} & \frac{4}{75} \\ \frac{3}{100} & \frac{9}{100} & \frac{9}{100} \\ \frac{4}{75} & \frac{9}{100} & \frac{4}{25} \end{bmatrix} \tag{39}$$

and the risk-free rate is 0.06. The portfolio that maximizes the slope of the line connecting $(0, 0.06)$ to an efficient portfolio can be solved for as shown below. Note that the slope will be obviously maximized for a portfolio on the efficient frontier. Hence, there is no need to add it as a constraint.

```
> Optimization:-Maximize((0.1*z[1]+0.12*z[2]+0.18*z[3]
  -0.06)/sqrt(add(add(z[i]*z[j]*Sigma[i,j],i=1..3),
  j=1..3)), {z[1]+z[2]+z[3]=1});
```

$$[0.302371578407381769, [z_1 = 4.81707351579053\,10^{-9}, \\ z_2 = -0.285714284732285, z_3 = 1.28571427991521]]. \tag{40}$$

Thus, the coordinate of the tangency point on the efficient frontier is given by

```
> subs(z[1]=4.81707351579053*10^(-9),
  z[2]=-.285714284732285,z[3]=1.28571427991521,
   [sqrt(add(add(z[i]*z[j]*Sigma[i,j],i=1..3),j=1..3)),
   0.1*z[1]+0.12*z[2]+0.18*z[3]]);
```

$$[0.4535573663, 0.1971428567]. \tag{41}$$

This point represents a portfolio with an expected value of 0.1971428567 and a standard deviation of 0.4535573663. Hence, the efficient frontier in this case will be a line connecting (0, 0.06) to [0.4535573663, 0.1971428567]. The slope of this line, as solved for above, is 0.302371578407381769. Hence, the equation of the line is 0.06 + 0.302371578407381769*sd as visualized in the following:

```
> plot([[3*sqrt(70)*(1/140),57/700],[.4535573663,
  .1971428567]],style=point,symbol=solidcircle,
  thickness=8,colour=black):

> plot([0.06+.302371578407381769*sd,57/700
  +3*sqrt(4200*sd^2-135)*(1/700)],sd=0..0.90,
  thickness=3,labels=[s,m],labelfont=[SYMBOL]):
  plots[display](%,%%);
```

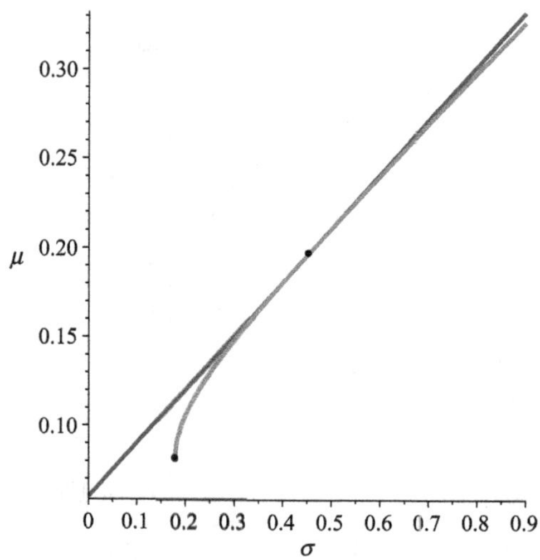

The portfolio represented by the tangency point (0.4535573663, 0.1971428567) in the above case is an essential portfolio. It is termed the *market portfolio.* The efficient frontier with a risk-free asset, R_f, becomes a line connecting the coordinates of the risk-free asset and the market portfolio, and it is termed the Capital Market Line (CML). The reasons for this terminology will become clearer as we proceed. The slope of the CML is connected to performance measures. The slope of the CML is $\frac{\mu_m - R_f}{\sigma_m}$, and by construction, it is greater than or equal to $\frac{\mu_i - R_f}{\sigma_i}$ for every portfolio in the market. The slope $\frac{\mu_i - R_f}{\sigma_i}$ is termed the *Sharpe ratio* of a security/portfolio. It measures the excess expected rate of return of a portfolio, over the risk-free rate per unit of standard deviations (risk) of the portfolio. Thus, it has a connotation of a measure of the performance of a portfolio per unit of risk, when the risk is measured by the standard deviation of the portfolio. Sharpe ratio has another interpretation related to *Post Modern Portfolio Theory* which (time permitting) will be explained later.

The market portfolio and, consequently, the CML will be determined by maximizing the slope of a line connecting $(0, R_f)$ to a portfolio on the efficient frontier, by solving the following equation:

$$\text{Maximize} \quad \frac{\sum_{i=1}^{N} x_i \mu_i - R_f}{\sqrt{\sum_{j=1}^{N} \left(\sum_{i=1}^{N} x_i \sigma_{ij} x_j \right)}}$$

$$\text{s.t.} \quad \sum_{i=1}^{N} x_i = 1.$$

Since $\sum_{i=1}^{N} x_i = 1$, we can write the objective function as

$$\frac{\sum_{i=1}^{N} x_i(\mu_i - R_f)}{\sqrt{\sum_{j=1}^{N} \left(\sum_{i=1}^{N} x_i \sigma_{ij} x_j \right)}}.$$

The objective function obtained is homogeneous of degree zero, that is, $f(k \cdot x) = k \cdot f(x)(k > 0)$. Hence, if x maximizes this function, so does $\frac{x}{k}$; therefore, we can ignore the constraint $\sum_{i=1}^{N} x_i = 1$ and solve the following unconstrained optimization:

$$\text{Max}_x \frac{\sum_{i=1}^N x_i(\mu_i - R_f)}{\sqrt{\sum_{j=1}^N \left(\sum_{i=1}^N x_i \sigma_{ij} x_j\right)}}.$$

Thus, the optimal portfolio can be found by equating to zero the derivatives of the function to be minimized with respect to x_i, $i = 1, \ldots, N$. After some algebraic manipulation (see the following hints), it can be shown that the optimal portfolio must satisfy the relations

$$\begin{aligned}\mu_i - R_f &= \lambda \cdot \sum_{j=1}^N x_j \sigma_{ij} = \lambda \sum_{j=1}^N x_j \text{Cov}(R_j, R_i) \\ &= \lambda \text{Cov}\left(\sum_{j=1}^N x_j R_j, R_i\right) \quad \text{for } i = 1, \ldots, N.\end{aligned}$$

where λ is a scalar. This is a very significant relation and its implications will be explored in the next lecture.

Denote by $(\sigma(x), \mu(x))$ the coordinate of the portfolio on the efficient frontier that maximizes the slope. Then the efficient frontier is the line connecting $(0, R_f)$ and $(\sigma(x), \mu(x))$. Therefore, portfolios on the efficient frontier are combinations of the risk-free asset and the optimal portfolio. Hence, every portfolio on the efficient frontier is composed of some proportion of the risky and non-risky portfolios. The composition of the risky portfolio (percentage wise) is the same for every portfolio on the efficient frontier and they all include the same set of risky securities. The efficient frontier is a line, which as we mentioned before, is called the Capital Market Line (CML).

Hints for Solving the Maximization of the Slope

Since $\sum_{i=1}^N x_i = 1$, we can write the objective function as follows:

$$\frac{\sum_{i=1}^N x_i(\mu_i - R_f)}{\sqrt{\sum_{j=1}^N \left(\sum_{i=1}^N x_i \sigma_{ij} x_j\right)}}$$

where σ_{ij} is the element in row i column j of the VarCov matrix $\mathbf{\Sigma}$, and since $\sum_{i=1}^{N} x_i = 1$, we have then $\sum_{i=1}^{N} x_i(\mu_i - R_f) = \sum_{i=1}^{N} x_i\mu_i - \sum_{i=1}^{N} x_i R_f = \sum_{i=1}^{N} x_i\mu_i - R_f \sum_{i=1}^{N} x_i = \sum_{i=1}^{N} x_i\mu_i - R_f$.

The objective function obtained is homogeneous of degree zero, that is, $f(k \cdot x) = k \cdot f(x)(k > 0)$. Hence, if x maximizes this function, so does $\frac{x}{k}$; therefore, we can ignore the constraint $\sum_{i=1}^{N} x_i = 1$ and solve the unconstrained optimization

$$\text{Max}_x \frac{\sum_{i=1}^{N} x_i(\mu_i - R_f)}{\sqrt{\sum_{j=1}^{N}\left(\sum_{i=1}^{N} x_i\sigma_{ij}x_j\right)}},$$

since we can always scale the optimal solution to satisfy the constraint.

The optimal portfolio is thus the solution of the set of equations

$$\frac{\partial}{\partial x}\left(\frac{\sum_{i=1}^{N} x_i(\mu_i - Rf)}{\sqrt{\sum_{j=1}^{N}\left(\sum_{i=1}^{N} x_i\sigma_{ij}x_j\right)}}\right) = 0.$$

A careful inspection of the above set of equations reveals that the ith equation is

$$\frac{\begin{array}{c}(\mu_i - R_f) \cdot \sqrt{\sum_{j=1}^{N}\left(\sum_{i=1}^{N} x_i\sigma x_j\right)} - \frac{1}{2}\left(\sum_{j=1}^{N}\sum_{i=1}^{N} x_i\sigma_{ij}x_j\right)^{-\frac{1}{2}} \\ \times 2 \cdot \sum_{i=1}^{N} x_i\sigma_{ij} \cdot \sum_{i=1}^{N} x_i(\mu_i - R_f)\end{array}}{\sum_{j=1}^{N}\left(\sum_{i=1}^{N} x_i\Sigma_{ij}x_j\right)}$$

$$= 0$$

which implies that

$$(\mu_i - R_f) = \lambda(x) \cdot \sum_{i=1}^{N} x_i\sigma_{ij}$$

where

$$\lambda(x) = \left(\frac{\left(\sum_{j=1}^{N}\sum_{i=1}^{N} x_i\sigma_{ij}x_j\right)^{-\frac{1}{2}} \cdot \sum_{i=1}^{N} x_i(\mu_i - R)}{\sqrt{\sum_{j=1}^{N}\left(\sum_{i=1}^{N} x_i\sigma_{ij}x_j\right)-}}\right).$$

Hence, in vector notations we can write the first-order conditions as

$$\mu - R_f = \lambda(x) \cdot \Sigma x$$

where μ is the vector of expected rates of return from each security and R_f is the vector $[R_f, \ldots, R_f]$.

Note, however, that if we solve

$$\mu - R_f = \Sigma y$$

where $y \in R^n$, the x that solves $\mu - R_f = \lambda(x) \cdot \Sigma x$ must be a constant (although unknown) multiplication of y. However, were we to solve for x to obtain our optimal portfolio, we would normalize the to obtain our optimal portfolio, we would normalize the x and our optimal portfolio would have been $\frac{x}{\sum_{i=1}^{N} x_i}$.

This same optimal portfolio would be obtained by solving the *linear set of equations* in y,

$$\mu - R_f = \Sigma y,$$

and scaling the solution y to satisfy $\sum_{i=1}^{N} y_i = 1$, which generates the optimal portfolio $x_i = \frac{y_i}{\sum_{i=1}^{N} y_i}$.

The optimal solution of the above problems, referred to as the market portfolio (the justification for this name will be given later), and the risk-free rate span the efficient frontier. The efficient frontier is the line connecting $(0, R_f)$ and $(\sigma(x), \mu(x))$. Therefore, portfolios on the efficient frontier are combinations of the risk-free asset and the optimal portfolio. Hence, as we mentioned earlier every portfolio on the efficient frontier is composed of some proportion of the risky and non-risky portfolios. The composition of the risky portfolio (percentage wise) is the same for every portfolio on the efficient frontier and they all include the same set of risky securities. The efficient frontier is a line, which as we mentioned before, is called the CML.

Chapter 7

The Capital Asset Pricing Model: CAPM

Introduction

The capital asset pricing model (CAPM) is an equilibrium model. Its conclusions are based on equilibrium analysis, among other things. While the CAPM employs certain assumptions, some more realistic than others, and suffers from some deficiencies, it is the first model to address the price of risk. The CAPM assumes that investors are risk averse, which implies that the value of a risky cash flow should be less than that of a sure cash flow. That is, given two cash flows one riskier than the other, the latter should be valued at less than the former. However, the questions of how risk is measured, and given the answer to this question, what the price of that risk should be and how to quantify this price, were open questions for quite a while.

These questions can also be refined looking at them from the point of view of the present value concept. If the present value of a non-risky \$1 in t units of time is $\frac{1}{1+r}$, one might conjecture that the discount factor for a risky dollar should be smaller than $\frac{1}{1+r}$ e.g., $\frac{1}{1+r+rp}$ where rp represents the risk premium, a positive number. The CAPM tells us how this rp is calculated. Putting it differently, if the rate of return on a sure dollar is r, the (expected) rate of return on a risky dollar should be $r + rp$, in order to compensate investors for taking on the risk.

The implications of the CAPM are useful not only in the investment field but also in the corporate finance field. Corporations aim to increase (maximize) the wealth of their shareholders. Following this strategy, corporations take on projects with positive net present values. How is the present value of risky projects being calculated? In order to calculate the present value, we must know the discount factors to be applied to projects with different risk characteristics. The importance of the mean–variance framework and the CAPM is now reinforced by the fact that the 1990 Economics noble prize was awarded to Professor Markowitz, Professor Miller, and Professor Sharpe "... for their pioneering work in the theory of financial economics."

In developing the CAPM, we will follow the steps as captioned in the following. First, we model the problem faced by an investor in choosing an optimal portfolio. Since a portfolio in the mean–variance framework is represented by its (σ, μ) coordinate and so is the feasible set, we need to investigate investors' ranking mechanisms of the feasible portfolios (efficient frontier) in the (σ, μ) plane. The ranking mechanism is presented by a function termed a utility function. It ranks the attractiveness of different portfolios based on their (σ, μ) characteristics, the higher the rank the more attractive the portfolio. The risk aversion assumption implies a certain property that must be fulfilled by the utility function defined over the (σ, μ) plane. We have already investigated the shape and characteristics of the feasible set under different scenarios (with and without short sales and with and without a risk free asset). Given the property of the utility function we can characterize the optimal portfolio. Once this is done, we can utilize market clearing conditions (supply = demand) to deduce the conclusions which would lead us to the way risk is measured in the CAPM, and consequently to the discount factors that should be applied to risky cash flows.

Mean–Variance and Utility Representation

There are a few variations of sets of assumptions under which the CAPM holds. One common possibility, adopted here, is to assume that the distribution of the rate of return of the securities in the market follows the Normal distribution and that all investors are risk averse. If $V(\sigma_Y, \mu_Y)$ is a utility function of a risk averse investor, our intuition tells us that since there is a tradeoff between risk and return, V should be decreasing in σ as the lower the risk the better, and increasing in μ as the higher the expected rate of return the better.

The appendix of this chapter elaborates on the definition of risk aversion and its implications to properties of utility functions.

A consequence of the risk–return tradeoff is that each given portfolio, like A in the following figure, divides the quadrant

$$\{(\sigma, \mu) \,|\, \sigma > 0, \mu > 0\}$$

into four regions.

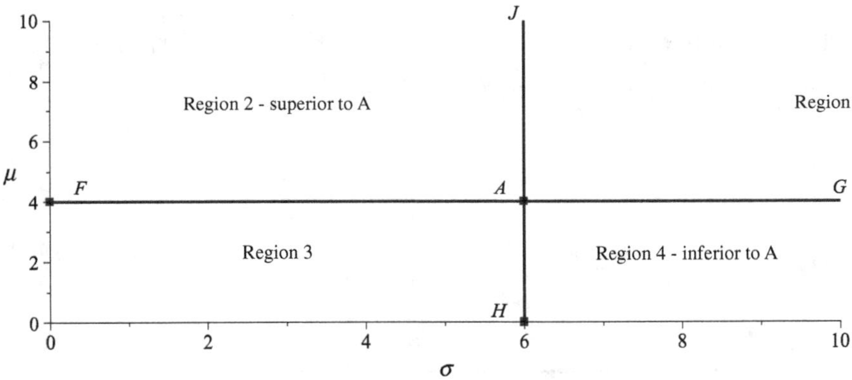

Region 4 is obviously inferior to A, as each portfolio in this region has a lower expected rate of return than A and a higher risk. Region 2 is superior to A, as each portfolio in this region has a higher expected rate or return than A and a lower risk. However, portfolios in regions 1 and 3 are not clearly superior or inferior to A. In these regions, there is a trade off between risk and return and things depend on the taste of the investor, which is expressed by the utility function.

Since the F portfolio is superior to A and the H portfolio inferior to A, it makes sense that there is portfolio in region 3, between F and H, that is equal to A. Such a portfolio has a lower risk than A but also a lower expected rate of return than A. It compensates the investor for the lower expected rate of return in terms of a lower risk. This portfolio between F and H is equal to A, in the sense that the utility function V at A, $V(\mu_A, \sigma_A)$ equals V at this portfolio between F and H. By the same argument, there will be a portfolio in region 1 that has the same utility as A. Such a portfolio has a higher expected rate of return but also a higher risk that compensates the investor enough to make the investor indifferent between this portfolio and

A. Hence, a utility function in terms of μ and σ, induces a curve, the collection of all portfolios that have the same utility as A, i.e.,

$$\{(\sigma, \mu) \mid V(\mu_A, \sigma_A) = V(\mu, \sigma)\}. \tag{1}$$

Such a curve, as in the following figure, is called an indifference curve as the investor is indifferent between all the portfolios on this curve. The curve passes via point A and the tradeoff argument implies that it increases in σ, the steeper the slope the more risk averse the investor. The shape of the curve (its convexity) is a consequence of the risk aversion of the investor (this is elaborated on in the "Utility and Uncertainty" appendix at the end of this file). Formally, these properties mean that $0 < \frac{\partial \mu(\sigma)}{\partial \sigma}$ and $0 < \frac{\partial^2 \mu(\sigma)}{\partial^2 \sigma}$.

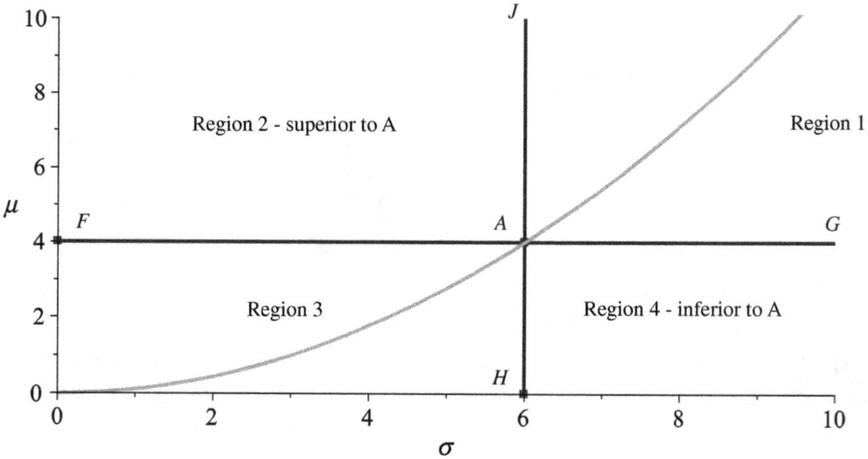

Of course, there are many indifference curves that correspond to the many different levels of utility. The higher the utility level the higher the curve e.g., an indifference curve that passes though portfolio H will be lower than the one that passes via A and an indifference curve passing via the portfolio F will be higher than the one that passes via A.

We conclude this section by commenting on the choice or the variance or standard deviation as a measure of risk. The risk measure intuitively should be concerned with a rate of return that is less than the expected value. If the variance is large due to the fact that the rate of return can be above the expected rate of return (i.e., the density function is skewed to the right), the variance is not a good measure for the risk. Having the possibility of realizing a rate of return above the expected value is not contributing to the risk of the portfolio. It will make more sense to use the semi-deviations as a risk measure, that is, the expression

$$\sum_{r_i<\mathrm{E}(r),\, i=1}^{n} Pr(r = r_i) \cdot (r_i - \mathrm{E}(r)), \tag{2}$$

where r is the random rate of return and $\Pr(r = r_i)$ is the probability that $(r = r_i)$. This however is not very attractive numerically. The literature contains a few models where the risk measure is defined differently, as well as models in which portfolios are also characterized by the third moment which measures how skewed the distribution is. Of course, under the assumption that the rate of return follows the Normal distribution, the μ and σ uniquely determine the distribution, thus the risk as well. Furthermore, for a symmetric distribution, the variance is indeed a good measure of risk.

Keep in mind that the variables in the decision problem are the percentage of the budget to be invested in each stock $(x_1, \ldots, x_n)$. Hence, $V(\mu, \sigma)$ is actually a function of $(x_1, \ldots, x_n)$. The investor, by choosing $x = (x_1, \ldots, x_n)$, determines the expected value and the standard deviation of the portfolio. The investor does it so as to maximize the utility function subject to the feasibility constraints, which are determined based on the existence of a risk-free rate and if short sales are allowed.

Choosing the Optimal Portfolio

We are now nearly at the point where we can invoke equilibrium-type arguments to obtain a few significant conclusions. We already established that when there is a risk-free asset in the market, the efficient frontier becomes a straight line, called the Capital Market Line (CML). We also mentioned that for a risk-averse investor the indifference curves, viewed as a function of σ in the (σ, μ) plane, are convex and monotone decreasing in σ.

Let us now look at a particular case illustrating the optimal portfolio for an investor with a utility function of the form $-\mathrm{e}^{\frac{1}{2}\sigma^2-\mu}$. Recall that investors choose the portfolio which, of course, determines μ and σ. However, under our assumption, choosing the portfolio is equivalent to choosing μ and σ. Let us define the utility function as a function in the following Maple.

```
> Utility:=(sigma, mu)->-exp((1/2)*sigma^2-mu);
```

$$\text{Utility} := (\sigma, \mu) \mapsto -\mathrm{e}^{\frac{\sigma^2}{2}-\mu}. \tag{3}$$

```
>
```

Thus, this utility function induces indifference curves which are monotone, increasing, and convex. For example the indifference curve that corresponds to -0.09 is graphed as follows.

```
> plots[implicitplot](Utility(sigma,mu)=-.9,
  sigma=0..0.54,mu=0..0.18);
```

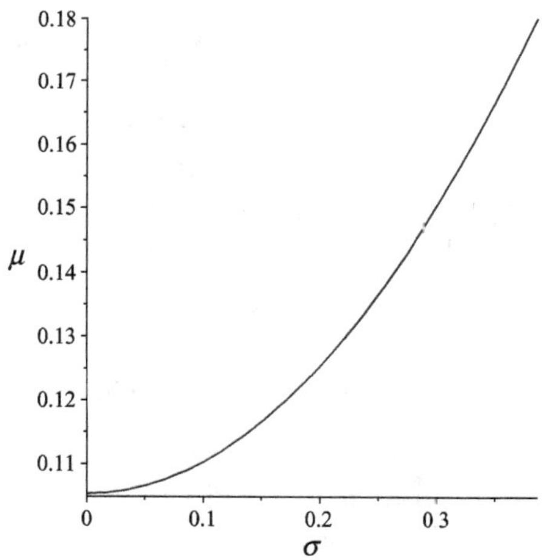

Assume that a risk-free asset exists and that short sales are allowed, thus the efficient frontier is a line, the CML line. If the risk-free rate is 0.07 and the market portfolio has the coordinate $\mu = 0.15$ and $\sigma = 0.2$, the CML is given by linear equation

$$\mu = 0.07 + \frac{0.15 - 0.07}{0.2} \cdot \sigma.$$

It is the equation of the line in the following figure which is superimposed on the indifference curve above that corresponds to a level of utility of -0.9. Note that the utility level is only a ranking mechanism and has no other meaning. The higher the level the higher the welfare of the investor.

```
> plots[implicitplot](Utility(sigma,mu)=-.9,sigma=0..1,
  mu=0..0.7):plot(0.07+((0.15-0.07)/0.2)*sigma,sigma=
  0..1,labels=[s,m],labelfont=[SYMBOL],thickness=3):
  plots[display](%,%%);
```

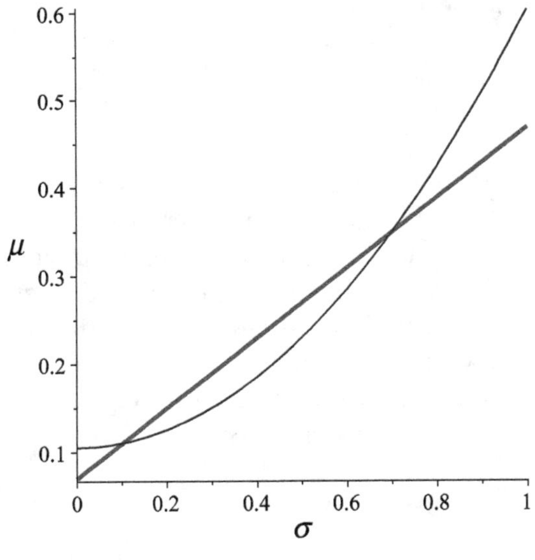

Clearly the investor can find a portfolio on the CML with a higher level of utility as a higher indifference curve will still intersect the CML. For example, the following figure displays the utility level of -0.9 and -0.87 together with the CML.

```
> seq(plots[implicitplot](Utility(sigma,mu)=-0.9+2*i/100,
  sigma=0..1,mu=0..0.58,labels=[s,m],labelfont=[SYMBOL],
  thickness=1,thickness=2),i=0..1):plot(0.07+((0.15-
  0.07)/0.2)*sigma,sigma=0..1,labels=[s,m],labelfont=
  [SYMBOL],thickness=3):plots[display](%,%%);
```

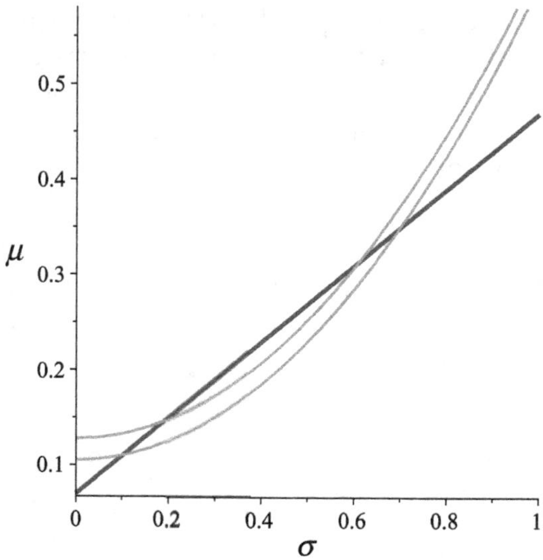

The above figure demonstrates that the investor can choose a portfolio on the CML that will have even a larger utility than −0.87. Every investor tries to maximize utility by choosing a portfolio on the CML that lies on the highest possible indifference curve. Let us now graph the CML and a few indifference curves, including the indifference curve that corresponds to the utility level above a level that could be reached, in one graph. We also place boxes at the coordinates of the optimal portfolio and the risk-free rate.

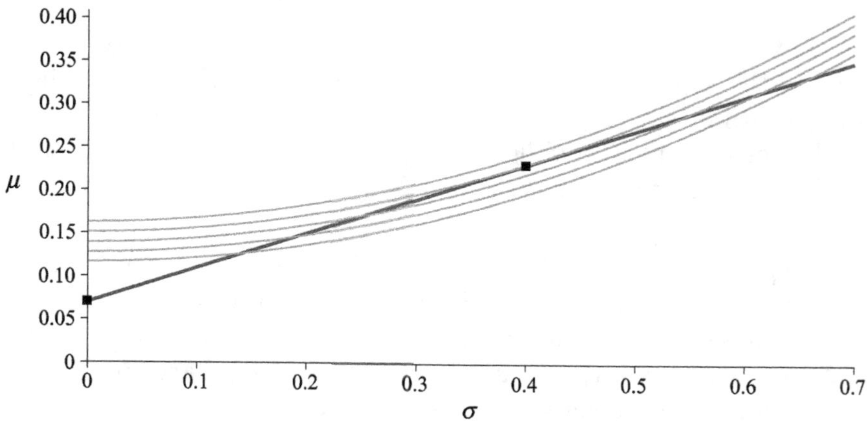

This visualization shows the process of the optimization. The portfolio on the CML that corresponds to the highest utility is the one at which the highest possible indifference curve tangents to the CML. While the discussion above was based on a specific utility function, the same conclusions would apply as long as the utility function is of a risk-averse investor and the risky rate of returns follow the normal distribution.

Hence, the optimal portfolio of every investor is somewhere on the CML. Since the CML is a combination of the risk-free asset and the market portfolio, the optimal portfolio of each investor is a combination of the risk-free asset and the market portfolio. The risky part in each investor's portfolio is the same and is the market portfolio. The different portfolios held by different investors differ only by the proportion of the risk-free asset and the market portfolio. Portfolios on the line segment between the risk-free rate and the market portfolio do not involve short positions. Portfolios on the CML with an expected rate of return above that of the market portfolios are composed of a short position in the risk-free rate (borrowing) and investing in the market portfolio.

Since the optimal portfolio is the tangency point between the CML and the indifference curve, their slopes at the optimal portfolio are equal. Furthermore, for every investor, the slope of the indifference curve at the optimal portfolio equals the slope of the CML. Consequently, the slopes of the indifference curve of every investor at the optimal portfolio is the same and equals the slope of the CML. This slope is termed the marginal rate of substitution. It is the compensation an investor requires for an infinitesimal increase in risk in terms of an additional expected rate of return.

Formally the maximization problem solved by the investor in order to find the optimal portfolio is

$$\text{Max} - e^{\left(\frac{\sigma^2}{2}-\mu\right)}$$

$$\text{s.t} \quad \mu = 0.07 + \frac{0.15 - 0.07}{0.2} \cdot \sigma.$$

Solving for the Optimal Portfolio

Note that in the optimization solved by the investor the constraint is the CML. That is done even though the feasible set of possible portfolios is not the CML, the CML is rather its upper envelope. Nevertheless this formulation is appropriate under the assumption of risk aversion (concave utility function), as the investor tries to be on the highest possible indifference curve.

Substituting for μ in terms of σ into the function to be maximized, and differentiating will yield the optimal μ and σ as follows.

```
> subs(mu=0.07+((0.15-0.07)/0.2)*sigma,
  -exp(-(-sigma^2+2*mu)/2));
```

$$-e^{\frac{1}{2}\sigma^2-0.07-0.4000000000\,\sigma} \tag{4}$$

```
>

> diff(%,sigma);
```

$$-(\sigma-0.4000000000)e^{\frac{1}{2}\sigma^2-0.07-0.4000000000\,\sigma} \tag{5}$$

```
>

> solve(%):subs(sigma=%,0.07+((0.15-0.07)/0.2)*sigma);
```

$$0.2300000000 \tag{6}$$

```
>
```

Thus, the optimal σ is 0.4 and the optimal μ is 0.23. Let us see what the value of the objective function is at this point.

```
> Utility(0.4,0.23);
```

$$-0.8607079764. \tag{7}$$

We end this section with a procedure that solves for the optimal portfolio given the risk-free rate, the expected rate of return and the standard deviation of the market portfolio, and the utility function (in fact the expected utility) of the investor in terms of μ and σ. The procedure solves for the optimal portfolio and prints its expected rate of return and standard deviation. It also plots a few indifference curves, the capital market line, and the optimal portfolio. The procedure, defined in the following, checks that the utility function specified satisfies our conditions, e.g., the indifference curves are convex and monotone increasing in σ. The utility function must be specified by the variable μ and σ. If this is not the case, an error message will be issued.

Here is how it works. If the risk-free rate is 0.10, the standard deviation of the market portfolio is 0.2, its expected rate of return is 0.12, and the utility function is $e^{\frac{(-\sigma^2+2\cdot\mu)}{2}}$ then the procedure will be executed as follows:

```
> EfficnIndif(0.10,0.2,0.12,-exp(-sigma^2+2*mu)/2);
```

The optimal (σ,μ) *is*, 0.1000000000, 0.1100000000

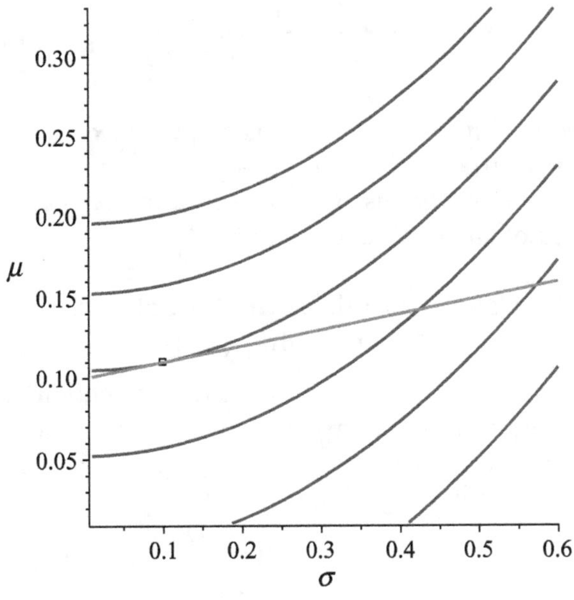

If the utility function is changed to be $\mu-\frac{3}{2}\sigma^2$, the result will be

```
> EfficnIndif(0.10,0.2,0.12,mu-(1/2)*3*sigma^2);
```

The optimal (σ,μ) *is*, 0.03333333333, 0.1033333333

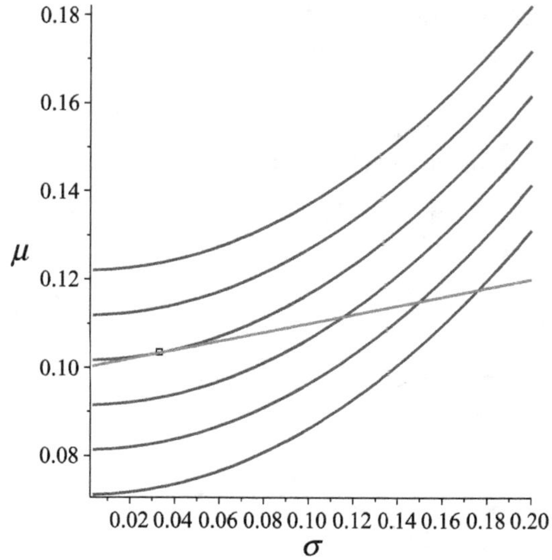

The next section utilizes the conclusions reached here in order to obtain an answer to questions we posed at the very beginning of this section: What should the discount factor for a risky cash flow be and how is the risk of the case flow measured?

The CAPM as an Equilibrium Model and the Security Market Line (SML)

The conclusion reached at the end of the last section was that the optimal portfolio of any investor would lie on the CML. The CML is a relation that is satisfied by all efficient portfolios in the market, and is sometimes stated as follows:

$$E[R_e] = R_f + \frac{E[R_M] - R_f}{\sigma_M}\sigma_e, \tag{8}$$

where the subscript e denotes an efficient portfolio on the CML, and

- R_f is the risk-free rate of return.
- R_M is the rate of return on the market portfolio.
- R_e is the rate of return on an efficient portfolio.
- σ_M is the standard deviation of the rate of return on the market portfolio.
- σ_e is the standard deviation of the rate of return on the efficient portfolio.

The CML is thus a line in the (σ, μ) plane that passes via $(0, R_f)$ and $(\sigma_M, E[R_M])$. Portfolios that are comprised of positive combinations of the risk-free rate and the market portfolio, lie on the line segment connecting $(0, R_f)$ and $(\sigma_M, E[R_M])$. This means that these are portfolios of investors dividing their investment between the risk-free rate and the market portfolio. However, some investors borrow at the risk-free rate in order to invest in the market portfolio. Such an investor holds a portfolio whereby the proportion invested in the market portfolio is greater than the proportion invested in the risk-free rate, with the latter being negative. The investor is taking a short position in the risk-free rate, adds it to the initial wealth, and invests it all in the market portfolio. Thus, such a portfolio lies on the CML but to the right of the market portfolio. In any event, since the portfolios of all investors are on the CML, every investor with a portion of a portfolio invested in the risky asset holds the same risky portfolio, the market portfolio.

Putting it differently, if an investor holding a portion of the money in the risky portfolio is chosen randomly, and the risky part of the portfolio is normalized, then the market portfolio is obtained. That is let $x_1, \ldots, x_N$ denote the holding of the ith risky security in the portfolio of such an investor and define $w_i = \frac{x_i}{\Sigma_{i=1}^N x_i}$, then the portfolio $(w_1, \ldots, w_N)$ must be the market portfolio.

In equilibrium, supply equals demand and the market clears. Thus, if all investors hold the same risky portfolio, the securities that exist in the market must be those that are in the market portfolio. If a security is not in the market portfolio nobody holds it, and thus it will not exist in the market. The market portfolio thus consists of all securities in the market. Consequently the w_i, $i = 1, \ldots, N$ must be the capitalization of each security in the market. That is, if the price of security i is P_i and there are N_i units of this security outstanding in the market, w_i must satisfy $w_i = \frac{Nx_i}{\Sigma_{i=1}^N Nx_i}$.

This conclusion might be surprising at first sight. However, if one examines the following list of the suppressed assumptions we have been working under, this result might not be as surprising as it first appears to be.

- No transaction costs.
- No taxes.

- Unlimited short sales are allowed.
- Assets are infinitely divisible.
- Perfect competition, i.e., an individual investor cannot affect the price of an asset by trading it. All investors are "price takers", however investors in aggregate determine the prices in equilibrium by their trading activities.
- Normal distribution of return and concave utility. That is, all investors are risk averse and thus portfolios are fully characterized by the mean and variance of the returns.
- Unlimited lending and borrowing at the risk-free rate.
- Homogeneous expectations and information.
- All assets are marketable, including human capital.

Our key question however is still not answered: What can we say about the price of risk? That is, can we show that a relation similar to the CML should be obeyed by every security in the market? Can we deduce the risk premium for every security in the market? This is going to be answered next.

Since the market portfolio is actually composed of the w_i, $i = 1, \ldots, N$ as defined above, we can conclude that the portfolio $(w_i, \ldots, w_N)$ satisfies the optimality condition of the optimization problem

$$\text{Max}_x \ \frac{\sum_{i=1}^{N} x_i(\mu_i - R_f)}{\sqrt{\sum_{j=1}^{N}\left(\sum_{i=1}^{N} x_i \sigma_{ij} x_j\right)}}$$

$$\text{s.t.} \sum_{i=1}^{N} x_i = 1 \tag{9}$$

that identifies the market portfolio by maximizing the slope of the CML. The optimality conditions were

$$\mu_i - R_f = \lambda \cdot \text{Cov}\left(\sum_{j=1}^{N} x_j R_j, R_i\right) \quad \text{for } i = 1, \ldots, N, \tag{10}$$

for a scalar λ. Thus, for $R_M = \sum_{i=1}^{N} w_i R_i$ the optimality conditions are satisfied and

$$\begin{aligned}\boldsymbol{\mu}_i - R_f &= \lambda \cdot \mathrm{Cov}\left(\sum_{j=1}^{N} w_j R_j, R_i\right) \\ &= \lambda \cdot \mathrm{Cov}(R_M, R_i) = \lambda \sigma_{Mi} \quad \text{for } i = 1, \ldots, N. \end{aligned} \tag{11}$$

Multiply the ith equation above by w_i and summing the equations yields

$$\begin{aligned}\sum_{i=1}^{N} w_i(\mu_i - R_f) &= \sum_{i=1}^{N} w_i\mu_i - \sum_{i=1}^{N} w_i R_f = \sum_{i=1}^{N} w_i\mu_i - R_f \\ &= \sum_{i=1}^{N} w_i\lambda \cdot \mathrm{Cov}(R_M, R_i) = \lambda \cdot \mathrm{Cov}\left(R_M, \sum_{i=1}^{N} w_i R_i\right). \end{aligned} \tag{12}$$

However,

$$\lambda \cdot \mathrm{Cov}\left(R_M, \sum_{i=1}^{N} w_i R_i\right) = \lambda \cdot \mathrm{Cov}(R_M, R_M) = \lambda \cdot \sigma_M^2. \tag{13}$$

Thus we obtain that

$$\sum_{i=1}^{N} w_i\mu_i - R_f = \lambda\sigma_M^2 \tag{14}$$

and since $\sum_{i=1}^{N} w_i\mu_i = \mu_M$ it follows that

$$\sum_{i=1}^{N} \mu_M - R_f = \lambda\sigma_M^2 \tag{15}$$

and thus

$$\frac{\mu_M - R_f}{\sigma_M^2} = \lambda. \tag{16}$$

Hence substitution of λ in $\mu_i - R_f = \lambda\sigma_{Mi}$, for $i = 1, \ldots, N$, yields

$$\mu_i - R_f = \frac{\mu_M - R_f}{\sigma_M^2}\sigma_{Mi}. \tag{17}$$

It is customary to denote $\frac{\sigma_{Mi}}{\sigma_M^2}$ by β_i and write this relation as:

$$\mu_i = R_f + \beta_i(\mu_M - R_f) \quad i = 1, \ldots, N. \tag{18}$$

This relation therefore must be satisfied by every security in the market and is called the Security Market Line (SML). If we graph this relation in the (μ, β) plane, it will be a linear relation. Its slope is $\mu_M - R_f$ and its y intercept is R_f.

Another Way of Proving the SML

All investors, by maximizing their utilities, arrived at an optimal point whereby the marginal rate of substitution equals the slope of the CML. Thus, in equilibrium, all investors have the same marginal rate of substitution, which equals the slope of the CML and hence is given by:

$$\frac{\mu_M - R_f}{\sigma_M}. \tag{19}$$

Thus in equilibrium, a marginal increase of the standard deviation of the market portfolio must be compensated by an increase in the expected rate of return of $\frac{\mu_M - R_f}{\sigma_M}$.

The expression $\mu_M - R_f$ is the market risk premium (or in short, the risk premium) and is of course always positive. Otherwise nobody would want to hold the market portfolio and everybody would invest in the risk-free rate. Notice that this is a relation between $\mu_M = E[R_M]$ and not the random variable R_M thus, it does not imply that $R_M - R_f > 0$ for every realization of R_M. Since all efficient portfolios are on the CML, $\frac{\mu_M - R_f}{\sigma_M}$ is the market price of risk (measured in units of σ_M) for all efficient portfolios — it expresses the compensation for taking risk in terms of the expected rate of return.

Let us investigate the affect on μ_M and σ_M of an infinitesimal change in the holding of asset i. Consider a portfolio where a proportion of a is invested in the risky asset i with mean μ_i and standard deviation σ_i, and $(1 - a)$ invested in the market portfolio. The expected return and standard deviation of such a portfolio are

$$\mu_P = a\mu_i + (1-a)\mu_M$$
$$\sigma_P = \left\{a^2\sigma^2 + (1-a)^2\,\sigma_M^2 + 2\,a(1-a)\sigma_{iM}\right\}^{\frac{1}{2}}. \tag{20}$$

Here $\sigma_{iM} = \rho_{iM}\sigma_i\sigma_M$, where ρ_{iM} is the correlation coefficient between the market portfolio and asset i. Since in equilibrium, the market portfolio contains an optimal allocation of assets, if a deviates from zero, the composed portfolio will not be a mean–variance efficient portfolio. A marginal increase in a will cause a change in the expected rate of return of the portfolio by $\mu_i - \mu_M$ and in the standard derivation of the portfolio by $\{a^2\sigma_i^2 + (1-a)^2\sigma_M^2 + 2\,a(1-a)\sigma_{iM}\}^{-\frac{1}{2}}\{a\sigma_i^2 - (1-a)\sigma_M^2 + (1-a)\sigma_{iM}\}$. This is verified by the fact that

$$\frac{\partial\mu_P}{\partial a} = \mu_i - \mu_M \tag{21}$$

and

$$\frac{\partial\sigma_P}{\partial a} = \frac{1}{2}\{a^2\sigma_i^2 + (1-a)^2\sigma_M^2 + 2\,a(1-a)\sigma_{iM}\}^{-\frac{1}{2}} \times \{2\,a\sigma_i^2 - 2(1-a)\sigma_M^2 + 2(1-a)\sigma_{iM}\}. \tag{22}$$

However, since in equilibrium $a = 0$, an increase of a from zero will cause a change of

$$\left.\frac{\partial\mu_P}{\partial a}\right|_{a=0} = \mu_i - \mu_M \tag{23}$$

in the expected rate of return and of

$$\left.\frac{\partial\sigma_P}{\partial a}\right|_{a=0} = \frac{\sigma_{iM} - \sigma_M^2}{\sigma_m} \tag{24}$$

in the standard derivation of the portfolio. Thus, the price of risk, the change in the expected rate of return per change in the standard deviation, is the ratio of

$$\left.\frac{\partial\mu_P}{\partial\sigma_P}\right|_{a=0} = \left.\frac{\frac{\partial\mu_P}{\partial a}}{\frac{\partial\sigma_P}{\partial a}}\right|_{a=0} = \frac{(\mu_i - \mu_M)}{\frac{\sigma_{iM}-\sigma_M^2}{\sigma_m}} = \frac{(\mu_i - \mu_M)\cdot\sigma_M}{\sigma_{iM} - \sigma_M^2}. \tag{25}$$

But in equilibrium the price of risk for the market portfolio (an efficient portfolio) is the slope of the CML, and hence

$$(\mu_i - \mu_M)\frac{\sigma_M}{\sigma_{iM} - \sigma_M^2} = \frac{\mu_M - r_f}{\sigma_M}. \tag{26}$$

Therefore,

$$\mu_i = \mu_M + \frac{\sigma_{iM} - \sigma_M^2}{\sigma_M^2}\{\mu_M - r_f\} = \mu_M + \left(\frac{\sigma_{iM}}{\sigma_M^2} - 1\right)\{\mu_M - r_f\} \tag{27}$$

or, equivalently,

$$\mu_i = r_f + \frac{\sigma_{iM}}{\sigma_M^2}(\mu_M - r_f) = r_f + \beta_i(\mu_M - r_f), \tag{28}$$

where $\beta_i = \frac{\sigma_{iM}}{\sigma_M^2}$.

An SML for the case where the risk free rate is 0.1, the expected value of the market is 0.15 and its standard deviation is 0.8 is displayed as follows:

```
> plot([[0,0.10],[0.8,0.15]],style=point,symbol=solidbox,
  thickness=8,title="SML for Rf=0.1,E(Rm)=0.15
  sigma(Rm)=0.8",titlefont =[TIMES,BOLD,10]):

> plot(0.10+beta*(0.15-0.10)/0.8,beta=0..1.5,
  labels=[b,m],labelfont=[SYMBOL],thickness=1):

> plots[display](%,%%);
```

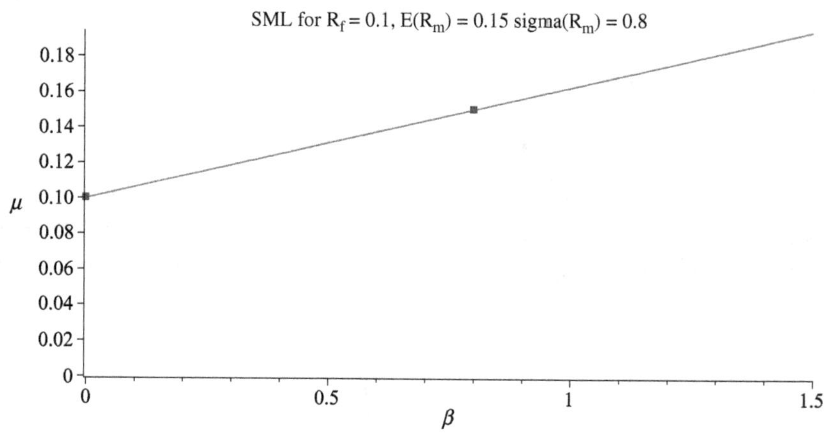

Note that for $\beta = 0$, $\mu = R_f$ and that for $\beta = 1$, $\mu = E(R_M)$. This can be confirmed from the definition of $\beta_i = \frac{\sigma_{Mi}}{\sigma_M^2}$. If i stands for R_f, $\sigma_{Mi} = 0$ and thus $\beta = 0$, and for $i = M$, $\sigma_{MM} = \sigma_M^2$ and thus β is 1.

The SML should hold in equilibrium for every security in the market. However, this is a relation *between the expected rate of return on a security and that of the market.* Thus, **observing a realization of the rates of return of the market and of the securities in the market that do not satisfy the SML, does not negate the SML**. The SML is not a relation between realization of random variables but rather the expected value of these variables.

Furthermore, since the SML relation holds for every security in the market, it must hold for every portfolio in this market with the β of the portfolio. Consider a portfolio defined by $(x_1, \ldots, x_N)$ and keep in mind that $\sum_{i=1}^{N} x_i = 1$. If we multiply the ith equation

$$\mu_i = R_f + \beta_i(E(R_m) - R_f) \quad i = 1, \ldots, N \tag{29}$$

by x_i and sum up the equations we obtain

$$\sum_{i=1}^{N} x_i\mu_i = R_f + (E(R_m) - R_f)\sum_{i=1}^{N} x_i\beta_i. \tag{30}$$

Let the expected rate of return on the portfolio i be denoted by $E(R_P) = \sum_{i=1}^{N} x_i\mu_i$ and denote by $\beta_P = \sum_{i=1}^{N} x_i\beta_i$. We thus have that

$$E(R_P) = R_f + \beta_P(E(R_m) - R_f). \tag{31}$$

Hence, we confirm that the SML is satisfied for every portfolio in the market, and that β of a portfolio is the weighted average of the β's of the securities in the portfolio.

It is important to be aware of the fact that the CML is satisfied by every *efficient portfolio* and that the SML is satisfied by every **security (and by every portfolio)**. The CML describes a relation in the (σ, μ) plane while the SML describes a relation in the (β, μ) plane. Interpreting the SML relation from an economic point of view revealing it to be the answer to our key questions, is the topic of the next section.

Properties of the SML

Let us observe again the SML (where we use μ_m instead of $E(R_m)$).

$$\mu_i = R_f + \beta_i \cdot (\mu_m - R_f). \tag{32}$$

The SML relates an expected return of a risky asset to its risk and stipulates the risk premium. Casual observation reveals that the SML presents the expected rate of return on a security as the sum of two components, one of which is the risk-free rate. Thus, it specifies the additional expected rate of return attributed to security i for being a risky security — that is the risk premium of security i.

In competitive markets, an investor holding a risky asset must be compensated for taking the risk, otherwise there would be no incentive to prefer it over the risk-free rate. This compensation is in the form of an expected rate of return. The expected rate of return on a risky asset, $E(R)$, must be greater than the rate of return offered by the risk-free asset, R_f. Hence, $E(R) > R_f$ and the difference $E(R) - R_f$ is termed the *risk premium.*

Furthermore, the CAPM stipulates the risk premium of security i as the product of the market risk premium $(\mu_m - R_f)$ and β of that security. Since the risk premium of security i is $\beta_i \cdot (\mu_m - R_f)$, the part that captures the risk of security i must be β_i. Before interpreting this risk measure and its use, we should realize what the CAPM provides us with. It shows us that the risk of a risky asset is measured by β. The compensation an investor needs in terms of expected rates of return, for holding a risky instead of a risk-free asset, is $\beta_i \cdot (\mu_m - R_f)$. Therefore, the CAPM provided an answer to the question: What should the risk-adjusted discount factor for a risk asset be?

In financial markets, a "fair" or a correct price of an asset or a financial instrument, is the present value of its future cash flows. In the Chapter 3, we investigated the risk-free environment, such as the debt market consisting of government bonds. In this case, the present value of the future cash flow of a bond is calculated by discounting it, at the risk-free rates, to obtain its present value.

The value or correct price of a risky asset that promises a risky cash flow, is also the present value of the cash flow. However, in a risky environment, a risk adjusted discount factor must be used. Obviously a future risky dollar is worth less than a sure dollar. Hence, if the discount factor for the sure dollar is $\frac{1}{(1+r)}$, the discount factor for a risky dollar must be $\frac{1}{(1+r+rp)}$, where rp is a positive constant representing the risk premium. One can argue that the major contribution of the CAPM is the specification of rp as $\beta_i \cdot (\mu_M - R_f)$.

In the CAPM, the risk of an asset is measured by its β. The β of an asset measures the sensitivity of the expected rate of return of a risky asset to the expected rate of return in the "market". The CAPM specifies the risk premium of an asset as a function of the excess expected rate of return of the market over the risk-free rate, i.e., $\mu_M - R_f$.

Since β is defined as the covariance of a security with the market divided by the variance of the market, it is evident that the risk of a security is no longer measured by its standard deviation. Rather, we see that the risk is measured by the covariance of the security with the market portfolio. We can therefore interpret the variance of the market as the unit of risk. Hence, the covariance when divided by the variance, measures how many units of risk are taken by an investor holding the security. This should sound familiar as we demonstrated that when a portfolio is naively diversified, and the number of securities in the market is large, the major factor in determining the risk is indeed the covariance.

In the context of the CAPM, everybody holds the market portfolio. Hence, the risk of a security is not its total risk (the variance). A portion of the variance is offset by the other securities in the market portfolio due to the covariance with other securities in the market portfolio. Thus, when an investor holds a risky security, the investor does not bear the full risk of the security, only the part that is not being offset by the other securities in the market portfolio.

The market "rewards" the investor only for the risk that the investor must bear. In other words, every firm in the market is affected by its own characteristics and by the conditions of the market. An investor cannot affect the market conditions overall but can eliminate the risk associated with a firm by holding a diversified portfolio. Thus, one can imagine splitting the risk of each security into two parts: one for which investors are compensated for a *systemic risk* and one for which there is no compensation, a *non-systematic risk*. This idea is presented more rigorously as follows.

The SML specifies a relationship between the expected value of the rate of return of the market portfolio and that of each security, namely $\mu_i = R_f + \beta(\mu_M - R_f)$. Of course, the same relation does not hold between the random variables, that is R_i does not equal $R_f + \beta(R_M - R_f)$. However, from the SML, we can infer something about the difference between the random variables R_i and $R_f + \beta \cdot (R_M - R_f)$.

Let us denote the difference between these variables by ε_i, hence

$$R_i = R_f + \beta_i \cdot (R_M - R_f) + \varepsilon_i. \tag{33}$$

Taking the expected value of both sides of this equation yields that the expected value of ε_i, $E(\varepsilon_i)$ must equal zero, otherwise the SML would be violated. Furthermore, the covariance of R_m with the left side of the equation and with the right side must be equal, that is

$$\text{Cov}(R_M, R_i) = \text{Cov}(R_M, R_f + \beta_i(R_M - R_f) + \varepsilon_i).$$

Since $\text{Cov}(R_M, R_f) = 0$ and $\text{Cov}(R_M, R_M) = \sigma_M^2$ following the covariance rules we have

$$\begin{aligned} \text{Cov}(R_m, R_i) &= \text{Cov}(R_m, \beta \cdot R_m) - \text{Cov}(R_m, \varepsilon_i) \\ &= \beta_i \cdot \text{Cov}(R_m, R_m) + \text{Cov}(R_m, \varepsilon_i) \end{aligned} \tag{34}$$

thus

$$\text{Cov}(R_m, R_i) = \beta_i \text{Cov}(R_m, R_m) + \text{Cov}(R_m, \varepsilon_i). \tag{35}$$

However, since $\beta_i = \frac{\text{Cov}(R_i, R_m)}{\text{Cov}(R_m, R_m)}$ we have that

$$\text{Cov}(R_m, R_i) = \text{Cov}(R_m, R_i) + \text{Cov}(R_m, \varepsilon_i) \tag{36}$$

and therefore that $\text{Cov}(R_m, \varepsilon_i) = 0$. Note that $\text{Cov}(R_m, R_m)$ is of course the variance of the market portfolio. Hence, using the relation

$$R_i = R_f + \beta_i \cdot (R_m - R_f) + \varepsilon_i \tag{37}$$

we can write

$$\text{Var}(R_i) = \text{Var}(R_f + \beta_i \cdot (R_m - R_f) + \varepsilon_i). \tag{38}$$

Following the rules of the variance and R_m and ε_i not being correlated imply:

$$\text{Var}(R_i) = \beta_i^2 \cdot \text{Var}(R_m) + \text{Var}(\varepsilon_i). \tag{39}$$

Therefore, the total risk of an asset can be divided into two parts:

$\beta_i^2 \cdot \text{Var}(R_m)$, essentially measured by β and referred to as the *systematic risk* or the *non-diversified risk*, and

$\text{Var}(\varepsilon_i)$, not correlated with the market and referred to as the *non-systematic*, the *specific risk* or the *idiosyncratic risk*.

$\text{Var}(\varepsilon_i)$ is the risk for which the investor is not rewarded.

An efficient portfolio on the CML is a combination of the risk-free rate and the market portfolio. Hence, the rate of return of an efficient portfolio can be written as

$$R_e = (1 - \beta_e) \cdot R_f + \beta_e \cdot R_m \tag{40}$$

where the subindex e stands for an efficient portfolio. Hence, $\text{Var}(R_e) = \beta_e^2 \cdot \text{Var}(R_m)$ and thus $\sigma_e = \beta_e \cdot \sigma_m$ confirms that assets on the CML are well diversified and their risks are composed only of systematic risks.

Note also that the standard deviation of such an asset is $\sigma_e = \beta_e \cdot \sigma_m = \frac{\sigma_{em}}{\sigma_m^2} \cdot \sigma_m = \frac{\sigma_{em}}{\sigma_m}$, which explains why some authors prefer to write the SML as

$$\mu_i = R_f + \frac{\sigma_{im}}{\sigma_m} \frac{\mu_m - R_f}{\sigma_m}. \tag{41}$$

This version of the SML can be interpreted as follow. The risk of a security is measured in units of σ_m. The risk of a security is σ_{im}, its covariance with the market portfolio. Thus, the security has $\frac{\sigma_{im}}{\sigma_m}$ units of risk. The compensation in terms of the expected rate of return per unit of risk is $\frac{\mu_m - R_f}{\sigma_m}$. Consequently, the total compensation in terms of expected rate of return is the product $\frac{\sigma_{im}}{\sigma_m} \frac{\mu_m - R_f}{\sigma_m}$. Securities with negative β are not common. Holding such a security in a portfolio reduces the overall risk of the portfolio and hence causes a reduction in its rate of return.

Concluding Remarks

The CAPM indeed presented a breakthrough in the analysis and understanding of the risk–return trade off. It has been used vastly in practical applications in spite of its deficiencies or biases caused by the way it has been applied. For example, in practical applications of the CAPM or for estimation purposes, the "market portfolio" is usually represented by an index which captures the market, such as the S&P 500. The academic literature reports significant biases that are due to the use of the proxy for the market portfolio. The CAPM is a one period model and the period is not specified by the model. Hence, in practical applications, one needs to decide about the "period" and accordingly estimate β and the return on the market. The CAPM also assumes that the β of a company is a constant, while empirical evidence seem to suggest otherwise. Furthermore, the CAPM assumes that the distributions and consequently the expected rate of return and variance of the market is stable, but this is also questionable.

There is no doubt that the CAPM is an elegant theory that is easily understood intuitively and perhaps this is why the CAPM, in spite of its caveats, is used in practical implications. Hence, the implementation of the CAPM presents practitioners with certain decisions that must be taken regarding the application of the CAPM to practical problems.

After the development of the CAPM, vast academic literature has sprung up that is devoted to all aspects of the CAPM. The literature includes techniques of estimating beta, the validity of the CAPM from an empirical point of view, efficient numerical procedures of calculating the efficient frontier, use of the CAPM in corporate finance, business valuation as well as judging the preference of various investment strategies, mutual funds etc.

Appendix A: Utility and Uncertainty

When we proceed to a model that captures uncertainty, the concavity of the utility functions will be used to describe risk attitudes of the investors. In uncertain situations, the wealth of the investor is a random variable, say X. The utility from a random event is commonly measured by the expected utility or the mean, e.g., by $E(U(X))$.

We say that an investor is risk averse if $U(E(X)) > E(U(X))$. This means that an investor for whom this inequality holds, prefers to receive the certain amount $E(X)$ to the random amount X. Since $E(X)$ is a convex combination of the possible realizations of X, $U(E(X)) > E(U(X))$ means that U is a concave function.

Let us illustrate this situation with a random variable that takes only two possible values: x_1, and x_2, where $x_1 < x_2$ with probabilities p_1 and p_2.

In this case, $E(U(X)) \leq U(E(X))$ is written as

$$p_1 U(x_1) + p_2 U(x_2) \leq U(p_1 x_1 + p_2 x_2) \tag{42}$$

which is satisfied by a concave utility function.

Let us illustrate this situation graphically. Assume that $x_1 = 2$ and $x_2 = 18$ and that $U(X)$ is the natural logarithm of x, i.e., $\ln(x)$. The line in the graph connects the points $(2, \ln(2))$ and $(18, \ln(18))$. The fact that the line lies underneath the graph of the function (the curve) is a consequence of the concavity of $\ln(x)$.

```
> plot([ln(x),[[2,ln(2)],[16,ln(16)]]],x=1..20,
  thickness=3);
```

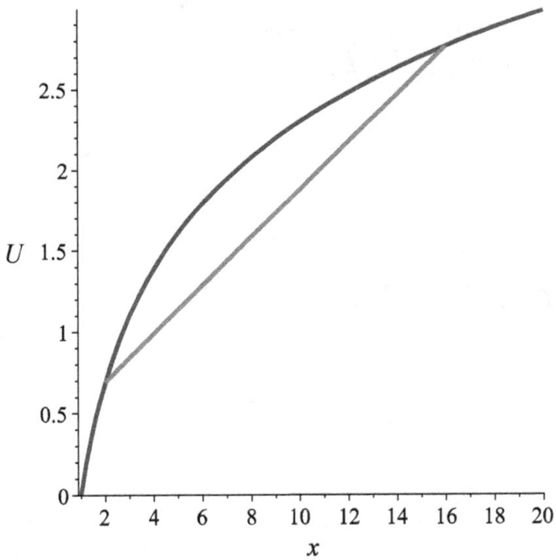

Now the point $(p_1 \cdot 2 + p_2 \cdot 16, p_1 \cdot \ln(2) + p_2 \cdot \ln(16))$ is somewhere on the line (the linear graph). The two extreme cases are: if $p_1 = 1$ then $p_2 = 0$ and the point is $(2, \ln(2))$ and, if $p_1 = 0$, $p_2 = 1$ the point is $(16, \ln(16))$. For any other value of p_1 that satisfies $0 < p_1 < 1$, the point is somewhere on the line. On the other hand, the point $(p_1 \cdot 2 + p_2 \cdot 16, \ln(p_1 \cdot 2 + p_2 \cdot 16))$ is somewhere on the curve, the graph of the function, and thus the utility associated with the expected value of the gamble $\ln(p_1 \cdot 2 + p_2 \cdot 16)$ is bigger than the expected value of the utility of the gamble, $\ln(2) + p_2 \cdot \ln(16)$.

We see that regardless of the value of p_1, a person with a utility function $\ln(x)$, or any concave utility function, is always prepared to receive the expected value of the gamble instead of taking the risk and facing the gamble. This is illustrated in the following where the vertical line intersects the **x-axis** at the expected value of the gamble. Hence, its intersection with the vertical line with the other line and the curve is $E(U(X))$ and $U(E(X))$, respectively.

```
> plots[textplot]([(1/3)*2+(2/3)*16,ln(1/3*2+2/3*16)
  +.1,'U(E(X))'],align=ABOVE):
> plot([ln(x),[[2,ln(2)],[16,ln(16)]],[[(1/3)*2+
  (2/3)*16,0],[(1/3)*2+(2/3)*16,ln(1/3*2+2/3*16)]]],
  x=1..20,thickness=3):
> plots[textplot]([(1/3)*2+(2/3)*16,1/3*ln(2)+
  2/3*ln(16),'E(U(X))'],align=RIGHT):
> plots[display](%,%%,%%%);
```

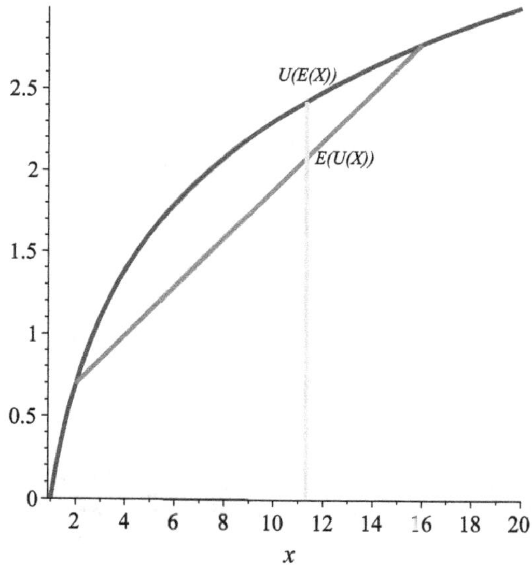

If on the other hand $U(E(X)) = E(U(X))$, the investor is termed risk neutral as he/she values the expected value the same as the random variable. For such an investor, U must be linear. Finally a risk lover is an investor with a convex utility function that implies that this investor derives utility from the risk.

As an illustration, let us reconsider a person with a utility function $\ln(x)$ that has been offered to choose between a random gamble that will yield a wealth of \$2 with a probability of $\frac{1}{3}$ and \$16 with a probability of $\frac{2}{3}$, or the expected value of gamble $\$\frac{34}{3}$.

The utility from the expected wealth $U(E(X))$ is

```
> ln(1/3*2 +2/3*16);
```

$$\ln\left(\frac{34}{3}\right). \tag{A.1}$$

The expected utility from the gamble $E(U(X))$ is

```
> 1/3*ln(2) +2/3*ln(16);
```

$$3\ln(2) \tag{A.2}$$

```
> evalf(%%)-evalf(%);
```

$$0.348306694. \tag{A.3}$$

Hence, the utility from the expected value is bigger, and the person will choose the non-risky situation of receiving the expected value instead of the risky situation.

To further justify the name risk averse, let us try to find out what will be the assured amount that generates, to a person with the above utility function, the same utility as the uncertain situation. Hence, we would like to solve for z such that:

```
> solve((1/3)*ln(2)+(2/3)*ln(16)=ln(z));
```

$$8. \tag{A.4}$$

The expected value of the gamble is

```
> 1/3*2 +2/3*16;
```

$$\frac{34}{3} \tag{A.5}$$

```
> 1/3*2.0 +2/3*16;
```

$$11.33333334. \tag{A.6}$$

Hence, this person is willing to forgo

```
> 34/3-8.0;
```

$$3.33333333 \tag{A.7}$$

dollars of the expected value in order to receive assured amount of \$8. This willingness to pay in order to avoid a risky situation, is the reason we term such a person "risk averse". This is visualized in the following graph, where the z for which $U(z)$ equals the expected utility of the gamble X, $E(U(X))$, is marked on the x-axis.

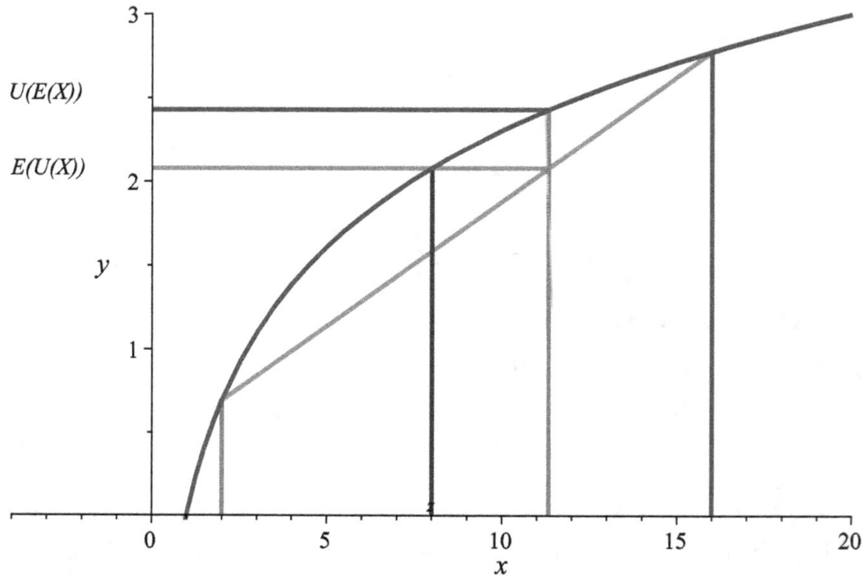

We utilized the expected utility framework when we investigate portfolio choices.

Appendix B: Safety First Models

The main purpose of this chapter is to introduce safety first models. The chapter also demonstrates measures of risk other than the variance which can be utilized to build an "efficient frontier" with respect to these measures. These types of models are not induced by equilibrium arguments like the CAPM.

The problem of portfolio choice or management falls into the general category of decision under uncertainty. Faced with a decision in an uncertain environment, in most cases, the decision is a solution to an optimization problem, albeit with some parameters that are random variables. Such optimization problems are classified as stochastic programming.

Consider an investor who would like to "maximize the return" on his/her portfolio. Since the return is a random variable "maximize the return" is not well defined, as it is a realization of random variables. By choosing a portfolio, an investor can of course affect the realization of the return, its volatility (variance) or the probability that a return above a certain value will be realized. However, by the nature of the problem at hand, the return is a random variable and thus the phrase "maximize the return" literally has no meaning.

In the CAPM, the portfolio decision problem is formulated by adopting the variance (standard deviation) as a measure of risk. The set of portfolio(s) for which the expected value of the return is maximized for a given variance is identified. Then a portfolio is chosen based on the trade off between the measure of risk and the expected return. Hence, the optimization problem which is solved in order to choose a portfolio, is defined in terms of deterministic parameters: the expected return and variance, which are functions of the portfolios.

The types of models we surveyed here, some of which were developed prior to the CAPM, are induced by the different philosophies (concepts) of converting the stochastic problem into a meaningful deterministic optimization. In these models, the risk is not captured directly by the variance but rather by a constraint of the type mentioned above, e.g., constraining the probability of achieving a return below a certain level. For these reasons, these methods are commonly referred to as safety first methods. In what follows, we investigate three different methods in this category and we will realize that there is an implicit but intimate relation between these methods and the CAPM.

We continue the analysis based on the assumption that the returns are distributed normally. The results obtained can be generalized and shown to be an approximation for other distributions based on Tchebyshev's inequality. Thus, we assume that there are N securities in the market and that the joint distribution of the return on the securities, R_i, $i = 1, \ldots, N$ follows the multinormal distribution with $\mu_i = E(R_i)$, Variance$(R_i) = \sigma_{ii}$ and Covariance$(R_i, R_j) = \sigma_{ij}$.

We use our usual notation and thus we let:

x_i be the percentage of the portfolio invested in security i,
$R_p = \sum_{i=i}^{N} x_i R_i$ be the rate of return on the portfolio,

$E(R_p) = \sum_{i=i}^{N} x_i\mu_i$ or μ_p be the expected rate of return on the portfolio, and

$\sigma_p = \sqrt{\sum_{i=1}^{N}\sum_{j=1}^{N} x_i x_j \sigma_{ij}}$ be the standard deviation of the return on the portfolio.

In order to visualize the feasible set of portfolios for some of the criteria, we need to define the following functions:

```
> ExpPortS:=(X::list,mu::list)->sum(X[i]*mu[i],
  i=1..nops(X)):
```

```
> VarPortS:=(X::list,Sigma::listlist)->sum(sum(X[i]*X[j]*
  Sigma[i][j],i=1..nops(X)),j=1..nops(X)):
```

Roy's Criterion

Roy's Criterion is obtained by converting the maximization of the "return", to a deterministic problem in which a certain return level L is given. The portfolio chosen is the one that minimizes the probability that the return will be below L. In his original paper, Roy[1] explained the philosophy behind his method as being related to a catastrophe that one would like to insure against. A person might assess that at least a level of L is needed for him/her to survive. Hence, their objective is to minimize the probability that the return will be less than L. Roy also motivates his method claiming that such an objective is practical and understood by investors rather than the concept of a utility function and the maximization of expected utility. Based on Roy's criterion, the optimal portfolio is the solution to the following optimization problem:

$$\text{Min}_{x_1,\ldots,x_N} \Pr(R_p \leq L) \tag{B.1}$$

$$\text{s.t.} \sum_{i=1}^{N} x_i = 1 \tag{B.2}$$

where Pr stands for the probability and, if short sales are not allowed, we add the constraint $0 \leq x_i$, for $i = 1, \ldots, N$.

[1]Roy Arthur D. (1952). "Safety First and the Holding of Assets". Econometrics 20 (July): 431–450.

Since

$$\Pr(R_p < L) = \Pr\left(\frac{R_p - E(R_p)}{\sigma_p} < \frac{L - E(R_p)}{\sigma_p}\right) \tag{B.3}$$

this probability will be minimized if $\frac{L-\mu_p}{\sigma_p}$ will be minimized.

The same objective will be obtained by solving

$$\text{Max}_{x_1,\ldots,x_N} - \frac{L - E(R_p)}{\sigma_p}$$
$$\text{s.t.} \sum_{i=1}^{N} x_i = 1. \tag{B.4}$$

or equivalently

$$\text{Max}_{x_1,\ldots,x_N} \frac{E(R_p) - L}{\sigma_p}$$
$$\text{s.t.} \sum_{i=1}^{N} x_i = 1. \tag{B.5}$$

The expression $\frac{E(R_p)-L}{\sigma_p} = \frac{\mu_p - L}{\sigma_p}$ should be familiar. It is the excess return per unit of risk. In this case, the excess return is measured with respect to L and the risk is measured by the σ of the portfolio. Given our assumption of the normal distribution, $\frac{R_p-\mu_p}{\sigma_p} \sim N(0,1)$, and thus the probability of obtaining a return less than L is determined by μ_p and σ_p.

We used the notation of μ_p instead of $E(R_p)$ as we would like to compare it to the CAPM soon. We should note however that, while suppressed, the direct variables of the optimization problems are the holding of each stock in the portfolio, i.e., $x_1, \ldots, x_N$ and not μ_p and σ_p. The values of μ_p and σ_p are consequences of the x's. Nevertheless the presentation in terms of μ_p and σ_p facilitates the comparison to the CAPM and efficient frontiers.

We already know that given μ_p there may be many portfolios with the same μ_p but with different σ_p. Hence, we can write the objective function of our optimization equivalently as if the optimization is done in two phases as follows:

$$\text{Max}_{s.t.\ \mu_p=\sum_{i=1}^{N} x_i\mu_i} \left\{ \text{Max} \frac{\mu_p - L}{\sigma_p} \middle| \sigma_p = \sqrt{\sum_{i=1}^{N}\sum_{j=1}^{N} x_i x_j \sigma_{ij}} \right\}$$

$$\sum_{i=1}^{N} x_i = 1 \tag{B.6}$$

First for each given μ_p satisfying $\mu_p = \sum_{i=1}^{N} x_i\mu_i$ and $\sum_{i=1}^{N} x_i = 1$, σ_p is chosen so as to maximize $\frac{\mu_p - L}{\sigma_p}$ and thus it is clear that the smallest possible σ_p will be chosen. In the second phase, the $x_1, \ldots, x_N$ and consequently μ_p for which $\frac{\mu_p - L}{\sigma_p}$ is the largest is chosen. This presentation makes it clear that the optimal portfolio will correspond to an efficient portfolio since the σ_p that corresponds to the optimal μ_p is the smallest possible.

The optimization problems above have the same structure as the problem solved to determine the market portfolio under the CAPM where short sales are allowed. This observation reinforces our conclusion that in a market without a risk-free asset, Roy's criterion will point to an efficient portfolio, as defined in the CAPM. In our formulation here, L plays the role of the risk-free rate in the CAPM.

Furthermore, it shows that if Roy's criterion is applied to a market without a risk-free asset, the chosen portfolio is the market portfolio under the CAPM in a market with a risk-free asset where the risk-free rate equals L. The geometric interpretation is therefore also the same as in the CAPM. In the (σ, μ) plane, the value of the objective function $\frac{\mu - L}{\sigma}$ equals C if $\frac{\mu - L}{\sigma} = C$ or $\mu = \sigma C + L$. C will be maximized by choosing the highest C for which there exists an admissible portfolio satisfying

$$\sum_{i=1}^{N} x_i E(R_i) = \sqrt{\sum_{j=1}^{N}\left(\sum_{i=1}^{N} x_i x_j \sigma_{ij}\right)} C + L. \tag{B.7}$$

Thus given L, we are looking for the highest C, the slope of the line $\mu = \sigma C + L$, for which the line has a point in common with the efficient frontier. The optimal C will thus be the slope of a line that crosses the μ axes (Y-axes) at L and is tangent to the efficient frontier at a point where the slope of the efficient frontier is C. The following animation demonstrates this process for $L = 15$ and an efficient frontier that is built from two portfolios $(\sigma_1, \mu_1) = (1, 10)$ and $(\sigma_2, \mu_2) = (2, 28)$.

```
> Prim:=plot([[1,10],[2,28]],style=point,symbol=box,
  thickness=5):
```

```
> Shortr5:=plot([sqrt(VarPortS([x,1-x],[[1,-0.8*2],
  [-0.8*2,4]])),ExpPortS([x,1-x],[10,28]),x=-2..1],
  thickness=3):
```

```
> Anil:=plots[animate](15+v*(ExpPortS([x,1-x],
  [10,28])-15)/sqrt(VarPortS([x,1-x],[[1,0.5*2],
  [0.5*2,4]])),v=0..4,x=-.5..1,thickness=2):
```

```
> plots[display](Prim,Anil,Shortr5,labelfont=[SYMBOL],
  labels=[s,m]);
```

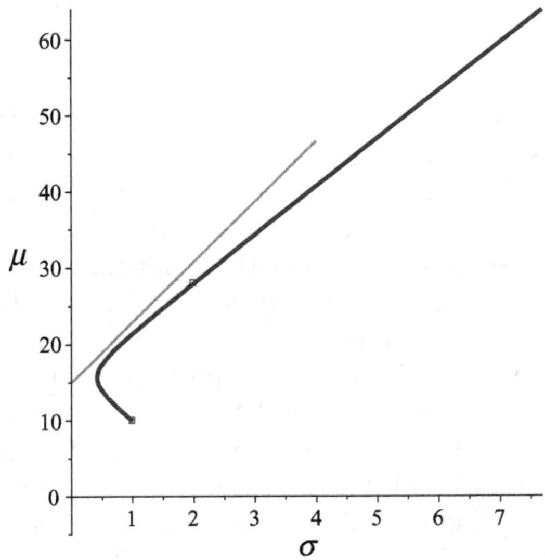

From the CAPM, we also know that the efficient frontier viewed as a function, $\mu(\sigma)$, is a concave function in σ. From the geometry, we know that the larger L is the larger the σ coordinate of the tangency point is, and due to the concavity, the smaller the slope is. Hence, the larger L is, the smaller is the optimal probability that we can obtain for the portfolio return not to be below L, which of course makes sense intuitively. Furthermore, the larger L is the larger the σ coordinate of the optimal portfolio, and the larger L the riskier the portfolio.

Roy does not intend his model to be used as related to the risk attitude of the investor, but rather as minimizing the probability of a catastrophe. The risk the investor is willing to take is communicated by the level of L. One may think that the larger L is the more risk averse the investor is, as the investor would like to minimize the probability of obtaining a return less than L. However, taking a second look at this issue one realizes that to obtain a larger return L, the larger the risk one would need to take to obtain this return. Hence, as our analysis indicated above, the larger L is the riskier the optimal portfolio is.

If a risk-free rate exists, the efficient frontier is the CML. In this case, it is easy to verify that if $L < R_f$, by choosing the optimal portfolio to be the risk-free rate, the probability of achieving a return less than L is minimized (it is zero). However, if $R_f < L$, the optimization problems defined above are unbounded and hence produce no optimal portfolio.

Given the above, it might be interesting to point out the following facts which shed some further light on the connection between this criterion and the CAPM. We see now that in a market where a risk-free rate exists, the criterion is meaningful only if L is the risk-free rate. In this case of course, the optimal portfolio is composed of only the risk-free asset since, for this portfolio, the probability of a return less than the risk-free is nil.

However, what will the optimal portfolio be under this criterion when L is the risk-free rate and there is an additional constraint requiring the portfolio to also include risky securities? The analysis above shows that an optimal portfolio will be the market portfolio. This is because the portfolio for which the probability of receiving a return less than L is the one which maximizes the slope of the line connecting $(0, L)$ and (σ, μ). This is exactly how we find the market portfolio. Hence, in the CAPM, there is another characterization of the market portfolio — a portfolio that does not include only the risk-free asset for which the probability of obtaining a return less than the risk-free rate is minimized.

The probability of obtaining a return less than L is in one to one correspondence with the slope of the line connecting $(0, L)$ and (σ, μ). The probability of receiving a return less than the risk-free rate is the same (and the least possible excluding the risk-free rate portfolio) for all portfolios on the efficient frontier — the CML.

Thus, there is another characterization of the efficient frontier. The efficient frontier in a market with a risk-free rate is composed of the risk-free rate and all the portfolios for which the probability of receiving a return less than the risk-free rate is minimized. We already mentioned that using Roy's criteria in a market with a risk-free asset is meaningful only if L is chosen to be the risk-free asset. In that case, however, Roy's criterion cannot be used for the risky portfolios. All risky portfolios on the CML have exactly the same probability of yielding a return less than the risk-free rate (which is the minimum possible for a risky portfolio) and the risk-free rate obviously has a zero probability for that event.

This point of view also sheds some new light on Sharpe's ratio of the portfolio x;

$$\frac{\sum_{i=1}^{N} x_i E(R_i) - R_f}{\sqrt{\sum_{j=1}^{N} \left(\sum_{i=1}^{N} x_i x_j \sigma_{ij}\right)}}. \tag{B.8}$$

Commonly it is interpreted as the reward for the risk taken i.e., as the excess rate of return over the risk-free rate per unit of standard deviation of the portfolio. Thus, the larger the ratio the better the portfolio since its risk reward tradeoff is larger. It can also be interpreted in view of the probability that this portfolio will generate a rate of return less than the risk-free rate. The larger the ratio the smaller this probability.

We can also interpret the SML in light of the above. The SML stipulates that for each asset (or portfolio) i,

$$\mu_i = R_f + \beta_i \cdot (\mu_m - R_f) \tag{B.9}$$

or since $\beta_i = \frac{\sigma_{im}}{\sigma_m^2}$ that

$$\mu_i - R_f = \frac{\sigma_{im}}{\sigma_m} \cdot \frac{\mu_m - R_f}{\sigma_m}. \tag{B.10}$$

However, since $\rho_{im} = \frac{\sigma_{im}}{\sigma_i \cdot \sigma_m}$, we can also write it as

$$\mu_i - R_f = \sigma_i \cdot \rho_{im} \cdot \frac{(\mu_m - R_f)}{\sigma_m} \tag{B.11}$$

or as

$$\left(\frac{\mu_i - R_f}{\sigma_i}\right) = \rho_{im} \cdot \left(\frac{\mu_m - R_f}{\sigma_m}\right) \text{ which implies } \rho_{im} = \frac{\left(\frac{\mu_i - R_f}{\sigma_i}\right)}{\left(\frac{\mu_m - R_f}{\sigma_m}\right)}. \tag{B.12}$$

There is a one-to-one correspondence between $\Pr(R_j < R_f)$ and $\frac{\mu_j - R_f}{\sigma_j}$ for each security j, such that the larger $\frac{\mu_j - R_f}{\sigma_j}$ the smaller $\Pr(R_j < R_f)$. Recall that $\frac{\mu_j - R_f}{\sigma_j}$ is the Sharpe ratio, or the slope of the lines connecting (σ_j, μ_j) to $(0, R_f)$. The market portfolio, as well as each security on the efficient frontier, minimizes the probability of obtaining a return less than the risk-free rate. Hence, ρ_{im} indicates a relation between the probability that the market rate of return will be less than the risk-free rate, and the probability that the rate of return of security i is less than the risk-free rate. Consequently, for all securities on the efficient frontier ρ_{im} equals one. This of course can be obtained from first principles since an efficient portfolio is a linear combination of the market portfolio and the risk-free rate. Thus, in the CAPM, if $\rho_{im} < 1$, the probability of security i having a return less than the risk-free rate is larger than the probability of the same event happening for the market portfolio. Alternatively, ρ_{im} can be interpreted as the ratio between the Sharpe ratios of security i and the market portfolio.

Kataoka's Criterion

Another way of formulating the ill-defined objective of "maximize the return" is provided by Kataoka's Criterion. In this criterion, a (maximum) probability α of not meeting a lower bound on the return, is provided by the investor and not minimized as it is in Roy's criteria. The optimal portfolio maximizes a lower bound L on the return, subject to the probability of the return being less than L, not exceeding the given probability of α. The optimization problem is formulated as follows:

$$\text{Max}_{L,x_1,\ldots,x_N} L$$

$$\text{s.t.} \quad \Pr\left(\sum_{i=i}^{N} x_i R_i \leq L\right) \leq \alpha$$

$$\sum_{i=1}^{N} x_i = 1. \tag{B.13}$$

As before, we can rewrite the constraint as

$$\Pr\left(\frac{R_p - \mu_p}{\sigma_p} \leq \frac{L - \mu_p}{\sigma_p}\right) \leq \alpha \tag{B.14}$$

and thus

$$Z = \frac{R_p - \mu_p}{\sigma_p} \sim N(0, 1). \tag{B.15}$$

We define by z_α the number such that $\Pr(Z \leq z_\alpha) = \alpha$. As long as

$$\frac{L - \mu_p}{\sigma_p} \leq z_\alpha \tag{B.16}$$

the constraint $\Pr(R_p < L) \leq \alpha$ will be satisfied.

An example of a calculation of z_α

The value of the standard normal cumulative density function (cdf) at a point say 0, can be calculated by

```
> stats[statevalf,cdf,normald](0);
```

$$0.5000000000. \tag{B.17}$$

To find the value of the cdf at the point -1, issue the command

```
> stats[statevalf,cdf,normald](-1);
```

$$0.1586552539. \tag{B.18}$$

In order to find the point $z_{0.05}$, that is the point such that $\Pr(Z < z_{0.05}) = 0.05$, one can use the inverse cdf (icdf) as follows:

```
> z05:=stats[statevalf,icdf,normald](0.05);
```

$$z_{0.05} := -1.644853627. \tag{B.19}$$

Geometrically, the $z_{0.05}$ can be visualized as the point such that the area under the pdf from negative infinity to $z_{0.05}$ is 0.05. We start by plotting the probability density function (pdf) of the standard normal distribution as follows:

```
> plot(stats[statevalf,pdf,normald],-3..3);
```

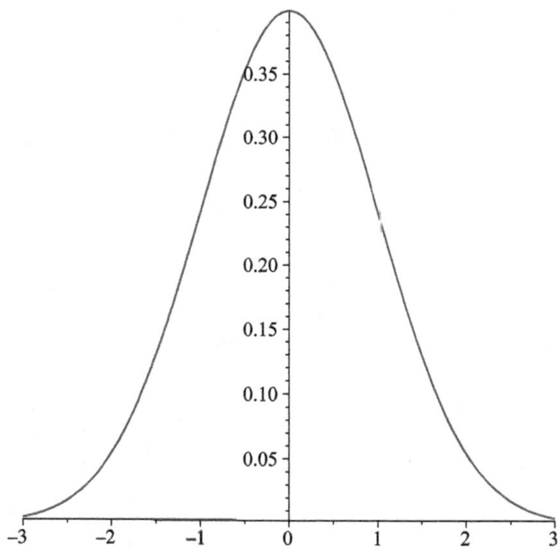

We now show the area under the graph to the point $z_{0.05}$ as gray.

```
> normal_curve:=plot(stats[statevalf,pdf,normald],-3..3):
```

```
> Areatoz05:=plot(stats[statevalf,pdf,normald],-3..z05,
filled=true):
```

```
> TxPloZ05:=plots[textplot]([z05,0,"z05"],align={ABOVE}):
```

```
> plots[display](normal_curve,Areatoz05,TxPloZ05);
```

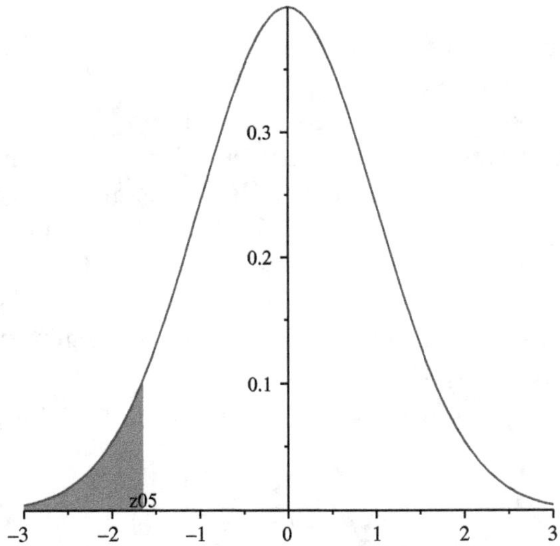

Hence, L must satisfy

$$L \leq z_\alpha \cdot \sigma_p + \mu_p \tag{B.20}$$

and we should remember that both μ_p and σ_p are functions of $x_1, \ldots, x_N$. Since we want to maximize L, the optimal L will satisfy the inequality as an equality and L will be chosen to satisfy $L = z_\alpha \sigma_p + \mu_p$.

In order to facilitate the comparison to the CAPM, in a market without a risk-free asset, we reformulate our optimization problem in an equivalent way:

$$\text{Max}_{x_1,\ldots,x_N} \;\; z_\alpha \sigma_p + \mu_p$$

$$\text{s.t.} \quad \sum_{i=i}^{N} x_i \mu_i = \mu_p$$

$$\sqrt{\sum_{i=1}^{N}\sum_{j=1}^{N} x_i x_j \sigma_{ij}} = \sigma_p$$

$$\sum_{i=1}^{N} x_i = 1. \tag{B.21}$$

The structure of this problem is exactly like the problem of maximizing the utility of an investor (as a function of σ_p, μ_p) subject to the constraints of choosing an admissible portfolio. Albeit in our formulation what replaces the utility function is a linear function, since $z_\alpha \sigma_p + \mu_p$ is linear in σ_p and μ_p. Hence, geometrically the situation can be described as in the CAPM where the indifference curves are replaced by the contours of the function $z_\alpha \sigma_p + \mu_p$.

The optimal portfolio will thus be the point on the efficient frontier at which the contour of $z_\alpha \sigma_p + \mu_p$ is tangent to the efficient frontier. To reiterate the above, recall that in the (σ, μ) plane (thinking about σ as X and μ as Y) the L contour of $z_\alpha \sigma_p + \mu_p$ is given by

$$\{(\sigma, \mu) \mid L = z_\alpha \sigma + \mu\}. \tag{B.22}$$

We are thus seeking the largest L, such that for a given α, there exists an admissible portfolio that lies on the line

$$\mu = L - z_\alpha \sigma. \tag{B.23}$$

L is the Y-intercept (μ-intercept) of this line. Hence, we are actually looking, given z_α which determines the slope of the line, for the portfolio that induces the above line with the highest Y-intercept point.

Keep in mind that it is reasonable to assume that $\alpha < 0.5$. The investor would probably not like to allow the likelihood of not meeting the lower bound, to be larger than 0.5. Thus, it is reasonable to assume that $z_\alpha < 0$, hence the slope of $L - z_\alpha \sigma$, is positive and $L - z_\alpha \sigma$ is increasing in σ. Thus, geometrically the illustration is exactly as in the CAPM where we are looking for the highest possible indifference curves, albeit they are linear and the optimal point will be a tangency point.

This is illustrated by the following animation for $z_\alpha = -0.7$ (that is for $\alpha = 0.2419$)

```
> stats[statevalf,cdf,normald](-0.7);
```

$$0.2419636522 \tag{B.24}$$

```
> stats[statevalf,icdf,normald](0.2419636522);
```

$$-0.7000000001 \tag{B.25}$$

and an efficient frontier that is built from two portfolios $(\sigma_1, \mu_1) = (1.5, 10)$ and $(\sigma_2, \mu_2) = (2, 12)$.

```
> Prim:=plot([[1.5,10],[2,12]],style=point,symbol=box,
  thickness=5):
```

```
> ExpPortS:=(X::list,mu::list)->sum(X[i]*mu[i],
  i=1..nops(X)):
```

```
> VarPortS:=(X::list,Sigma::listlist)->sum(sum(X[i]*X[j]*
  Sigma[i][j],i=1..nops(X)),j=1..nops(X)):
```

```
> Shortr5:=plot([sqrt(VarPortS([x,1-x],
  [[1.5^2,-.9*2*1.5],[-.9*2*1.5,4]])),ExpPortS([x,1-x],
  [10,12]),x=-2..1],thickness=3):
```

```
> Anil:=plots[animate](L+.7*s,s=0..10,L=9..11,
  thickness=2):
```

```
> plots[display](Prim,Anil,Shortr5,labelfont=[SYMBOL],
  labels=[s,m]);
```

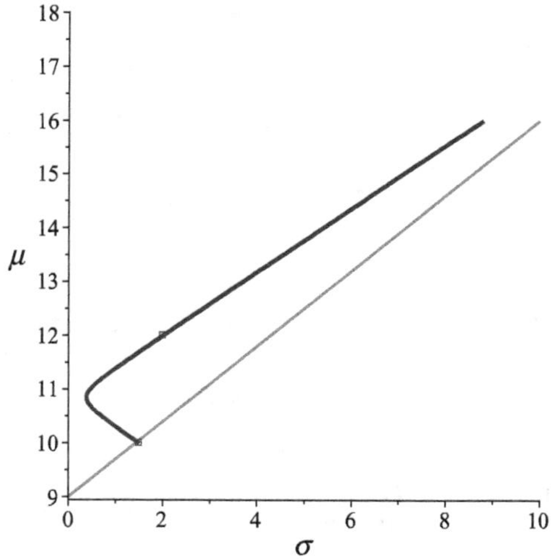

Assume that there is a risk-free rate in the market. In this case, the efficient frontier is the CML. The optimal portfolio is an efficient portfolio, the one that is the tangency point of the line that corresponds to the maximum L and the linear efficient frontier. It is therefore easy to determine now that if $-z_\alpha$ happens to be equal to the slope of the CML, every point on the efficient frontier is an optimal portfolio. If on the other hand $-z_\alpha$ is larger than the slope of the CML, the optimal portfolio includes only the risk-free asset, while if $-z_\alpha$ is smaller than the slope of the CML, the problem is unbounded. No optimal portfolio exists.

Before we move to the next criterion in this section, let us examine again how the investor input is related to the risk attitudes in a market with no risk-free asset. The smaller the α is the larger the slope of the linear contours. We have already mentioned that the efficient frontier is concave and hence its slope is decreasing in σ. That is, the smaller σ is the larger the slope of the efficient frontier. The optimal portfolio is the tangency point of the contour and the efficient frontier. Hence, they have the same slope at the tangency point. This means that the smaller α is, the smaller the σ of the optimal portfolio. Conversely, the larger α is the larger the σ of the optimal portfolio. Hence, the smaller α is the more risk averse the investor is. A smaller α will cause an optimal portfolio with a smaller σ and, of course, a smaller expected value but with the probability of the "tail" being as required by α.

Tesler's Criterion

Tesler's criterion is another way of generating a deterministic optimization problem from the "ill-defined" stochastic problem of "maximizing return". This suggestion is very similar to the one we just introduced. However, in this criteria, the investor inputs to the optimization process both α and L, where L is still the lower bound on the return, and α the probability of the return being less than L. As we shall soon see, this criteria is also different than the other two, in that here the investor provides not only a mechanism to choose the optimal portfolio, but actually shrinks the original set of feasible portfolios.

The inputs provided by the investor "cut" a slice from the original set of possible portfolios, and the objective function maximized in this criteria is $E(R_p)$. The formulation of the problem is given as follows:

$$\begin{aligned} &\text{Max} E(R_p) \\ \text{s.t.}\quad &\Pr(R_p \leq L) \leq \alpha. \end{aligned} \tag{B.26}$$

Our previous analysis, of the constraint under the assumption of the normal distribution, still holds. Hence, given z_α and L, we are looking for an admissible portfolio that satisfies

$$L \leq z_\alpha \sigma_p + \mu_p. \tag{B.27}$$

In the (σ, μ) plane, we look at the intersection of the set $\{(\sigma, \mu) \,|\, L \leq z_\alpha \sigma + \mu\}$ with the set of possible portfolios. As we know, the equation $\mu_p = L - z_\alpha \sigma_p$ specifies a line in the (σ, μ) plane. However, here the investor's inputs, $-z_\alpha$ (the slope) and L (the μ-intercept), completely determine the line.

With the aid of the functions defined in the initialization section above, given two securities on the efficient frontier, their variances, and the correlation coefficient between them, the complete frontier can be determined. Assume for example that we are given two securities on the efficient frontier (one even on the non-efficient part) such that

$$\begin{aligned} &\mu_1 = 5 \quad \sigma_1 = 2 \\ &\mu_2 = 13 \quad \sigma_2 = 3 \quad \rho_{1,2} = -0.9 \end{aligned} \tag{B.28}$$

The graph of the efficient frontier, the rotated U graph, is illustrated below. It has three dots on it. One is labeled "optimal" and the other two are the given portfolios.

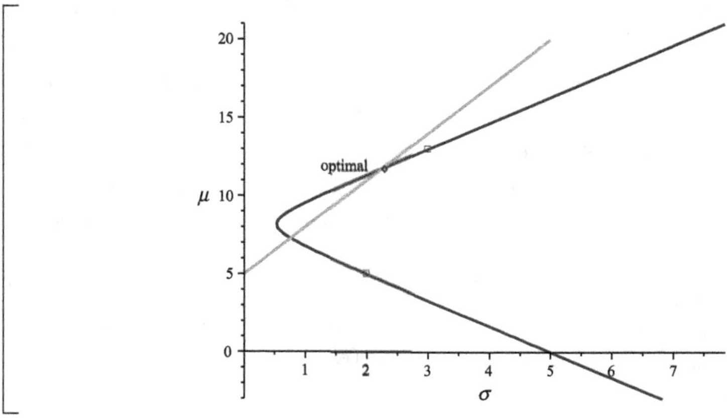

In the above figure, the linear line represents the line $\mu_p = L - z_\alpha \sigma_p$. Hence, L is 5 and the slope of the line is $-z_\alpha$. The feasible portfolios for this investor are thus those that are between the two graphs. As opposed to the first two criteria mentioned above, in this criteria the investor actually "shrinks" the feasible set.

Since the constraint is $\mu_p \leq L - z_\alpha \cdot \sigma_p$, maximizing μ_p implies that the optimal portfolio will be on the line. Furthermore, in choosing a portfolio so as to maximize μ_p it is clear that the optimal portfolio is the intersection of the line and the efficient part of the frontier.

In general the optimal portfolio, if one exists, will correspond to the higher intersection point of the line and the efficient frontier in the (σ, μ) plane. The optimization problem to be solved in terms of the portfolio composition, $x_1, \ldots, x_N$ is thus:

$$\text{Max}_{x_1,\ldots,x_N} \sum_{i=i}^{N} x_i \mu_i$$

$$\text{s.t.} \quad z_\alpha \cdot \sqrt{\sum_{i=1}^{N} \sum_{j=1}^{N} x_i x_j \sigma_{ij}} + \sum_{i=i}^{N} x_i \mu_i \geq L$$

$$\sum_{i=1}^{N} x_i = 1. \tag{B.29}$$

Our graphical illustration also shows that the line $\mu = L - z_\alpha \sigma$ which is specified by the investor, may not intersect the efficient frontier. In such a case, there would be no feasible solution for this criterion.

Given L we can find the market portfolio as in the CAPM for a risk-free rate of L. If the investor specifies an L with an α such that $-z_\alpha$ is larger than the slope of the CML (for this market when L is the risk-free rate), there will be no feasible portfolio for this criterion.

If a risk-free rate exists, the efficient frontier is the CML. Now, if L and α are such that $\mu = L - z_\alpha \sigma$ coincides with the CML, all the portfolios on the efficient frontiers are optimal. If on the other hand L is smaller than the risk-free rate and $-z_\alpha$ is bigger than the slope of the CML, a unique optimal portfolio will exist. However, if L is smaller than the risk-free rate and $-z_\alpha$ smaller than the slope of the CML, the optimization problem is unbounded and no optimal portfolio will exist. If L is bigger than the risk-free rate, $-z_\alpha$ is bigger than the slope of the CML, no feasible portfolio exists, but if $-z_\alpha$ is smaller than the slope of the CML, the optimization problem is unbounded and no optimal portfolio exists. These conditions are very easy to verify graphically.

Chapter 8

The Security Market Line, Estimations and Single Index Models

Introduction

The capital asset pricing model (CAPM) is an equilibrium model. The security market line (SML) is probably the main contribution of the CAPM. This relation connects the expected rate of return of each security in the market to the market portfolio. It also stipulates the price of risk and the risk measure as the coefficient in the linear regression of each security on the market.

These conclusions of the CAPM are supported by equilibrium arguments. The CAPM is a one factor model as the risk is measured and defined relative to the market portfolio — the one factor. However, one can look at the CAPM model and adopt some of its conclusions as assumptions (not as consequences of equilibrium arguments). This is the topic of the present chapter. It starts by investigating the estimation of the SML and continues by assuming a linear relation between the rate of return of each security and a factor or an Index. This assumed relation is between the random variables, the rate of return on the securities and the Index, and not only between the expected values of the securities and the Index (as in the SML).

Estimation of the SML and β

Having estimated all the expected values, variances, and covariances, the variance–covariance matrix can be estimated. Consequently, the composition of the market portfolio R_M can be solved for as explained above, i.e., R_M is specified as $R_M = \sum_{i=1}^{S} x_i R_i$, where x_i is the proportion of security i in the market portfolio. Once the composition of R_M is known, its variance and covariance with each security can be estimated by the formulas

$$\text{Var}(R_M) = \text{Var}\left(\sum_{i=1}^{S} x_i R_i\right) = \sum_{i=1}^{S}\sum_{j=1}^{S} x_i x_j \,\text{Cov}(R_i R_i) \quad \text{and}$$

$$\text{Cov}(R_M, R_n) = \text{Cov}\left(\sum_{i=1}^{S} x_i R_i, R_n\right) = \sum_{i=1}^{S} x_i \,\text{Cov}(R_i, R_n).$$

It follows that the β of security n can be estimated as $\beta_n = \frac{\text{Cov}(R_M, R_n)}{\text{Var}(R_M)}$.

This, however, is not the conventional way of estimating beta since simplifying models, as we shall soon see, replaces the market portfolio with a proxy and avoids calculating directly the variances and covariances of all the securities in the market.

Rewriting the SML as

$$\mu_i = R_f + \beta_i(\mu_m - R_f) = R_f(1 - \beta_i) + \beta_i \cdot \mu_m$$

and defining $\alpha_i = (1 - \beta_i)R_f$ yield the relation

$$\mu_i = \alpha_i + \beta_i \cdot \mu_m.$$

Thus, β_i can be estimated by running a regression of the rate of return of security i against the rate of return on the market portfolio over the last N periods. See the Appendix section of Chapter 5 regarding running a regression with Maple. The alpha in the above regression is used for performance measures. If $\alpha_i = R_f(1-\beta_i)$ it means indeed, that during the period of the regression

$$(\mu_i - R_f) = \beta_i \cdot (\mu_m - R_f).$$

That is, the ith security performance was as predicted by the CAPM.

If on the other hand $\alpha_i > R_f(1-\beta_i)$, then $\mu_i > R_f - \beta_i \cdot R_f + \beta_i \cdot \mu_m$ and hence

$$(\mu_i - R_f) > \beta_i \cdot (\mu_m - R_f).$$

That is, the security did better than as predicted by the CAPM since the risk compensation was above the prediction of the CAPM.

Similarly, if $\alpha_i < R_f(1-\beta_i)$, then μ_i, $R_f - \beta_i \cdot R_f + \beta_i \cdot \mu_m$ thus

$$(\mu_i - R_f) < \beta \cdot (\mu_m - R_f)$$

which means that the security performed is less than as predicted by the CAPM. The difference, $\alpha_i - R_f(1-\beta_i)$, is ***Jensen***'s measure of performance and is usually referred to as *Jensen's alpha.* A regression property is that the realized average of a security's rate of return μ_i equals $\alpha_i + \beta_i \cdot \mu_m$, where μ_m is the realized average of the market portfolio. Thus, Jensen's alpha can be calculated without running a regression and α_i is estimated as $\mu_i - \beta_i \cdot \mu_m$. Consequently, *Jensen's alpha* can be estimated as $\mu_i - \beta_i \cdot \mu_m - R_f(1-\beta_i) = \mu_i - R_f - \beta_i \cdot (\mu_m - R_f)$ when β_i is estimated by $\frac{\sigma_{iRm}}{\sigma^2_{Rm}}$.

Solving the Regression Algebraically

The regression is solved for by minimizing the sum of squared deviations of r_{ij} from the linear relation $\alpha + \beta \cdot r_{mj}$ i.e., by solving the minimization problem

$$\text{Minimize}_{\alpha,\beta} \sum_{j=1}^{N} (r_{ij} - \alpha_i + \beta_i r_{mj})^2$$

where r_{ij} and r_{mj} are the rates of return over the jth month of the security and the market, respectively.

Indeed solving this minimization, as explained in the following, produces an optimal β which satisfies

$$\beta_i = \frac{\sum_{j=1}^{N} \frac{r_{ij} \cdot r_{mj}}{N} - \sum_{i=1}^{N} \frac{r_{ij}}{N} \cdot \sum_{i=1}^{N} \frac{r_{mj}}{N}}{\sum_{j=1}^{N} \frac{r_{mj}^2}{N} - \left(\sum_{i=1}^{N} \frac{r_{mj}}{N}\right)^2}, \quad i = 1, \ldots, S.$$

If you look carefully at the above expression for the optimal β, you can see that it can be written as

$$\beta_i = \frac{\text{Cov}(R_i, R_m)}{\text{Var}(R_m)}$$

where in the above, Var and Cov stand for the estimator of the Covariance and Variance, respectively.

The optimal α, as explained in the following is given by

$$\alpha_i = -\frac{\left(\sum_{j=1}^{N} r_{ij} rm_j\right)\left(\sum_{j=1}^{N} rm_j\right) - \left(\sum_{j=1}^{N} rm_j^2\right)\left(\sum_{j=1}^{N} r_{ij}\right)}{N\left(\sum_{j=1}^{N} rm_j{}^2\right) - \left(\sum_{j=1}^{N} rm_j\right)^2},$$

$i = 1, \ldots, S.$

Alternatively solving for β, α can be determined from the fact that $\sum_{i=1}^{N} \frac{r_{ij}}{N}$ and $\frac{r_{mj}}{N}$ satisfy $\sum_{i=1}^{N} \frac{r_{ij}}{N} = \alpha_i + \beta_i \cdot \frac{r_{mj}}{N}$, hence $\alpha_i = \sum_{i=1}^{N} \frac{r_{ij}}{N} - \beta_i \cdot \frac{r_{mj}}{N}$. α also plays a role in performance valuations as discussed above.

Algebraically the regression is a solution to the following optimization:

$$\text{Minimize}_{\alpha,\beta} \sum_{j=1}^{N} (r_{ij} - \alpha_i + \beta_i r_{mj})^2.$$

Hence, the first-order conditions, of the above optimization, are given by

$$\frac{\partial}{\partial \alpha} \sum_{j=1}^{N} (r_{ij} - \alpha_i + \beta_i r_{mj})^2 = 0 \quad \text{and} \quad \frac{\partial}{\partial \beta} \sum_{j=1}^{N} (r_{ij} - \alpha_i + \beta_i r_{mj})^2 = 0.$$

We can solve for the optimal α and β with Maple as follows:

```
> diff(sum((r[i]-(alpha +beta*rm[i]))^2,i=1..N),beta);
```

$$\sum_{i=1}^{N} (2\,\beta\, rm_i{}^2 + 2\,\alpha\, rm_i - 2\, r_i rm_i) \tag{1}$$

```
>
```

```
> diff(sum((r[i]-(alpha +beta*rm[i]))^2,i=1..N),alpha);
```

$$2\,N\alpha + \sum_{i=1}^{N} (2\,\beta\, rm_i - 2\, r_i) \tag{2}$$

```
>
```

Thus, the optimal α and β are given by

```
> solve({%=0,%%=0},{alpha,beta});
```

$$\left\{\alpha = -\frac{\left(\sum_{i=1}^{N} r_i rm_i\right)\left(\sum_{i=1}^{N} rm_i\right) - \left(\sum_{i=1}^{N} rm_i^2\right)\left(\sum_{i=1}^{N} r_i\right)}{N\left(\sum_{i=1}^{N} rm_i^2\right) - \left(\sum_{i=1}^{N} rm_i\right)^2}, \beta = \frac{N\left(\sum_{i=1}^{N} r_i rm_i\right) - \left(\sum_{i=1}^{N} r_i\right)\left(\sum_{i=1}^{N} rm_i\right)}{N\left(\sum_{i=1}^{N} rm_i^2\right) - \left(\sum_{i=1}^{N} rm_i\right)^2}\right\} \quad (3)$$

```
>
```

```
> select(has, %, beta);
```

$$\left\{\beta = \frac{N\left(\sum_{i=1}^{N} r_i rm_i\right) - \left(\sum_{i=1}^{N} r_i\right)\left(\sum_{i=1}^{N} rm_i\right)}{N\left(\sum_{i=1}^{N} rm_i^2\right) - \left(\sum_{i=1}^{N} rm_i\right)^2}\right\} \quad (4)$$

```
> select(has, %%, alpha);
```

$$\left\{\alpha = -\frac{\left(\sum_{i=1}^{N} r_i rm_i\right)\left(\sum_{i=1}^{N} rm_i\right) - \left(\sum_{i=1}^{N} {rm_i}^2\right)\left(\sum_{i=1}^{N} r_i\right)}{N\left(\sum_{i=1}^{N} rm_i^2\right) - \left(\sum_{i=1}^{N} rm_i\right)^2}\right\} \quad (5)$$

```
>
```

The use of β in Corporate Finance

The use of β is very common in practical applications such as valuing risky cash flows in order to decide if a risky project is worth taking or not (i.e., if its present value is positive). β plays an important role in the valuation of a corporation, the estimation of the cost of capital for a firm, etc. Indeed Bloomberg and other financial companies do report estimates of β.

One must remember that when a β is estimated for a company, it is in fact a β of a portfolio. If the company is financed by some debts, the riskiness of the company is a function of its debt and equity. We already know that the β of a portfolio is the weighted average of the β of the securities in the portfolio. Thus, if we assume a company that is financed by both equity and debt, where its debt value is D and its equity value E, the estimated β of the company will be

$$\beta = \frac{E}{D+E}\beta_E + \frac{D}{D+E}\beta_D,$$

where β_E is the β of the equity of the firm and β_D is the β of the debt of the firm.

The Single Index Model

The Single Index Model (SIM) initiation point is certain assumptions about the rate of return of a security and its relation to an Index or Indices. Given these assumptions, we can estimate the parameters of the models and thereby get a simplified and numerically more tractable process of estimation of the variance–covariance matrix. Having established this, we can utilize the methods we used to generate the efficient frontier.

The SIM is in spirit similar to the CAPM or at least to the way the CAPM is implemented in practice. We mention at the end of this chapter that practically when the CAPM is used, an Index is chosen to represent the market portfolio. Thus, β estimates are done by running a regression of each stock against this Index. The SIM takes it a step further by assuming certain properties that significantly simplify the estimation process.

The Single and Multi indices were developed for a number of reasons. Most importantly, they simplify the numerical calculation of the efficient frontier and they allow separating the analysis of the stock market into different categories. We will be dealing with the simplification soon while the separation allowed will become apparent as we introduce the following model.

With no simplifying assumptions, in order to solve for the efficient frontier, one needs to estimate the corresponding variance–covariance matrix and the expected return of each stock that is being considered. Hence, if N stocks are being followed, one needs to estimate N

expected returns plus N variances plus $\frac{N(N-1)}{2}$ covariances (due to the symmetry). Thus, total estimated parameters are

$$N + N + \frac{N(N-1)}{2} = N\left(2 + \frac{N-1}{2}\right).$$

We can see in the following how this number increases as a function of the number of stocks followed.

```
> seq(N*(2+(N-1)/2),N=1..200);
```

2, 5, 9, 14, 20, 27, 35, 44, 54, 65, 77, 90, 104, 119, 135, 152, 170, 189, 209, 230, 252, 275, 299, 324, 350, 377, 405, 434, 464, 495, 527, 560, 594, 629, 665, 702, 740, 779, 819, 860, 902, 945, 989, 1034, 1080, 1127, 1175, 1224, 1274, 1325, 1377, 1430, 1484, 1539, 1595, 1652, 1710, 1769, 1829, 1890, 1952, 2015, 2079, 2144, 2210, 2277, 2345, 2414, 2484, 2555, 2627, 2700, 2774, 2849, 2925, 3002, 3080, 3159, 3239, 3320, 3402, 3485, 3569, 3654, 3740, 3827, 3915, 4004, 4094, 4185, 4277, 4370, 4464, 4559, 4655, 4752, 4850, 4949, 5049, 5150, 5252, 5355, 5459, 5564, 5670, 5777, 5885, 5994, 6104, 6215, 6327, 6440, 6554, 6669, 6785, 6902, 7020, 7139, 7259, 7380, 7502, 7625, 7749, 7874, 8000, 8127, 8255, 8384, 8514, 8645, 8777, 8910, 9044, 9179, 9315, 9452, 9590, 9729, 9869, 10010, 10152, 10295, 10439, 10584, 10730, 10877, 11025, 11174, 11324, 11475, 11627, 11780, 11934, 12089, 12245, 12402, 12560, 12719, 12879, 13040, 13202, 13365, 13529, 13694, 13860, 14027, 14195, 14364, 14534, 14705, 14877, 15050, 15224, 15399, 15575, 15752, 15930, 16109, 16289, 16470, 16652, 16835, 17019, 17204, 17390, 17577, 17765, 17954, 18144, 18335, 18527, 18720, 18914, 19109, 19305, 19502, 19700, 19899, 20099, 20300

(6)

```
>
```

What motivates the SIM is the observation that the rate of return of a stock depends, in some manner, on the "overall" performance of the stock market. This overall performance is measured by one of the stock market Indices. This dependency, of part of the rate of return of the stock that is correlated with the market, was labeled in the CAPM as the systemic risk.

Mathematically speaking, the SIM takes the approach that the return on each stock can be decomposed into two parts:

- a part that is specific to the particular stock (referred to as the non-systematic risk in the CAPM), plus
- another part that is related directly to the overall market performance (the systemic or non-diversifiable risk in the CAPM).

Thus, the random variable, R_i, denoting the rate of return on a stock can be written as

$$R_i = a_i + \beta_i \cdot R_m,$$

where

a_i is the (random) part in the rate of return that is specific to the stock in question,
R_m the rate of return on a stock market index, and
β_i the sensitivity of the individual stock to the market performance.

β_i can also be presented as the increase/decrease in the return of the specific stock for an increase/decrease by one percentage of the Index. The a_i and R_m are random variables, while β_i is a deterministic constant.

The equation $R_i = a_i + \beta_i \cdot R_m$ thus describes a relation between random variables. a_i, like every random variable, can be written as the sum of its expected value α_i and a random variable (the deviation from the expected value) with an expected value of zero, e_i, i.e., as $a_i = \alpha_i + e_i$.

Hence, we can represent the rate of return on the stock R_i as

$$R_i = \alpha_i + \beta_i \cdot R_m + e_i,$$

where $\alpha_i = E(a_i)$ is a deterministic constant and e_i a random variable such that $E(e_i) = 0$.

The appealing tractability of the SIM stems from the following assumptions:

The random variables e_i and R_m are uncorrelated, i.e., $\text{Cov}(e_i, R_m) = 0$. This is the formal consequence of the assumption that a_i captures the part of the rate of return on the stock that is not related to the performance of the market. Recall that if we write a relation like the SML in the CAPM between R_i and R_m (not between $E(R_i)$ and $E(R_m)$), we also obtain a similar result. Thus, the assumption of the SIM stipulates that

$$\text{Cov}(e_i, R_m) = 0 \quad \text{for every } i.$$

The SIM also assumes that the interrelation between two stocks is induced only via the Index and not via the part that is specific to each stock, i.e. not via e_i, in the current presentation.That is, since each security is affected by the market, R_m, there must be some correlation between the securities (unless β_i is zero for at least one of the securities). This essential assumption is that the component in the return, which is stock-specific, is uncorrelated across stocks. Hence, mathematically, this assumption states that

$$\text{Cov}(e_i, e_j) = 0 \quad \text{for } i \neq j.$$

but since $E(e_i)$ is by construction zero, and

$$\text{Cov}(e_i, e_j) = E(e_i, e_j) - E(e_i) \cdot E(E_j)$$

this assumption can also be stated as

$$E(e_i \cdot e_j) = 0.$$

Let us see what the implications are of these assumptions on a number of parameters that are needed to be estimated and how this facilitates the separation between analysts that are grouped according to market segments.

Applying the formula for the variance of a sum of random variables, we have

$$\begin{aligned}\text{Var}(R_i) &= \text{Var}(\alpha_i + \beta_i R_m + e_i) = \text{Var}(\beta_i R_m) + \text{Var}(e_i)\\ &= \beta_i^2 \text{Var}(R_m) + \text{Var}(e_i).\end{aligned}$$

Since $\text{Cov}(e_i, R_m) = 0$ and α_i is a deterministic constant we have, as explained in the following, that

$$\text{Cov}(R_i, R_j) = \beta_i \beta_j \text{Var}(R_m).$$

Explanation for the Covariance Formula

Furthermore,

$$\mathrm{Cov}(R_i, R_j) = \mathrm{Cov}(\alpha_i + \beta_i R_m + e_i, \alpha_j + \beta_j R_m + e_j)$$

but since α_i is a deterministic constant we have that

$$\begin{aligned}\mathrm{Cov}(\beta_i R_m + e_i, \beta_j R_m + e_j) &= \mathrm{Cov}(\beta_i R_m, \beta_j R_m) + \mathrm{Cov}(\beta_i R_m, e_j)\\ &\quad + \mathrm{Cov}(\beta_j R_m, e_i) + \mathrm{Cov}(e_i, e_j).\end{aligned}$$

By our assumptions, the last three elements vanish and hence

$$\mathrm{Cov}(R_i, R_j) = \beta_i \beta_j \mathrm{Cov}(R_m, R_m)$$

but since $\mathrm{Cov}(R_m, R_m) = \mathrm{Var}(R_m)$.

Therefore, estimating the variance–covariance matrix, which involves $\frac{N(N-1)}{2}$ covariances plus N variances, is reduced now to estimating one variance, that of the index, and N β's.

Moreover, the SIM introduces a separation between the analysts who follow different stocks or segments of the industry. Rather than estimating the covariance of the securities followed, with each of the other securities followed by the institution, only the covariance with the Index should be estimated. We will soon turn to the estimation of the β's, but let us first see what the assumptions above imply with respect to a portfolio.

It is easy to verify that

$$E\left(\sum_{i=1}^{N} x_i R_i\right) = E\left(\sum_{i=1}^{N} x_i \alpha_i\right) + E\left(\sum_{i=1}^{N} x_i \beta_i R_m\right).$$

Denoting $\sum_{i=1}^{N} x_i \alpha_i$ by α_P and $\sum_{i=1}^{N} x_i \beta_i$ by β_P, that is, β_P and α_P are the weighted average α and β of the securities in the portfolio, we have that

$$E\left(\sum_{i=1}^{N} x_i R_i\right) = \alpha_P + \beta_P E(R_m).$$

Thus, the expected value of the portfolio follows the same equation that applies to a security, with the parameters being the average of the parameters in the portfolio. This is virtually the same result that we obtained with regards to the SML in the CAPM, i.e., that it must be satisfied by each security or a portfolio in the market.

The variance of a portfolio, as explained in the following, is

$$\text{Var}\left(\sum_{i=1}^{N} x_i R_i\right) = \sum_{i=1}^{N} x_i^2 \text{ Var}(e_i) + \beta_p^2 \text{ Var}(R_m)$$

where

$$\beta_p = \sum_{i=1}^{N} x_i \beta_i \quad \text{and} \quad \beta_p^2 = \sum_{j=1}^{N} \sum_{i=1}^{N} x_i \beta_i \beta_j x_j$$

Explanation for the Variance Formula

$$\text{Var}\left(\sum_{i=1}^{N} x_i R_i\right) = \sum_{j=1}^{N} \sum_{i=1}^{N} x_i \text{ Cov}(R_i, R_j) x_j = \sum_{i=1}^{N} x_i^2 \text{ Var}(R_i)$$
$$+ \sum_{j=1}^{N} \sum_{i=1, i\neq j}^{N} x_i x_j \text{ Cov}(R_i, R_j).$$

Based on our assumptions,

$$\text{Var}(R_i) = {\beta_i}^2 \text{ Var}(Rm) + \text{Var}(e_i), \quad \text{and}$$
$$\text{Cov}(R_i, R_j) = \beta_i \beta_j \text{ Var}(R_m)$$

and hence

$$\sum_{i=1}^{N} x_i^2 \text{ Var}(R_i) = \text{Var}(R_m) \left(\sum_{i=1}^{N} x_i^2 {\beta_i}^2\right) + \sum_{i=1}^{N} x_i^2 \text{ Var}(e_i)$$

and

$$\sum_{j=1}^{N} \sum_{i=1, i\neq j}^{N} \text{Cov}(x_i \; R_i, x_j \; R_j) = \text{Var}(R_m) \sum_{j=1}^{N} \sum_{i=1, i\neq 1}^{N} x_i \beta_i \beta_j x_j.$$

Putting it together yields

$$\text{Var}\left(\sum_{i=1}^{N} x_i R_i\right) = \sum_{i=1}^{N} x_i^2 \text{ Var}(e_i) + \text{Var}(R_m) \sum_{j=1}^{N} \sum_{i=1}^{N} x_i \beta_i \beta_j x_j.$$

However, $\beta_p = \sum_{i=1}^{N} x_i \beta_i$ and thus $\beta_p^2 = \sum_{j=1}^{N} \sum_{i=1}^{N} x_i \beta_i \beta_j x_j$ and therefore we have the result that the variance of the portfolio is given by

$$\text{Var}\left(\sum_{i=1}^{N} x_i R_i\right) = \sum_{i=1}^{N} x_i^2 \text{Var}(e_i) + \beta_p^2 \ \text{Var}(R_m).$$

Recall our investigation of the variance when $x_i = \frac{1}{N}$ and N approaches infinity of the non-systematic risk in the CAPM. A similar conclusion is obtained here. The variance in this case will approach

$$\beta_{av}^2 \ \text{Var}(R_m) + \frac{\text{Var}_{av}}{N}$$

where β_{av} is the arithmetic mean of the β in the portfolio and Var_{av} is the arithmetic mean of the $\text{Var}(e_i)$. Hence as N approaches infinity and assuming the Var_{av} and β_{av} approach some constant, the variance of the portfolio approaches $\beta_p^2 \ \text{Var}(R_m)$ and thus the portfolio measure of risk, **the standard deviation, approaches** $\beta_p \sigma(R_m)$.

This is virtually the same result we obtained in the CAPM for the systemic risk of each portfolio or security. The expression $\text{Var}(e_i)$, part of the variance (risk), also here can be referred to as either a *diversifiable risk* or a *non-systematic risk*. It is the risk that an investor with a "well" diversified portfolio should not care about since it can be diversified away. As such, the risk of a well-diversified portfolio is $\beta_p \sigma(R_m)$ and **hence could actually be measured by its** β_p since the risk of a well-diversified portfolio is simply a scalar, $\sigma(R_m)$, multiplied by β_p.

Note the similarity of the SML and the SIM. Although the SML is a relation between expected values and the SIM is between random variables, the estimation of α and β is the same for the SML and the SIM. **The SIM β and α of each stock are estimated in the same manner as explained above for the SML.** This is demonstrated in the following example where the SIM is implemented.

Example: Implementing the SIM

Consider the following data of a market with three securities where a no risk-free asset exists, and short sales are allowed. This market is analyzed based on the SIM and compared to its analysis using the CAPM. The efficient frontier is solved for by generating its equation, e.g., μ (of an efficient portfolio) as a function of its σ and the minimum σ portfolio is identified. There are 12 equally spaced observations for the monthly rates of return of three stocks ($\text{In}_1, \text{In}_2, \text{In}_3$) and of the Index ($R_M$) as given in the following:

```
> In1 := [0.46084996e-1, 3.314024388, 9.536860570,
-4.135758840, 1.026763259, 3.252547687, 1.568706112,
10.55913510, 4.125557156, -2.606338513, -6.265079250,
-3.226822390];
```

$$In_1 := [0.046084996, 3.314024388, 9.536860570, -4.135758840, 1.026763259, 3.252547687, 1.568706112, 10.55913510, 4.125557156, -2.606338513, -6.265079250, -3.226822390] \quad (7)$$

```
> In2 := [-7.76308905, -16.23578942, -19.17368386,
-14.53825238, 7.954982304, 20.99654536, 62.32509250,
-12.68043177, -5.434588552, 23.30842738, 11.48982678,
-6.77906627];
```

$$In_2 := [-7.76308905, -16.23578942, -19.17368386, -14.53825238, 7.954982304, 20.99654536, 62.32509250, -12.68043177, -5.434588552, 23.30842738, 11.48982678, -6.77906627] \quad (8)$$

```
> In3 := [33.33949669, 11.72516476, 5.452432682,
6.324806212, 22.99779302, -1.413364074, -1.037708370,
2.494561939, 7.747052708, .967134896, -12.62572076,
11.01172354];
```

$$In_3 := [33.33949669, 11.72516476, 5.452432682, 6.324806212, 22.99779302, -1.413364074, -1.037708370, 2.494561939, 7.747052708, 0.967134896, -12.62572076, 11.01172354] \quad (9)$$

```
> Rm := [8.540830875, -.398866758, -1.394796869,
  -4.116401670, 10.65984620, 7.611909657, 20.95203008,
  .1244217563, 2.146007105, 7.223074588, -2.466991077,
  .335278293];
```

$$Rm := [8.540830875,\ -0.398866758,\ -1.394796869,\ -4.116401670,\ 10.65984620,\ 7.611909657,\ 20.95203008,\ 0.1244217563,\ 2.146007105,\ 7.223074588,\ -2.466991077,\ 0.335278293] \tag{10}$$

The analysis is divided into three steps:

1. estimating the expected value and the variance of the Index,
2. running the regressions needed to estimate the β of each security and the variance of the residuals in each regression, and
3. utilizing the following equations (that hold in the SIM) to estimate the expected values and variances of the securities as well as the covariances between each of the two securities.

$$\begin{aligned} E(R_i) &= \alpha_i + \beta_i\, E(R_m) \\ \mathrm{Var}(R_i) &= \mathrm{Var}(\alpha_i + \beta_i R_m + e_i) = \mathrm{Var}(\beta_i R_m) + \mathrm{Var}(e_i) \\ &= \beta_i^2\ \mathrm{Var}(R_m) + \mathrm{Var}(e_i) \\ \mathrm{Cov}(R_i, R_j) &= \beta_i \beta_j\ \mathrm{Var}(R_m). \end{aligned}$$

   In_i represents the rate of return of security i, and R_m the rate of return on the index.

Once these there steps are completed, the efficient frontier can be solved for, as was done in the CAPM, based on the following command. Note that σ, A and b are redefined based on the equations above that hold in the SIM and not in the CAPM.

```
> Sigma:=Matrix(3,3,[[sigma11,sigma12,sigma13],[sigma21,
  sigma22,sigma23],[sigma31,sigma32,sigma13]]);
```

(σ_i is the variance of security i and σ_j the covariance between securities i and j. The matrix A is defined by

```
> A:=Matrix(3,2,[[mu1,1],[mu2,1],[mu3,1]]);
```

where μ_i is the expected value of security i and vector b is defined by

```
> b:=Vector(2,1,[e,1]);
```

where e represents the expected value of an efficient portfolio. Then the efficient frontier is solved for by following command are as done in the CAPM.

```
> with(LinearAlgebra):XV:=MatrixInverse(Sigma).A.
  MatrixInverse(Transpose(A).MatrixInverse(Sigma).A).b
```

We start by estimating the variance and expected value of the index (R_m) as follows:

```
> VarRm:=stats[describe,variance](Rm);#
  The Variance of RM
```

$$\text{VarRm} := 46.97451866 \tag{11}$$

```
> MuRm:=stats[describe,mean](Rm);#
  The expected Value of Rm
```

$$\text{MuRm} := 4.101361848. \tag{12}$$

In order to use the Eqs. (13) and (14), we need to run three regressions and determine the value of the β's and the variances of the residuals in each regression.

This is done in a compact way as follows:

```
> seq(stats[fit,leastsquare[[SIM,S||i]]]([Rm,In||i]),
  i=1..3);
```

$$S1 = 0.01162831544\,SIM + 1.385281427,\ S2 = 2.702591350\,SIM - 7.461807299,\ S3 = 0.2857803354\,SIM + 6.076525877 \quad (13)$$

Therefore, the β's values are

```
> beta1:=0.01162831544
```

$$\beta_1 := 0.01162831544 \quad (14)$$

```
> beta2:=2.702591350;
```

$$\beta_2 := 2.702591350 \quad (15)$$

```
> beta3:=0.2857803354;
```

$$\beta_3 := 0.2857803354 \quad (16)$$

Consequently, we can assign the values of the covariances as follows:

```
> Cov12:=beta1*beta2*VarRm;
```

$$\mathrm{Cov}_{12} := 1.476248690 \quad (17)$$

```
> Cov13:=beta1*beta3*VarRm;
```

$$\mathrm{Cov}_{13} := 0.1561030845 \quad (18)$$

```
> Cov23:=beta2*beta3*VarRm;
```

$$\mathrm{Cov}_{23} := 36.28065029 \quad (19)$$

The α's values are

```
> alpha1:=1.385281427;
```

$$\alpha_1 := 1.385281427 \quad (20)$$

```
> alpha2:=-7.461807299;
```

$$\alpha_2 := -7.461807299 \tag{21}$$

```
> alpha3:=6.076525877;
```

$$\alpha_3 := 6.076525877 \tag{22}$$

In order to calculate the variances of the residuals in each regression, we first have to determine the residuals' values, i.e., $\text{In}_i - (\alpha_i + \beta_i R_m)$, $i = 1, \ldots, 3$. However, since we are only interested in the variance of the residuals, and $\text{Var}(\text{In}_i - (\alpha_i + \beta_i R_m)) = \text{Var}(\text{In}_i - \beta_i R_m)$ it is sufficient to calculate the values of $\text{In}_i - \beta_i R_m$, $i = 1, \ldots, 3$. This is done as follows:

```
> e1:=In1-beta1*Rm;Vare1:=stats[describe,variance](e1);
  #NOTE 2 COMMANDS ON THIS LINE
```

$$e1 := [-0.05323047953,\ 3.318662536,\ 9.553079708, -4.087892023,\ 0.9028072048,\ 3.164034000, 1.325069297,\ 10.55768828,\ 4.100602708,\ -2.690330703,\ -6.236392300, -3.230721112]$$

$$\text{Var}_1 := 24.44918535 \tag{23}$$

```
> e1:=map (x->x+alpha1,In1+beta1*Rm);#
  no need to add alpha
```

$$e1 := [1.530681898, 4.694667667,\ 10.90592286, -2.798344230,\ 2.536000740, 4.726342801,\ 3.197624354, 11.94586335,\ 5.535793031,\ -1.137064896,\ -4.908484773,\ -1.837642241] \tag{24}$$

```
> Vare1:=stats[describe,variance](e1);
```

$$\text{Var}_1 := 24.47459252 \tag{25}$$

```
> e2:=In2+beta2*Rm;Vare2:=stats[describe,variance](e2);
  #NOTE 2 COMMANDS ON THIS LINE
```

$$e2 := [15.31928659, -17.31376327, -22.94324981, -25.66320393, 36.76419043, 41.56842656, 118.9498678, -12.34417061, 0.365191687, 42.82944628, 4.822558035, -5.872946056]$$

$$\mathrm{Var}_2 := 1533.099322 \tag{26}$$

```
> e3:=In3+beta3*Rm;Vare3:=stats[describe,variance](e3);
  #NOTE 2 COMMANDS ON THIS LINE
```

$$e3 := [35.78029820, 11.61117648, 5.053827165, 5.148419562, 26.04416744, 0.761970021, 4.949969814, 2.530119230, 8.360339338, 3.031347574, -13.33073830, 11.10753948]$$

$$\mathrm{Var}_3 := 142.1792502 \tag{27}$$

The variances of the securities can now be calculated as

```
> VarIn1:=(beta1**2)*VarRm+Vare1;
```

$$\mathrm{VarIn}_1 := 24.48094431 \tag{28}$$

```
> VarIn2:=(beta2**2)*VarRm+Vare2;
```

$$\mathrm{VarIn}_2 := 1876.201206 \tag{29}$$

```
> VarIn3:=(beta3**2)*VarRm+Vare3;
```

$$\mathrm{VarIn}_3 := 146.0156779 \tag{30}$$

and the covariances are

```
> Cov12:=beta1*beta2*VarRm;
```

$$\mathrm{Cov12} := 1.476248690 \tag{31}$$

```
> Cov13:=beta1*beta3*VarRm;
```

$$\text{Cov13} := 0.1561030845 \tag{32}$$

```
> Cov23:=beta2*beta3*VarRm;
```

$$\text{Cov23} := 36.28065029. \tag{33}$$

The Var–Covr matrix can therefore be defined by

```
> Sigma:=Matrix(3,3,[[VarIn1,Cov12,Cov13],[Cov12,
  VarIn2,Cov23],[Cov13,Cov23,VarIn3]]);
```

$$\Sigma := \begin{bmatrix} 24.48094431 & 1.476248690 & 0.1561030845 \\ 1.476248690 & 1876.201206 & 36.28065029 \\ 0.1561030845 & 36.28065029 & 146.0156779 \end{bmatrix} \tag{34}$$

Once the expected value of each stock is calculated, the matrix A can be defined. **Note that the expected value is calculated under the assumption of the SIM**, hence

$$\mu_i = \alpha_i + \beta_i \mu Rm$$

```
> mu1:=alpha1+beta1*MuRm;mu2:=alpha2+beta2*MuRm;
  mu3:=alpha3+beta3*MuRm;
```

$$\mu_1 := 1.432973356$$

$$\mu_2 := 3.622497751$$

$$\mu_3 := 7.248614442 \tag{35}$$

Recall that the regression line passes via the average of the dependent and independent variables. Due to this property, the expected value estimation directly from the data and the expected value estimation assuming the SIM are identical.

```
> In1 := [0.046084996, 3.314024388, 9.536860570,
  -4.135758840, 1.026763259, 3.252547687, 1.568706112,
```

```
10.55913510, 4.125557156, -2.606338513, -6.265079250,
-3.226822390];
```

$$In_1 := [0.046084996, 3.314024388, 9.536860570, -4.135758840, 1.026763259, 3.252547687, 1.568706112, 10.55913510, 4.125557156, -2.606338513, -6.265079250, -3.226822390] \quad (36)$$

```
> stats[describe,mean](In1);
```

$$1.432973357 \quad (37)$$

```
> A:=Matrix(3,2,[[mu1,1],[mu2,1],[mu3,1]]);
```

$$A := \begin{bmatrix} 1.432973356 & 1 \\ 3.622497751 & 1 \\ 7.248614442 & 1 \end{bmatrix}, \quad (38)$$

and the vector b is as defined in the following:

```
> b:=Vector(2,1,[e,1]);
```

$$b := \begin{bmatrix} e \\ 1 \end{bmatrix} \quad (39)$$

It is now possible to utilize the following command (see the explanations in Chapter 6), to solve for the efficient frontier, e.g., for the composition of an efficient portfolio given its expected value.

```
> with(LinearAlgebra):XV:=MatrixInverse(Sigma).A.
  MatrixInverse(Transpose(A).MatrixInverse(Sigma).A).b;
```

$$XV := \begin{bmatrix} -0.172232396724515\,e + 1.24220558980130 \\ 0.000452771620784953\,e + 0.00672691442975752 \\ 0.171779625103730\,e - 0.248932504231062 \end{bmatrix} \quad (40)$$

```
> XV[1];
```

$$-0.172232396724515\,e + 1.24220558980130 \quad (41)$$

Continuing as explained in the development of the CAPM, the minimum variance as a function of the expected value is

```
> MinVar:=simplify(add(add(XV[j]*Sigma[i,j]*XV[i],
  j=1..3),i=1..3));
```

$$\mathrm{MinVar} := 5.03142934655477\, e^2 - 22.7976643519103\, e + 46.7156601300276 \tag{42}$$

The standard deviation is thus

```
sqrt(MinVar);
```

$$\sqrt{5.03142934655477\, e^2 - 22.7976643519103\, e + 46.7156601300276} \tag{43}$$

The standard deviation as a function of e is plotted as follows:

```
> plot(sqrt(MinVar),e=0.0..4,labels=[m,s],
  labelfont=[SYMBOL]);
```

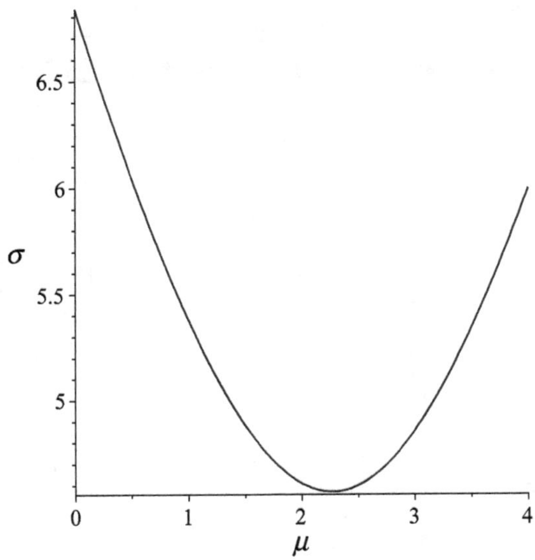

The expected rate of return as a function of the standard deviation is the inverse of the above function. It is solved for the following case:

```
> Sol_e:=solve({sqrt(MinVar)=sd},{e});
```

$$Sol\_e := \{e = 2.265525637 + 3.530521283\,10^{-16} \sqrt{1.594523608 \times 10^{30}\,\mathrm{sd}^2 - 3.331169274\,10^{31}}\}, \{e = 2.265525637 - 3.530521283 \times 10^{-16} \sqrt{1.594523608 \times 10^{30}\,\mathrm{sd}^2 - 3.331169274 \times 10^{31}}\} \quad (44)$$

The minimum standard deviation is therefore the sd for which $1.594523608\,10^{30}\,\mathrm{sd}^2 - 3.331169274\,10^{31} = 0$, i.e.,

```
> solve(1.594523608*10^30*sd^2-3.331169274*10^31=0);
```

$$4.570701653, \ -4.570701653 \quad (45)$$

Plotting the efficient and inefficient part of the frontier can be done by choosing both solutions using the following command (or can just be copied and pasted)

```
> plot([rhs(op(Sol_e[1])),rhs(op(Sol_e[2]))],sd=4..11,
  thickness=3,labels=[s,m],labelfont=[SYMBOL]);
```

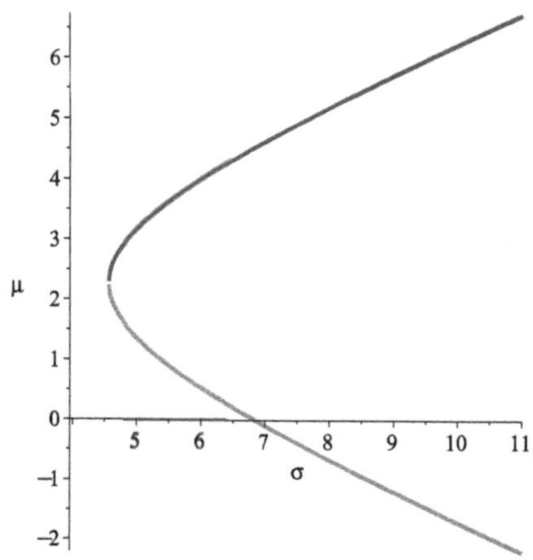

Observing the two solutions of e as a function of sd, it is clear that the efficient frontier function is the solution with the larger e, that is

$$e = 2.265525637 + 3.530521283\,10^{-16} \times \sqrt{1.594523608\,10^{30}\,\mathrm{sd}^2 - 3.331169274\,10^{31}}.$$

The function SimEf defined in the following is the efficient frontier, i.e., the expected value as a function of σ under the SIM

```
> SimEf:=e->2.265525637+3.530521283*10^(-16)*
  sqrt(1.594523608*10^30*sd^2-3.331169274*10^31);
```

$$\mathrm{SimEf} := e \mapsto 2.265525637 + 3.530521283\left(\frac{1}{10000000000000000}\right) \times \sqrt{1.594523608\,10^{30}\,\mathrm{sd}^2 - 3.331169274\,10^{31}} \quad (46)$$

```
> plot(SimEf(sd),sd=4.570701653..8);
```

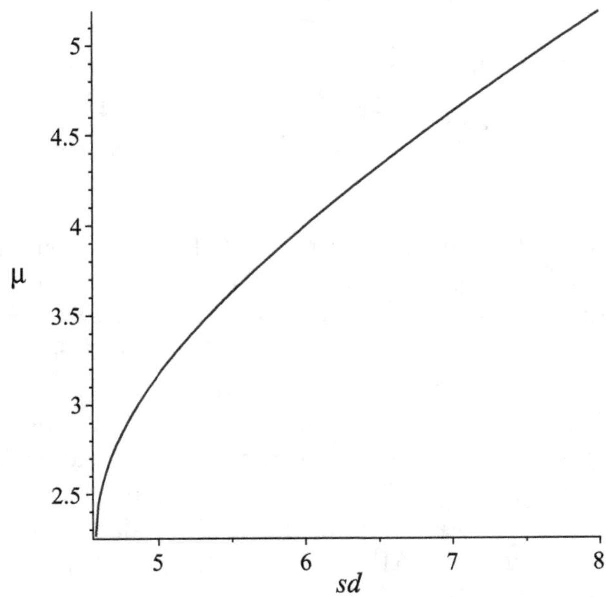

The efficient frontier based on the CAPM as was solved for in Lab 8 is

```
> EffCAPM:=sd->2.640763709+4.660062176*10^(-16)
*sqrt(1.208030992*10^30*sd^2-1.904680973*10^31);
```

$$\text{EffCAPM} := \text{sd} \mapsto 2.640763709 + 4.660062176\left(\frac{1}{10000000000000000}\right) \times \sqrt{1.208030992\,10^{30}\,\text{sd}^2 - 1.904680973\,10^{31}} \quad (47)$$

Hence, the two efficient frontiers can be presented together by

```
> plot([SimEf(sd),EffCAPM(sd)],sd=4..20);
```

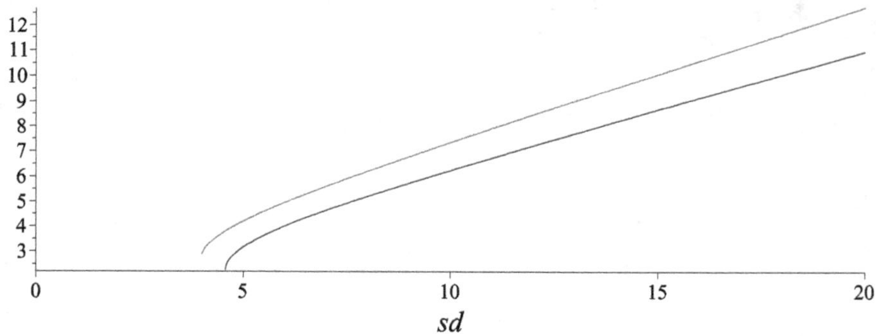

The advantages of using a SIM were cited before as being the separation introduced to the organization and the reduction in the number of parameters needed to be estimated. There is, of course, another issue regarding the computation of the efficient frontier. While given the advances of the computers' hardware and software in the last decade, this may not be a significant advantage. The SIM does induce a very simple rule based on which the efficient frontier can be constructed. This rule emphasizes and conveys the notion of risk being measured by the systematic risk, the undiversifiable risk.

As we show in the CAPM, given a diversified portfolio, its risk should be measured by β. The development in the appendix shows how the SIM (after some tedious algebraic manipulations which, thanks to Maple, are not so horrendous) reinforces this notion of risk. The SIM induces a criteria that ranks securities based on their excess return over the risk-free rate per "unit" of β, named *Treynor Ratio.* That is, a security will be ranked based on its expected rate of return minus the risk-free rate of return divided by its β, i.e., by

$$\frac{E(R_i) - R_f}{\beta_i} = \text{Exe}Rf_i$$

which can be interpreted as the expected return over the risk-free rate per unit of risk. Thus, the larger the expression, the more attractive the security. The optimal market portfolio in the SIM is composed of a long position in each security for which $\text{Exe}Rf_i$ is greater than a cut-off value C and a short position in each security for which $\text{Exe}Rf_i$ is less than the cut-off C. What determines if security i will be held in a long position in the portfolio, is if its excess return over the risk-free rate exceeds a certain cut-off-value which is C.

If $0 < \text{Exe}Rf_i - C$, security i will be held long, and if $\text{Exec}_1 - C < 0$ it will be held short. A security will be excluded from the portfolio if $\text{Exe}Rf_i - C = 0$. The interesting point, however, is that such an equation will hold true for every security in the portfolio and the excess return of each security will be compared to the same value; to C. Thus, implicit in this model is the measurement of excess return per unit of risk, where risk is measured by the β of the portfolio. The value of the cut-off point C can be determined without the knowledge of the composition of the market portfolio. Thus, this property can improve the procedure for finding the optimal market portfolio. *Furthermore, if the Index is one of the traded assets in the market, the cut-off point C satisfies* $C = E(RI) - Rf$, where RI is the expected rate of return on the index.

A model simpler than the SIM is the constant correlation model, where the correlation coefficient between each two securities is the same, $\rho_{ij} = \rho$. In such a model, the optimal market portfolio can be determined as in the SIM where *Sharpe ratio,* $\frac{E(R_i)-R_f}{\sigma_{R_i}}$, replaces $\frac{E(R_i)-R_f}{\beta_i}$. The Sharpe ratio of a security (or a portfolio) is the ratio between the excess rate of return of a security above the risk-free rate, to the standard deviation of the security. Note that $\frac{(\mu_i-R_f)}{\sigma_i}$ is the slope of the line connecting (σ_i, μ_i) to $(0, R_f)$. Therefore, when i stands for the market portfolio it is the slope of the CML. However, this slope can be measured given any efficient portfolio on the CML as $\frac{\mu_e-R_f}{\sigma_e}$, where μ_e, σ_e are the expected value and standard deviation of a portfolio on the CML. Hence, the Sharpe ratio of every security (or a portfolio) on the CML is the same and equals the slope of the CML, i.e., to $\frac{(\mu_m - R_f)}{\sigma_m}$. Furthermore, based on the construction of the CML, there exists no security or a portfolio in the market for which $\frac{(\mu_i - R_f)}{\sigma_i} > \frac{(\mu_m - R_f)}{\sigma_m}$, as the CML was constructed by maximizing the ratio $\frac{(\mu_i - R_f)}{\sigma_i}$. Hence, the Sharpe ratio of every security (or a portfolio) on the CML is the same and equals $\frac{(\mu_m - R_f)}{\sigma_m}$ i.e., the slope of the CML. Apropos the *Sharpe ratio*, it is interesting to mention a related performance measures dubbed the ***M^2-Measure***.

This measure allows the interpretation of the difference between the M^2 ranking of two portfolios. The M^2 uses the total risk of a portfolio that is the σ of the portfolio. The M^2 of a portfolio is the difference in the expected rate of return of the market portfolio and the given portfolio, after the given portfolio risk σ was adjusted to equal to the the market portfolio σ_m. Hence, given a portfolio p with a risk of $\sigma_p \neq \sigma_m$, the first step is to combine the given portfolio with a position in the risk-free rate such that the σ of the new portfolio will equal σ_m. Since $\sigma_{Rf} = 0$ and $\text{Cov}(R_f, p) = 0$, the following equation determines the position in the risk-free rate to be $1 - x$

$$x \cdot \sigma_p + (1 - x) \cdot \sigma_{Rf} = \sigma_m \text{ which implies that } x = \frac{\sigma_m}{\sigma_p}.$$

Consequently, if $\sigma_p < \sigma_m$ then $x > 1$ and a short portion is taken in the risk-free asset. That is, to obtain a portfolio such that its $\sigma = \sigma_m$, one borrows at the risk-free rate and invests in the portfolio p. If $\sigma_p > \sigma_m$, then $x < 1$ and the portfolio p is scaled down by x, and $(1 - x)$ is invested in the risk-free asset. Denote the obtained new portfolio by e, the M_p^2 of p is $\mu_e - \mu_m$. Thus, there is a meaning to the difference between the M^2 measure of two portfolios p_1 and p_2. If $M_{p_1}^2 > M_{p_1}^2$, then

$$M_{p_1}^2 - M_{p_1}^2 = \mu_{e1} - \mu_m - (\mu_{e2} - \mu_m) = \mu_{e1} - \mu_{e_2},$$

which means that $M_{p_1}^2 - M_{p_1}^2 > 0$ is the difference in expected values of the two adjusted portfolios and both have the same σ which equals σ_m.

Note that geometrically M^2 requires finding a portfolio with σ_m that is on the line connecting the coordinate of the risk-free rate and the given portfolio p. The expected value of a portfolio on this line cannot be higher than the expected value of the market portfolio since to have a higher expected value, the slope of this line must be steeper than that of the CML. However, the CML slope is the maximum slope of any line that connects the risk-free asset R_f to any security or portfolio in this market. Hence, in the CAPM, the maximum M^2 of any portfolio is zero and is obtained for any portfolio on the CML. M^2 of any other portfolio is negative. The M^2 was suggested by Leah **M**odigliani and Franco **M**odigliani (**MM doubt** M^2). To exemplify the M^2 measure, it is evaluated for a portfolio p with $\sigma_p = 5$ and $\mu_p = 8.5$, in a market in which the risk-free rate is 6 and a market portfolio (m) with $\sigma_m = 8$ and $\mu_m = 12$. The equation above is utilized to value the M^2 of the portfolio p. Hence, a portfolio X, where a percentage $x = \frac{8}{5} = \frac{\sigma_m}{\sigma_p}$ is invested in the portfolio p and $1 - x = -\frac{3}{8}$ is invested in the risk-free asset, is composed. Consequently, the standard deviation of the portfolio is $\frac{8}{5} \cdot 5 + \frac{3}{8} \cdot 0 = 8$ and its expected value is $\frac{8}{5} \cdot 8.5 - \frac{3}{8} \cdot 6 = 10$.

```
> 8.5*(8/5)-6*3/5;
```

$$10.00000000. \tag{48}$$

Hence, M^2 of p is $10 - 12 = -2$. The geometric interpretation M^2 is shown in the following figure. The M^2 measure of the portfolio p is the negative of the length of the segment $[X, m]$. This is the expected value of the rate of return of m minus that of X. The portfolio X was generated by combining the portfolio p with the risk-free asset to generate a portfolio with the same standard deviation as the market portfolio m. Geometrically, it means that X is on the line connecting p and the risk-free assets as shown in the following figure:

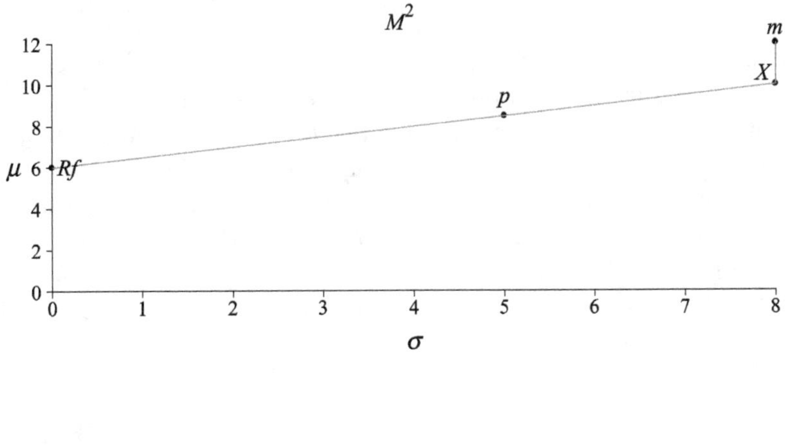

Practitioners' Form of the CAPM

The market model is very similar to the SIM but the assumption of $\text{Cov}(e_i, e_j) = 0$ for $i \neq j$ is not made. Thus, the interaction (covariance) between two securities exists not only because the return on each security depends on the Index, but also due to a direct interaction. Hence, the variance of a portfolio is no longer the simple expression given in the SIM and the separation that exists in the SIM model is lost.

Let us review the SIM formulas and revise them when the assumption of $\text{Cov}(e_i, e_j) = 0$ for $i \neq j$ is not made. We still assume that the rate of return on each security in the market follows the process

$$R_i = \alpha_i + \beta_i R_m + e_i.$$

As well, we still think about e_i as representing the non-systematic risk and hence keep the assumption that $\text{Cov}(e_i, R_m) = 0$. Thus, the variance of each security will be given by

$$\begin{aligned}\text{Var}(R_i) &= \text{Var}(\alpha_i + \beta_i\ R_m + e_i) = \text{Var}(\beta_i\ R_m) + \text{Var}(e_i)\\ &= \beta_i^2\ \text{Var}(R_m) + \text{Var}(e_i).\end{aligned}$$

Note that when we estimate the α and β of a security with a rate of return R by running the regression

$$R = \alpha + \beta\ R_m + e,$$

the estimated covariance between e and R_m is always zero.We will first explain the intuition behind this phenomena and will follow up with a visualized geometric example in the following subsection. The regression above attempts to explain the changes in the rate of return R, by a combination of a factor multiplying the rate of return R[m] and a constant alpha. The variable R[m] can explain part of the variability in R, only if there is a "connection" between the two variables. More precisely, the meaning of this "connection" is that the covariance between R and R[m] is different than zero. The regression tries to explain the maximum variability in R and as a result determines the best value of β and α. If the variability in R can be fully explained by $\beta * R[\text{m}] + \alpha$, then there will be no unexplained residuals and e will be zero. If ϵ is not zero, it means that the best value of α and β did not manage to explain the full variability of R, and there is a residual. However, α and β are chosen such as to explain the maximum variability in R. If, however, there is still a connection between R and e, it means that it is still possible to explain part of the variability in R, by choosing better values for α and β. Thus, for the best possible α and β, e cannot explain any part of the variability of R. Consequently, there is no connection between e and R or more precisely, $\text{Cov}(e_i, R_m) = 0$.

A Visualized Example

Given $r = (r_1, \ldots r_n)$ the vector of observations on R, the vector $r_m = (r_{m_1}, \ldots, r_{m_n})$ of observations on R_m and the vector $\mathbf{1} = (1, 1, \ldots, 1)$, we try to see if r satisfies

$$(r_1, \ldots, r_n) = \alpha \cdot (1, 1, \ldots, 1) + \beta \cdot (r_{m_1}, \ldots, r_{m_n})$$

or in a scalar notation if

$$r_i = \alpha \cdot 1 + \beta \cdot r_{m_i} \quad \text{for } i = 1, \ldots, n.$$

If this is the case, r is a linear combination of $\mathbf{1}$ and r_m and the vector of realized deviations

$$\begin{aligned}\epsilon &= (\varepsilon_1, \ldots, \varepsilon_n) = (r_1 - \alpha + \beta \cdot r_{m_1}, \ldots, r_n - \alpha + \beta \cdot r_{m_n}) \\ &= (0, \ldots, 0)\end{aligned}$$

is zero. Thus the estimated covariance, $\text{Cov}(e_i, R_m)$, $\frac{\sum_{j=1}^n \epsilon_j r_{m_j}}{n} - \frac{\sum_{j=1}^n \epsilon_j}{n} \cdot \frac{\sum_{j=1}^n r_{m_j}}{n}$, is trivially zero and indeed $\left(\sum_{j=1}^n \epsilon_j^2\right) = \sum_{j=1}^n (r_j - \alpha + \beta \cdot r_{m_j})^2 = 0$ was minimized.

However, if r is not a linear combination of 1 and r_m, by minimizing $\left(\sum_{j=1}^n \varepsilon_j^2\right)$ we are in fact searching for α and β such that $\alpha + \beta\, r_m$ is the closest to r, as the distance (Euclidian norm) between r_m and $\alpha + \beta\, r_m$ is $\left(\sum_{j=1}^n \epsilon_j^2\right)$. In this case, we are looking for vector generated by a linear combination of $(1, 1, \ldots, 1)$ and $(r_{m_1}, \ldots, r_{m_n})$ which is the closest to $r_1, \ldots, r_n$, i.e., a vector in the subspace generated by 1 and r_m which is the closest to r. This will result in splitting r

into two vectors: one in the subspace generated by 1 and r_m, that is $\alpha + \beta r_m$ (for the optimal α and β) and the other orthogonal to this subspace. The orthogonal vector is ϵ.

Since ϵ is orthogonal to the subspace generated by 1 and r_m, it satisfies $\sum_{j=1}^{n} \epsilon_j r_{m_j} = 0$ and $\sum_{j=1}^{n} \epsilon_j \cdot 1 = 0$. Therefore, the estimated covariance, between ϵ and r_m, is zero.

Let us now look at an example assuming we have three observations of the rate of return on the market and on a security. Let the rate of return on the market be [2,1,1.5] and the rate of return on the security be [0.5,1.5,3].

Let us plot the vector of the rate of return on the market and the vector of [1,1,1] together with the subspace they spanned. Recall that if the relation between the rate of return on the security and the market is linear, then the vector of observations on the security will be in this subspace.

```
> VecM:=plots[arrow](<2,1,1.5>,width=[0.02,relative],
  head_length=[0.04, relative],axes=normal,
  view=[-.5..2.6,-.5..2.6,-.5..2.6]):

>

> VecOne:=plots[arrow](<1,1,1>, width=[0.02,relative],
  head_length=[0.04, relative],axes=normal,
  view=[-.5..2.6,-.5..2.6,-.5..2.6]):

>

> SubSpace:=plot3d([alpha+2*beta,alpha+beta,alpha+
  1.5*beta],alpha=-5..3, beta=-5..3,axes=box,
  style=patchnogrid,orientation=[46,38],
  transparency=0.1):

>

> plots[display](VecM,VecOne,SubSpace);
```

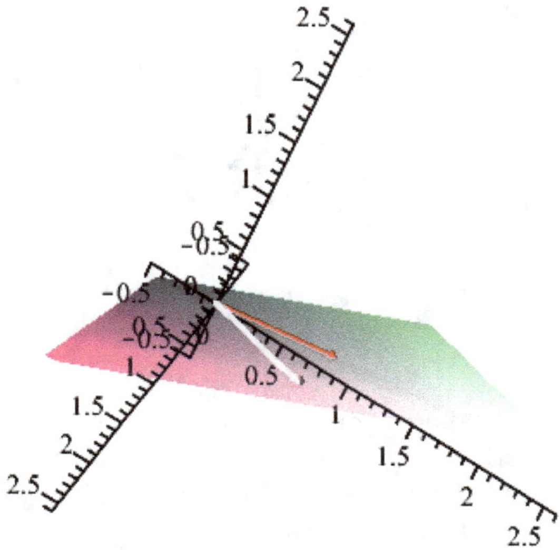


```
>
```

There are two vectors in the above graphs. One vector is [1,1,1] and the other is the rate of return on the market. We see the subspace generated by these two vectors. Next we are going to add the vector of observations on the security so we can see if it is in the subspace or not. If it is in the subspace, we empirically have a perfect linear relation between the rate of return on the market and on the security. Otherwise we will search the closest possible vector to the vector of observations that is in the subspace.

Below we plot the vector of observations on the rate of return on the security and plot it as a green vector.

```
> VecR:=plots[arrow]({<.5,1.5,3>}, width=[0.02,relative],
  head_length=[0.04, relative], color=green,axes=normal,
  view=[-.5..2.6,-.5..2.6,-.5..2.6]):
```

```
>
```

```
> plots[display](VecM,VecOne,SubSpace,VecR);
```

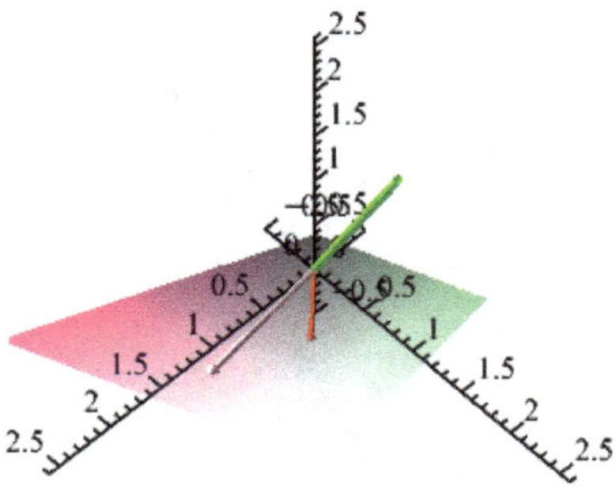

```
>
```

It is apparent that the vector of observations is not in the subspace and cannot be written as a linear combination of the other two vectors that generate the subspace. Thus, we now try to find a vector that is a linear combination of the rate of return on the market and the vector [1,1,1], that is as close as possible to the vector of the rate of return on the security. We solve for this vector in the following and define it to be ProjVec

```
> (alpha+2*beta-.5)^2+(alpha+beta-1.5)^2
  +(alpha+1.5*beta-3)^2;
```

$$(\alpha + 2\,\beta - 0.5)^2 + (\alpha + \beta - 1.5)^2 + (\alpha + 1.5\,\beta - 3)^2 \qquad (49)$$

```
>
```

```
> solve({diff(%,alpha)=0,diff(%,beta)=0});
```

$$\{\alpha = 3.166666667, \beta = -1.\} \qquad (50)$$

```
>
```

```
> ProjVec:=subs(op(%),[alpha+2*beta,alpha+beta,
  alpha+1.5*beta]);;
```

$$\text{ProjVec} := [1.166666667,\ 2.166666667,\ 1.666666667] \qquad (51)$$

```
>
```

```
> Proj:=plots[arrow]({<ProjVec[1],ProjVec[2],
  ProjVec[3]>}, width=[0.02,relative], head_length=
  [0.04, relative], color=blue,axes=normal):
```

```
>
```

We are now in a position to visualize the closest vector (which must be a vector in the subspace) to the vector of observations. This vector is the blue vector.

```
> plots[display](VecM,VecOne,SubSpace,VecR,Proj);
```

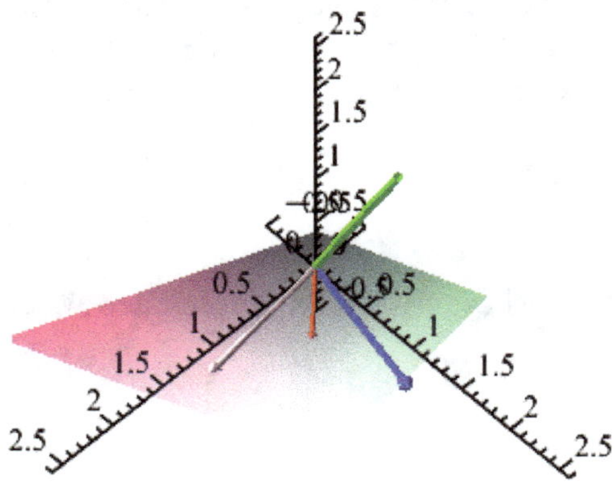


```
>
```

We can now visualize that this blue vector is indeed the projection of the vector of observations on the rate of return on the security onto the subspace. In other words, the closest vector in the subspace to the vector of observations on the rate of return on the security, is obtained via the following operation. Find two vectors one which is in the subspace and one which is perpendicular to the subspace such that their sum is the vector of observations on the rate of return of the security. The perpendicular vector is the vector of deviations from the linear relation. We again visualize this operation where the vector of deviation, epsilon is shown in black.

```
> epsilon:=[.5,1.5,3]-ProjVec;
```

$$\varepsilon := [-0.666666667,\ -0.666666667,\ 1.333333333] \quad (52)$$

```
>
```

```
> epsilon+ProjVec;
```

$$[0.500000000,\ 1.500000000,\ 3.000000000] \quad (53)$$

```
>
```

```
> Epsilon:=plots[arrow](<op(epsilon)>,width=[0.013,
  relative],head_length=[0.004, relative],
  color=black,axes=normal):
```

```
>
```

```
> plots[display](VecM,VecOne,SubSpace,VecR,Proj,Epsilon);
```

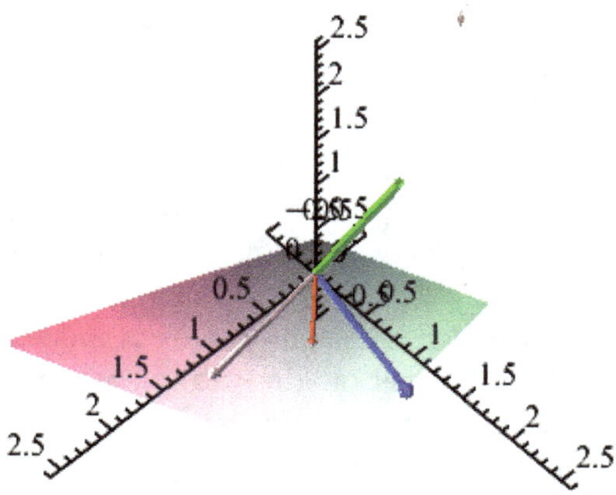


```
>
```

It is now apparent that the vector epsilon, denoted by e_i in the following, is perpendicular to the vector of observations on the market R_m, and also to the vector [1,1,1]. Hence, $\sum_{j=1}^{n} e_{ij} = 0$ and

$\sum_{j=1}^{n} e_{ij} \cdot R_{mj} = 0$ where the index j denotes the jth observation. Thus, empirically we will always have that $\text{Cov}(e_i, R_m) = 0$.

The market model actually assumes that $\text{Cov}(e_i, R_m) = 0$ and thus we have, as in the SIM that

$$\begin{aligned}\text{Cov}(R_i, R_j) &= \text{Cov}(\alpha_i + \beta_i R_m + e_i, \alpha_j + \beta_j R_m + e_j)\\ &= \text{Cov}(\beta_i R_m + e_i, \beta_j R_m + e_j)\end{aligned}$$

which equals

$$\text{Cov}(\beta_i R_m, \beta_j R_m) + \text{Cov}(\beta_i R_m, e_j) + \text{Cov}(\beta_j R_m, e_i) + \text{Cov}(e_i, e_j).$$

By the assumption that $\text{Cov}(e_i, R_m) = 0$, the middle two elements vanish and hence $\text{Cov}(R_i, R_j) = \beta_i\ \beta_j\ \text{Cov}(R_m, R_m) + \text{Cov}(e_i, e_j)$, but since $\text{Cov}(R_m, R_m) = \text{Var}(R_m)$ we have $\text{Cov}(R_i, R_j) = \beta_i \beta_j\ \text{Var}(R_m) + \text{Cov}(e_i, e_j)$.

Note that the market model is in fact the way "practitioners" work with the CAPM. Most practitioners will choose an Index to represent the market portfolio and will estimate α and β with the regression. Since as we demonstrated above, the assumption made by the Market model namely $\text{Cov}(e_i, R_m) = 0$ is always satisfied empirically by the estimated $\text{Cov}(e_i, R_m)$, the market model can be regarded as the practical application of the CAPM.

Appendix: SIM, Constant Correlation, and the Efficient Frontier

Below we demonstrate the dependency of the optimal market portfolio in the SIM on the measure $\frac{E(R_i)-R_f}{\beta_i}$. We start by assuming that there are only four securities in the market, and assigning the value 4 to N — the number of securities in the market. It is apparent that this number was chosen arbitrarily and if the reader assigns a different value for N the result demonstrated in the following will be unchanged.

```
> N:=4;
```

$$N := 4 \tag{A.1}$$

```
>
```

The variance–covariance matrix under the SIM will be defined as follows:

```
> MapSi:=(i,j)->if i<>j then beta[i]*beta[j]*VarRm
  else (beta[i]^2)*VarRm+Vare[i] fi;
```

$$\text{Map}Si := (i,j) \to \textbf{if } i \neq j \textbf{ then } \beta_i \beta_j \text{ Var}Rm \textbf{ else } \beta_i^2 \text{ Var}Rm + \text{Vare}_i \textbf{ end if} \tag{A.2}$$

```
>
```

```
> Sigma:= Matrix(N,N,MapSi);
```

$$\Sigma := \big[\big[\beta_1^2 \text{ Var}Rm + \text{Vare}_1, \beta_1 \beta_2 \text{ Var}Rm, \beta_1 \beta_3 \text{ Var}Rm, \beta_1 \beta_4 \text{Var}Rm\big], \big[\beta_1 \beta_2 \text{ Var}Rm, \beta_2^2 \text{ Var}Rm + \text{Vare}_2, \beta_2 \beta_3 \text{ Var}Rm, \beta_2 \beta_4 \text{Var}Rm\big], \big[\beta_1 \beta_3 \text{ Var}Rm, \beta_2 \beta_3 \text{ Var}Rm, \beta_3^2 \text{ Var}Rm + \text{Vare}_3, \beta_3 \beta_4 \text{Var}Rm\big], \big[\beta_1 \beta_4 \text{ Var}Rm, \beta_2 \beta_4 \text{ Var}Rm, \beta_3 \beta_4 \text{ Var}Rm, \beta_4^2 \text{ Var}Rm + \text{Vare}_4\big]\big] \tag{A.3}$$

```
>
```

When short sales are allowed and a risk-free asset exists, the market portfolio is the solution to the system of equations in the following:

$$E_i - R_f = \sum_{j=1}^{N} X_i \sigma_{i,j} \quad i = 1, \ldots, N.$$

We shall set this system of equations using matrix notation.

```
> Ri_rf:=Vector(N,x->r||x-rf);
```

$$Ri\_rf := \begin{bmatrix} r1 - rf \\ r2 - rf \\ r3 - rf \\ r4 - rf \end{bmatrix} \tag{A.4}$$

```
>
```

The solution for x_1 is produced in the following.

```
> LinearAlgebra[LinearSolve](Sigma,Ri_rf)[1];
```

$$\begin{aligned}&\big(-\mathrm{Var}e_4\ \mathrm{Var}e_3\,\beta_1\,\beta_2\ \mathrm{Var}Rm\ r2+\mathrm{Var}e_4\ \mathrm{Var}e_3\,\beta_1\,\beta_2\ \mathrm{Var}Rm\ rf\\&\quad+\mathrm{Var}e_3\ \mathrm{Var}e_2\,\beta_4\ \mathrm{Var}Rm\,\beta_1 rf+\mathrm{Var}e_4\ \mathrm{Var}e_3\,\beta_2^2\ \mathrm{Var}Rm\ r1\\&\quad-\mathrm{Var}e_4\ \mathrm{Var}e_3\,\beta_2^2\ \mathrm{Var}Rm\ rf-\mathrm{Var}e_3\ \mathrm{Var}e_2\,\beta_4^2\ \mathrm{Var}Rm\ rf\\&\quad+\mathrm{Var}e_4\ \mathrm{Var}e_2\,\beta_3\ \mathrm{Var}Rm\,\beta_1\ rf+\mathrm{Var}e_4\ \mathrm{Var}e_3\ \mathrm{Var}e_2\,r_1\\&\quad-\mathrm{Var}e_4\ \mathrm{Var}e_3\ \mathrm{Var}e_2 rf-\mathrm{Var}e_4\ \mathrm{Var}e_2\,\beta_3\ \mathrm{Var}Rm\,\beta_1\,r_3\\&\quad-\mathrm{Var}e_3\ \mathrm{Var}e_2\,\beta_4\ \mathrm{Var}Rm\,\beta_1\,r_4+\mathrm{Var}e_4\ \mathrm{Var}e_2\,\beta_3^2\ \mathrm{Var}Rm\,r_1\\&\quad-\mathrm{Var}e_4\ \mathrm{Var}e_2\,\beta_3^2\ \mathrm{Var}Rm\ rf+\mathrm{Var}e_3\ \mathrm{Var}e_2\,\beta_4^2\ \mathrm{Var}Rm r_1\big)\big/\\&\quad\big(\mathrm{Var}e_4\ \mathrm{Var}e_3\,\beta_2^2\ \mathrm{Var}Rm\ \mathrm{Var}e_1+\mathrm{Var}e_4\ \mathrm{Var}e_3\ \mathrm{Var}e_2\,\beta_1^2\ \mathrm{Var}Rm\\&\quad+\mathrm{Var}e_4\ \mathrm{Var}e_3\ \mathrm{Var}e_2\ \mathrm{Var}e_1+\mathrm{Var}e_4\ \mathrm{Var}e_2\,\beta_3^2\ \mathrm{Var}Rm\ \mathrm{Var}e_1\\&\quad+\mathrm{Var}e_3\ \mathrm{Var}e_2\,\beta_4^2\ \mathrm{Var}Rm\ \mathrm{Var}e_1\big)\end{aligned}\tag{A.5}$$

```
>
```

As we see, the system can be solved even symbolically when the SIM is assumed, so the advantage may not be of significant importance but it does add a flavor to our understanding. To this end, let us move to a scalar notation and generate each equation.

```
> X:=Vector(N,symbol=x);
```

$$X := \begin{bmatrix} x_1 \\ x_2 \\ x_3 \\ x_4 \end{bmatrix} \tag{A.6}$$

```
>
```

```
> i='i':for i from 1 to 4 do;
> eq(i):=(Sigma.X)[i]-Ri_rf[i];
> od; i:='i':
```

$$\begin{aligned}
\mathrm{eq}(1) := {} & (\beta_1^2\ \mathrm{Var}Rm + \mathrm{Vare}_1)x_1 + \beta_1\,\beta_2\ \mathrm{Var}Rm\,x_2 \\
& + \beta_1\,\beta_3\ \mathrm{Var}Rm\,x_3 + \beta_1\,\beta_4\ \mathrm{Var}Rm\,x_4 - r1 + rf \\
\mathrm{eq}(2) := {} & \beta_1\,\beta_2\ \mathrm{Var}Rm\,x_1 + (\beta_2^2\ \mathrm{Var}Rm + \mathrm{Vare}_2)x_2 \\
& + \beta_2\,\beta_3\ \mathrm{Var}Rm\,x_3 + \beta_2\,\beta_4\ \mathrm{Var}Rm\,x_4 - r2 + rf \\
\mathrm{eq}(3) := {} & \beta_1\,\beta_3\ \mathrm{Var}Rm\,x_1 + \beta_2\,\beta_3\ \mathrm{Var}Rm\,x_2 \\
& + (\beta_3^2\ \mathrm{Var}Rm + \mathrm{Vare}_3)x_3 + \beta_3\,\beta_4\ \mathrm{Var}Rm\,x_4 - r3 + rf \\
\mathrm{eq}(4) := {} & \beta_1\,\beta_4\ \mathrm{Var}Rm\,x_1 + \beta_2\,\beta_4\ \mathrm{Var}Rm\,x_2 + \beta_3\,\beta_4\ \mathrm{Var}Rm\,x_3 \\
& + (\beta_4^2\ \mathrm{Var}Rm + \mathrm{Vare}_4)x_4 - r4 + rf
\end{aligned} \tag{A.7}$$

```
>
```

Again, we can solve it with Maple but we would like to generate a specific form for the solution to demonstrate a certain point. Hence, rather than using the following command for the solution, we continue to manipulate the equations.

```
> solve({seq(eq(i),i=1..N)},{seq(x[i],i=1..N)}):
```

```
>
```

Consider Eq. (1):

```
> eq(1);
```

$$\begin{aligned}
& (\beta_1^2\ \mathrm{Var}Rm + \mathrm{Vare}_1)x_1 + \beta_1\,\beta_2\ \mathrm{Var}Rm\,x_2 + \beta_1\,\beta_3\ \mathrm{Var}Rm\,x_3 \\
& + \beta_1\,\beta_4\ \mathrm{Var}Rm\,x_4 - r1 + rf
\end{aligned} \tag{A.8}$$

```
>
```

We divide both sides of the equation by β_1 and expand it

```
> expand((eq(1)/beta[1]));
```

$$\begin{aligned}
& \beta_1\,x_1\ \mathrm{Var}Rm + \frac{x_1\ \mathrm{Vare}_1}{\beta_1} + \beta_2\ \mathrm{Var}Rm\,x_2 + \beta_3\ \mathrm{Var}Rm\,x_3 \\
& + \beta_4\ \mathrm{Var}Rm\,x_4 - \frac{r1}{\beta_1} + \frac{rf}{\beta_1}
\end{aligned} \tag{A.9}$$

```
>
```

and solve for $\frac{X_1 \text{ Vare}_1}{\beta_1}$.

```
> expand(solve({%},{X[1]*Vare[1]/beta[1]}));
Warning, solving for expressions other than names or
functions is not recommended.
```

$$\left\{\frac{x_1 \text{ Vare}_1}{\beta_1} = -\beta_1\, x_1 \text{ Var}Rm + \frac{r1}{\beta_1} - \beta_2 \text{ Var}Rm\, x_2 - \beta_3 \text{ Var}Rm\, x_3 - \beta_4 \text{ Var}Rm\, x_4 - \frac{rf}{\beta_1}\right\} \tag{A.10}$$

```
>
```

The expression

$$\frac{r1}{\beta_1} - \frac{rf}{\beta_1} = \frac{r1 - rf}{\beta_1}$$

appears in the equation above. This is indeed the excess return we spoke about earlier. We thus define $\frac{r_1 - r_f}{\beta_1}$ as Exec_1 the excess return on security one and substitute it in the equation.

```
> algsubs(r1/beta[1]-(rf/beta[1])=Exec[1],op(%));
```

$$\frac{x_1 \text{ Vare}_1}{\beta_1} = -\beta_1\, x_1 \text{ Var}Rm + \text{Exec}_1 - \beta_2 \text{ Var}Rm\, x_2 - \beta_3 \text{ Var}Rm\, x_3 - \beta_4 \text{ Var}Rm\, x_4 \tag{A.11}$$

```
>
```

A careful inspection of the obtained equation reveals a certain property of its structure. Its right-hand side is composed of two expressions: an expression that is individual to Eq. (1) the Exec_1, and

$$-\beta_1\, X_1 \text{ Var}Rm - \beta_2 \text{ Var}Rm\, X_2 - \beta_3 \text{ Var}Rm\, X_3 - \beta_4 \text{ Var}Rm\, X_4$$

which will appear in each of the equations above.

This should be apparent but we will explicitly show it very shortly.

Defining this latter expression as $SbXV$, (i.e., in general $SbXV = \mathrm{Var}Rm\left(\sum_{i=1}^{N}\beta_i X_i\right)$, and substituting it in the equation yields

```
> algsubs(sum(beta[i]*x[i]*VarRm,i=1..N)=SbXV,%);
```

$$\frac{x_1\ \mathrm{Vare}_1}{\beta_1} = -SbXV + \mathrm{Exec}_1 \tag{A.12}$$

```
>
```

Solving for x_1 in this term produces our desired form for the solution.

```
> solve({%},{x[1]});
```

$$\left\{x_1 = -\frac{(SbXV - \mathrm{Exec}_1)\beta_1}{\mathrm{Vare}_1}\right\} \tag{A.13}$$

```
>
```

Let us take a look at this solution (assuming the common case of β_1 being positive)

$$X_1 = [\mathrm{Exec}_1 - SbXV]\left[\frac{\beta_1}{\mathrm{Vare}_1}\right].$$

What determines if X_1 will be held in a long position in the portfolio is if its excess return exceeds a certain cut-off value which is $SbXV$. If $0 < \mathrm{Exec}_1 - SbXV$, X_1 will be held long and if $\mathrm{Exec}_1 - SbXV < 0$ it will be held short. X_1 will be excluded from the portfolio if $\mathrm{Exec}_1 - SbXV = 0$. The interesting point, however, is that such an equation will hold true for every security in the portfolio and the excess return of each security will be compared to the same value; to $SbXV$. Thus, implicit in this model is the **measurement of excess return per unit of risk where risk is measured by the beta** of the portfolio. Below we show that our analysis indeed holds for every security.

```
> i:='i': for i from 1 to N do:
  expand((eq(i)/beta[i])):
  expand(solve({%},{X[i]*Vare[i]/beta[i]})):
```

```
algsubs(r||i/beta[i]-(rf/beta[i])=Exec[i],op(%)):
algsubs(rhs(%)-Exec[i]=-SbXV,%);
eq(i):=op(solve({%},{X[i]})):
od;i:='i':
```

$$\beta_1\, x_1\, \mathrm{Var}Rm + \frac{x_1\, \mathrm{Vare}_1}{\beta_1} + \beta_2\, \mathrm{Var}Rm\, x_2 + \beta_3\, \mathrm{Var}Rm\, x_3 + \beta_4\, \mathrm{Var}Rm\, x_4 - \frac{r1}{\beta_1} + \frac{rf}{\beta_1}$$

Warning, solving for expressions other than names or functions is not recommended.

$$\left\{\frac{x_1\, \mathrm{Vare}_1}{\beta_1} = -\beta_1\, x_1\, \mathrm{Var}Rm + \frac{r1}{\beta_1} - \beta_2\, \mathrm{Var}Rm\, x_2 - \beta_3\, \mathrm{Var}Rm\, x_3 - \beta_4\, \mathrm{Var}Rm\, x_4 - \frac{rf}{\beta_1}\right\}$$

$$\frac{x_1\, \mathrm{Vare}_1}{\beta_1} = -\beta_1\, x_1\, \mathrm{Var}Rm + \mathrm{Exec}_1 - \beta_2\, \mathrm{Var}Rm\, x_2 - \beta_3\, \mathrm{Var}Rm\, x_3 - \beta_4\, \mathrm{Var}Rm\, x_4$$

$$\frac{x_1\, \mathrm{Vare}_1}{\beta_1} = -SbXV + \mathrm{Exec}_1$$

$$\mathrm{eq}(1) := x_1 = -\frac{(SbXV - \mathrm{Exec}_1)\beta_1}{\mathrm{Vare}_1}$$

$$\beta_1\, x_1\, \mathrm{Var}Rm + \beta_2\, \mathrm{Var}Rm\, x_2 + \frac{x_2\, \mathrm{Vare}_2}{\beta_2} + \beta_3\, \mathrm{Var}Rm\, x_3 + \beta_4\, \mathrm{Var}Rm\, x_4 - \frac{r2}{\beta_2} + \frac{rf}{\beta_2}$$

Warning, solving for expressions other than names or functions is not recommended.

$$\left\{\frac{x_2\, \mathrm{Vare}_2}{\beta_2} = -\beta_1\, x_1\, \mathrm{Var}Rm - \beta_2\, \mathrm{Var}Rm\, x_2 - \frac{rf}{\beta_2} - \beta_3\, \mathrm{Var}Rm\, x_3 - \beta_4\, \mathrm{Var}Rm\, x_4 + \frac{r2}{\beta_2}\right\}$$

$$\frac{x_2 \operatorname{Var}e_2}{\beta_2} = -\beta_1 x_1 \operatorname{Var}Rm - \beta_2 \operatorname{Var}Rm\, x_2 - \beta_3 \operatorname{Var}Rm\, x_3 - \beta_4 \operatorname{Var}Rm\, x_4 + \operatorname{Exec}_2$$

$$\frac{x_2 \operatorname{Var}e_2}{\beta_2} = -SbXV + \operatorname{Exec}_2$$

$$\operatorname{eq}(2) := x_2 = -\frac{(SbXV - \operatorname{Exec}_2)\beta_2}{\operatorname{Var}e_2}$$

$$\beta_1 x_1 \operatorname{Var}Rm + \beta_2 \operatorname{Var}Rm\, x_2 + \beta_3 \operatorname{Var}Rm\, x_3 + \frac{x_3 \operatorname{Var}e_3}{\beta_3} + \beta_4 \operatorname{Var}Rm\, x_4 - \frac{r3}{\beta_3} + \frac{rf}{\beta_3}$$

Warning, solving for expressions other than names or functions is not recommended.

$$\left\{\frac{x_3 \operatorname{Var}e_3}{\beta_3} = -\beta_1 x_1 \operatorname{Var}Rm - \beta_2 \operatorname{Var}Rm\, x_2 - \beta_3 \operatorname{Var}Rm\, x_3 - \beta_4 \operatorname{Var}Rm\, x_4 + \frac{r3}{\beta_3} - \frac{rf}{\beta_3}\right\}$$

$$\frac{x_3 \operatorname{Var}e_3}{\beta_3} = -\beta_1 x_1 \operatorname{Var}Rm - \beta_2 \operatorname{Var}Rm\, x_2 - \beta_3 \operatorname{Var}Rm\, x_3 - \beta_4 \operatorname{Var}Rm\, x_4 + \operatorname{Exec}_3$$

$$\frac{x_3 \operatorname{Var}e_3}{\beta_3} = -SbXV + \operatorname{Exec}_3$$

$$\operatorname{eq}(3) := x_3 = -\frac{(SbXV - \operatorname{Exec}_3)\beta_3}{\operatorname{Var}e_3}$$

$$\beta_1 x_1 \operatorname{Var}Rm + \beta_2 \operatorname{Var}Rm\, x_2 + \beta_3 \operatorname{Var}Rm\, x_3 + \beta_4 \operatorname{Var}Rm\, x_4 + \frac{x_4 \operatorname{Var}e_4}{\beta_4} - \frac{r4}{\beta_4} + \frac{rf}{\beta_4}$$

```
Warning, solving for expressions other than names or
functions is not recommended.
```

$$\left\{\frac{x_4\ \mathrm{Vare}_4}{\beta_4} = -\beta_1\, x_1\ \mathrm{Var}Rm - \beta_2\ \mathrm{Var}Rm\, x_2 - \beta_3\ \mathrm{Var}Rm\, x_3 - \beta_4\ \mathrm{Var}Rm\, x_4 + \frac{r4}{\beta_4} - \frac{rf}{\beta_4}\right\}$$

$$\frac{x_4\ \mathrm{Vare}_4}{\beta_4} = -\beta_1\, x_1\ \mathrm{Var}Rm - \beta_2\ \mathrm{Var}Rm\, x_2 - \beta_3\ \mathrm{Var}Rm\, x_3 - \beta_4\ \mathrm{Var}Rm\, x_4 + \mathrm{Exec}_4$$

$$\frac{x_4\ \mathrm{Vare}_4}{\beta_4} = -SbXV + \mathrm{Exec}_4$$

$$\mathrm{eq}(4) := x_4 = -\frac{(SbXV - \mathrm{Exec}_4)\beta_4}{\mathrm{Vare}_4} \tag{A.14}$$

```
>
```

In order to solve for the optimal portfolio based on

$$X_i = [\mathrm{Exec}_i - SbXV]\left[\frac{\beta_i}{\mathrm{Vare}_i}\right] \quad \text{for } i =, \ldots, N$$

we need to solve for the value of $SbXV$. However $SbXV$ itself is a function of the optimal X_i, so it seems that we have a vicious circle here. There is however a way to find the value of $SbXV$ without knowing the value of X. This is demonstrated by the following steps.

```
> sum(beta[i]*eq(i),i=1..N);
```

$$\beta_1\, x_1 + \beta_2\, x_2 + \beta_3\, x_3 + \beta_4\, x_4 = -\frac{\beta_1^2\,(SbXV - \mathrm{Exec}_1)}{\mathrm{Vare}_1} - \frac{\beta_2^2\,(SbXV - \mathrm{Exec}_2)}{\mathrm{Vare}_2} - \frac{\beta_3^2\,(SbXV - \mathrm{Exec}_3)}{\mathrm{Vare}_3} - \frac{\beta_4^2\,(SbXV - \mathrm{Exec}_4)}{\mathrm{Vare}_4} \tag{A.15}$$

```
>
```

```
> subs(X[1]*beta[1]+beta[2]*X[2]+beta[3]*X[3]
  +beta[4]*X[4]= SbXV/VarRm,%);
```

$$\frac{SbXV}{\mathrm{Var}Rm} = -\frac{\beta_1^2\,(SbXV - \mathrm{Exec}_1)}{\mathrm{Vare}_1} - \frac{\beta_2^2\,(SbXV - \mathrm{Exec}_2)}{\mathrm{Vare}_2} - \frac{\beta_3^2\,(SbXV - \mathrm{Exec}_3)}{\mathrm{Vare}_3} - \frac{\beta_4^2\,(SbXV - \mathrm{Exec}_4)}{\mathrm{Vare}_4} \tag{A.16}$$

```
>
```

```
> solve(%,SbXV);
```

$$\big((\beta_1^2\,\mathrm{Exec}_1\ \mathrm{Vare}_2\ \mathrm{Vare}_3\ \mathrm{Vare}_4 + \beta_2^2\,\mathrm{Exec}_2\ \mathrm{Vare}_1\ \mathrm{Vare}_3\ \mathrm{Vare}_4 + \beta_3^2\,\mathrm{Exec}_3\ \mathrm{Vare}_1\ \mathrm{Vare}_2\ \mathrm{Vare}_4 + \beta_4^2\,\mathrm{Exec}_4\ \mathrm{Vare}_1\ \mathrm{Vare}_2\ \mathrm{Vare}_3)\mathrm{Var}Rm\big)/ \big(\mathrm{Vare}_4\ \mathrm{Vare}_3\beta_2^2\ \mathrm{Var}Rm\,\mathrm{Vare}_1 + \mathrm{Vare}_4\ \mathrm{Vare}_3\ \mathrm{Vare}_2\,\beta_1^2\ \mathrm{Var}Rm + \mathrm{Vare}_4\ \mathrm{Vare}_3\ \mathrm{Vare}_2\ \mathrm{Vare}_1 + \mathrm{Vare}_4\ \mathrm{Vare}_2\,\beta_3^2\ \mathrm{Var}Rm\ \mathrm{Vare}_1 + \mathrm{Vare}_3\ \mathrm{Vare}_2\,\beta_4^2\ \mathrm{Var}Rm\ \mathrm{Vare}_1\big) \tag{A.17}$$

which equals

```
> (Exec[1]*Vare[2]*Vare[3]*Vare[4]*beta[1]^2+Exec[2]*
   Vare[1]*Vare[3]*Vare[4]*beta[2]^2+Exec[3]*Vare[1]*
   Vare[2]*Vare[4]*beta[3]^2+Exec[4]*Vare[1]*Vare[2]*
   Vare[3]*beta[4]^2)/(Vare[1]*Vare[2]*Vare[3]*
   beta[4]^2+Vare[1]*Vare[2]*Vare[4]*beta[3]^2+Vare[1]*
   Vare[3]*Vare[4]*beta[2]^2+Vare[2]*Vare[3]*Vare[4]*
   beta[1]^2+Vare[1]*Vare[2]*Vare[3]*Vare[4]);
```

$$\big(\mathrm{Exec}_1\ \mathrm{Vare}_2\ \mathrm{Vare}_3\mathrm{Vare}_4\,\beta_1^2 + \mathrm{Exec}_2\ \mathrm{Vare}_1\ \mathrm{Vare}_3\ \mathrm{Vare}_4\,\beta_2^2 + \mathrm{Exec}_3\ \mathrm{Vare}_1\ \mathrm{Vare}_2\ \mathrm{Vare}_4\,\beta_3^2 + \mathrm{Exec}_4\ \mathrm{Vare}_1\ \mathrm{Vare}_2\ \mathrm{Vare}_3\,\beta_4^2\big)/ \big(\mathrm{Vare}_1\ \mathrm{Vare}_2\ \mathrm{Vare}_3\,\beta_4^2 + \mathrm{Vare}_1\ \mathrm{Vare}_2\ \mathrm{Vare}_4\,\beta_3^2 + \mathrm{Vare}_1\ \mathrm{Vare}_3\ \mathrm{Vare}_4\,\beta_2^2 + \mathrm{Vare}_2\ \mathrm{Vare}_3\ \mathrm{Vare}_4\,\beta_1^2 + \mathrm{Vare}_1\ \mathrm{Vare}_2\ \mathrm{Vare}_3\ \mathrm{Vare}_4\big) \tag{A.18}$$

We thus have managed to solve for $SbXV$ in terms of known constants and we have a well-defined rule to guide us in composing the portfolio defined by

$$X_i = [\text{Exec}_i - SbXV]\left[\frac{\beta_i}{\text{Vare}_i}\right].$$

We could have solved directly for the value of each X_i utilizing K.T. conditions and the linear equations it induces (as demonstrated at the beginning of this section). This method of solution enhances the notation of a return per unit risk. Once the X_i are solved for we still need to normalize it, i.e., to define the optimal solution as $x_i = \frac{X_i}{\sum_{i=1}^{N} X_i}$.

One of the end of chapter questions will ask you to solve for the optimal portfolio in the SIM in both ways and rank the securities based on excess rate of return, i.e., based on $\text{Exec}_i - SbXV$. You may want to use a spreadsheet for solving the problem based on excess return.

If one of the securities that is traded in the market is the Index, the procedure is even simpler. The generic SIM equation that determines the market portfolios is

```
> (beta[1]^2*VarRm+Vare[1])*X[1]+beta[1]*beta[2]*
  VarRm*X[2]+beta[1]*beta[3]*VarRm*X[3]+beta[1]*
  beta[4]*VarRm*X[4]-r1+rf = 0;
```

$$(\beta_1^2 \,\text{Var}Rm + \text{Vare}_1)x_1 + \beta_1\,\beta_2\,\text{Var}Rm\,x_2 + \beta_1\,\beta_3\,\text{Var}Rm\,x_3 + \beta_1\,\beta_4\,\text{Var}Rm\,x_4 - r1 + rf = 0 \quad (\text{A.19})$$

```
>
```

Assume that indeed asset 1 is the Index, then $\beta_1 = 1$ and $\text{Vare}_1 = 0$. Substituting these in the equation above yields:

```
> subs(beta[1]=1,Vare[1]=0,%);
```

$$x_1\,\text{Var}Rm + \beta_2\,\text{Var}Rm\,x_2 + \beta_3\,\text{Var}Rm\,x_3 + \beta_4\,\text{Var}Rm\,x_4 - r1 + rf = 0 \quad (\text{A.20})$$

```
>
```

```
> collect(%,VarRm);
```

$$(\beta_3\, x_3 + \beta_4\, x_4 + x_1 + \beta_2\, x_2)\mathrm{Var}Rm - r1 + rf = 0 \quad \text{(A.21)}$$

Recall our conclusion from above

$$X_i = [\mathrm{Exec}_i - SbXV]\left[\frac{\beta_i}{\mathrm{Var}e_i}\right]$$

where $SbXV$ was defined to be

$$\mathrm{Var}Rm\left(\sum_{i=1}^{N} x_i \beta_i\right)$$

which as seen above is equal to

```
> solve(%,(X[3]*beta[3]+beta[4]*X[4]+X[1]
  +beta[2]*X[2])*VarRm);
Warning, solving for expressions other than names or
functions is not recommended.
```

$$r1 - rf \quad \text{(A.22)}$$

```
>
```

Hence, if asset one is the Index, we can simply follow the derivation of the SIM with $SbXV = r1 - rf$.

Constant Correlation Coefficient

Under this assumption, the covariance between any two securities is given by $\rho\,\sigma_i\sigma_j$

```
> MapSi:=(i,j)->if i<>j then rho*sigma||i*sigma||j
  else sigma||i^2 fi;
```

$$\mathrm{Map}Si := (i,j) \mapsto \textbf{if } i \neq j \textbf{ then } \rho\,\sigma\|i\,\sigma\|j \textbf{ else } \sigma\|i^2 \textbf{ end if} \quad \text{(A.23)}$$

```
>
```

```
> N:=4;
```

$$N := 4 \tag{A.24}$$

```
> Sigma:= Matrix(N,N,MapSi);
```

$$\Sigma := \begin{bmatrix} \sigma 1^2 & \rho\,\sigma 1\,\sigma 2 & \rho\,\sigma 1 \sigma 3 & \rho\,\sigma 1\,\sigma 4 \\ \rho\,\sigma 1\,\sigma 2 & \sigma 2^2 & \rho\,\sigma 2\,\sigma 3 & \rho\,\sigma 2\,\sigma 4 \\ \rho\,\sigma 1\,\sigma 3 & \rho\,\sigma 2\,\sigma 3 & \sigma 3^2 & \rho\,\sigma 3\,\sigma 4 \\ \rho\,\sigma 1\,\sigma 4 & \rho\,\sigma 2\,\sigma 4 & \rho\,\sigma 3\,\sigma 4 & \sigma 4^2 \end{bmatrix} \tag{A.25}$$

```
>
```

but the same system of equations needs to be solved for the optimal portfolio. That is

```
> i='i':Vector(N,symbol=x):for i from 1 to 4 do;
> eq(i):=(Sigma.X)[i]=Ri_rf[i];
> od; i:='i':
```

$$\begin{aligned} \mathrm{eq}(1) &:= \rho\,\sigma 1\,\sigma 2\,x_2 + \rho\,\sigma 1\,\sigma 3\,x_3 + \rho\,\sigma 1\,\sigma 4\,x_4 + \sigma 1^2 x_1 = r1 - rf \\ \mathrm{eq}(2) &:= \rho\,\sigma 1\,\sigma 2\,x_1 + \rho\,\sigma 2\,\sigma 3\,x_3 + \rho\,\sigma 2\,\sigma 4\,x_4 + \sigma 2^2 x_2 = r2 - rf \\ \mathrm{eq}(3) &:= \rho\,\sigma 1\,\sigma 3\,x_1 + \rho\,\sigma 2\,\sigma 3\,x_2 + \rho\,\sigma 3\,\sigma 4\,x_4 + \sigma 3^2 x_3 = r3 - rf \\ \mathrm{eq}(4) &:= \rho\,\sigma 1\,\sigma 4\,x_1 + \rho\,\sigma 2\,\sigma 4\,x_2 + \rho\,\sigma 3\,\sigma 4\,x_3 + \sigma 4^2 x_4 = r4 - rf \end{aligned} \tag{A.26}$$

```
>
```

The solution to this system of equations can be presented in terms of excess rate of return per unit risk, where in this context the risk is measured by the standard deviation. That is securities will be ranked based on

$$\frac{\mu_i - R_f}{\sigma_i}.$$

Chapter 9

Multi-Index Models and Arbitrage Pricing Theory

Introduction

The multi-index model (MIM) is an extension of the single index model (SIM). The relation between the SIM and the MIM is similar to the relation between a single and multi-variable regression. The MIM introduces the thought that there are a few sources of risk, identified by the model, and thus risk is no longer captured only by the variance of a security or the beta of a security. The idea behind the MIM stems from the premise that there are few common factors (indices) that affect the prices of securities in the market.

The Arbitrage Pricing Theory (APT) is in fact a MIM. It assumes a return process for the securities in the market which is virtually identical to the MIM. The APT does not identify the indices or factors, as they are referred to in the APT. It offers a theory which is midway between equilibrium models, like the capital asset pricing model (CAPM) and the MIM. While the MIM simply assumes the statistical process of the rate of return process, the APT offers some insight into the factors by assuming that arbitrage opportunities do not exist in financial markets.

This last assumption is the cornerstone of modern financial theory and is employed extensively for pricing financial instruments, e.g., of derivative securities. This assumption gave rise to an equivalent of the beta in the CAPM. However here, because of the multiplicity of the index and consequently the multiple sources of risk, there are multiple prices of risks and hence, multiple betas. The beta in the CAPM was derived based on equilibrium arguments. Here, however, the existence of the betas and their values are derived by applying arbitrage arguments.

We were exposed to arbitrage arguments albeit in a non-risky environment, proving that the risk-free discount factors are monotone decreasing in time. The arbitrage arguments applied here are conceptually the same. In fact, one of the questions asked the reader to develop the security market line (SML), under some assumptions, from arbitrage. The same type of arguments will work here. However, the multiplicity of factors should be adhered to, since the CAPM is essentially a one factor model. In the CAPM, the expected value of the rate of return of each security is explained by the risk premium with respect to only one risky portfolio — the market portfolio. The beta in the CAPM is virtually the price of the risk, by which the risk premium is determined. This is the "message" of the SML which was derived there again based on equilibrium arguments.

The APT starts by assuming a multi-factor process and shows that by invoking arbitrage arguments, we can discover the price of risks and generate an equivalent of the SML for the multi-factors world. While conclusions derived by the APT (when done in a rigorous way) require limiting arguments and assume an infinite number of securities, with some simplifications, a sound derivation that motivates the APT can be demonstrated.

The APT Model

The APT assumes that the return on security i can be stipulated as a function of s factors (random variables) $F_1, \ldots, F_s$. The Fs are factors (indices) that explain the rate of return of each security. Thus, in the APT, the rate of return of a security i, R_i $i = 1, \ldots, N$, is stipulated as a linear combination of a constant a_i, the factors and a residual term, a random variable e_i, as stipulated in the following:

$$R_i = a_i + \sum_{j=1}^{s} a_{i,j} F_j + e_i \quad i = 1, \ldots, N. \tag{1}$$

As we will show, the factors F_j $j = 1, \ldots, K$, can be assumed without loss of generality (WLG) to be not correlated. This is also referred to by saying that the factors are orthogonal and the justification is provided henceforth. Intuitively, this means that the change in say the index F_k affects the rate of return of the security only directly. That is, no changes occur because when F_k changes, it affects another index which also affects the rate of return on the security. Thus, there is no interaction between the indices or no correlations between them.

The e_i is denoted as a "residual" since, as explained in the following, by construction, $E(e_i) = 0$ for all i and thus we have

$$E(R_i) = a_i + \sum_{j=1}^{s} a_{i,j} E(F_j) \quad i = 1, \ldots, N. \tag{2}$$

The a_i can be interpreted as the expected value of R_i, if the indices have a value of zero. In fact, the random variable $\eta_i = a_i + e_i$, like in the SIM, can be interpreted as the part of the rate of return that is specific to the security. It is written as $\eta_i = a_i + e_i$ with a_i being $E(\eta_i)$ and thus $E(e_i) = 0$.

The APT also assumes that e_i is specific to each security and there is no connection between terms that are specific to each security, that is

$$\text{Cov}(e_i, e_j) = 0 \quad \text{for all } i \text{ and } j. \tag{3}$$

As well, it assumes that the relation between the securities is only due to the fact that they are all affected by the factors, but yet there is no relation between the e_i and the factors. That is, APT also assumes that

$$\text{Cov}(e_i, F_j) = 0 \quad \text{for all } i \text{ and } j. \tag{4}$$

APT exposes the price of risk by investigating riskless portfolios and their characteristics in this framework.

Consider a portfolio denoted by $x = (x_1, \ldots, x_N)$, where x_i is the fraction of initial wealth invested in security i, hence $\sum_{i=1}^{N} x_i = 1$. The rate of return on a portfolio is thus characterized by

$$\sum_{i=1}^{N} x_i R_i = \sum_{i=1}^{N} x_i a_i + \sum_{i=1}^{N} x_i \left(\sum_{j=1}^{s} a_{i,j} F_j \right) + \sum_{i=1}^{N} x_i e_i. \tag{5}$$

Interchanging the order of the double summation to be $\sum_{j=1}^{s} F_j \left(\sum_{i=1}^{N} x_i a_{i,j}\right)$ and denoting by

$$a_j(x) = \sum_{i=1}^{N} x_i a_{ij}$$

$$a(x) = \sum_{J=1}^{N} x_j a_j, \tag{6}$$

we have

$$\sum_{i=1}^{N} x_i R_i = a(x) + \sum_{j=1}^{s} a_j(x) F_j + \sum_{i=1}^{N} x_i e_i. \tag{7}$$

Thus, when the F_j are all zero, the expected rate of return on the portfolio is the weighted average of the expected rates of return of the securities when the F_j are all zero. Also the sensitivity of the portfolio to change in the jth factor $a_j(x)$, is the weighted average, by x, of the a_{ij} $j = 1, \ldots, s$. Hence, the sensitivity of the portfolio to the jth factor is a weighted average of the sensitivity of the securities in the portfolio to the jth factor. Thus, in this setting, a portfolio x is characterized by $a(x), a_1(x), \ldots, a_s(x)$ and by $\sum_{i=1}^{N} x_i e_i$.

Our exposition of the APT also makes the assumption that it is feasible to have a portfolio with any given set of characteristics such that $\sum_{i=1}^{N} x_i e_i = 0$. In other words, it assumes that given a portfolio that is characterized by the values of $a(x), a_1(x), \ldots, a_s(x)$, it is always possible, as explained in the following subsection, to find an x with the same values of the a's with $\sum_{i=1}^{N} x_i e_i = 0$. Hence, it is assumed to hold, and together with the assumptions that F_j are orthogonal and the e_i are not correlated we have that

$$\operatorname{Var}\left(\sum_{i=1}^{N} x_i\ R_i\right) = \operatorname{Var}\left(\sum_{j=1}^{s} a_j(x)\ F_j\right) + \operatorname{Var}\left(\sum_{i=1}^{N} x_i\ e_i\right)$$

$$= \operatorname{Var}\left(\sum_{j=1}^{s} a_j(x)\ F_j\right) = \sum_{j=1}^{s} a_j(x)^2 \operatorname{Var}(F_j). \tag{8}$$

Consequently, a portfolio x for which $[a_j(x)] = 0$ for every j is riskless. The return on such a portfolio is "nearly" a deterministic constant.

Why is $\sum_{i=1}^{N} x_i e_i = 0$ not a Binding Constraint?

Indeed the rigorous proof of this model assumes that the number of securities in the market is infinite. In such an environment, since we assume that $\text{cov}(e_i, e_j) = 0$, we have that

$$\text{Var}\left(\sum_{i=1}^{N} x_i e_i\right) = \sum_{i=1}^{N} x_i^2 \text{Var}(e_i) \tag{9}$$

and as N approaches infinity x_i is very small and x_i^2 is even smaller and thus

$$\lim_{N\to\infty}\left(\sum_{i=1}^{N} x_i^2 \text{Var}(e_i)\right) = 0. \tag{10}$$

The rigorous claim is that in an economy with an infinite number of securities, we can construct a sequence of portfolios that satisfy certain (risk) characteristics and

$$\lim_{n\to\infty}\left(\sum_{i=1}^{N} x_i^2 \text{Var}(e_i)\right) = 0. \tag{11}$$

Roughly speaking, it is claimed that $\sum_{i=1}^{N} x_i^2 \text{Var}(e_i)$ can be ignored as we can always get it to zero. Therefore, a portfolio is actually characterized by $a(x)$ and $a_j(x)$ for $j, \ldots, s$.

Comparing $\sum_{i=1}^{N} x_i e_i$ to the CAPM (or to diversification in the SIM) one can think about $\sum_{i=1}^{N} x_i e_i$ as a diversifiable risk. A well-diversified portfolio would not be affected by the e_i. Since $E\left(\sum_{i=1}^{N} x_i e_i\right) = 0$ and $\text{Var}\left(\sum_{i=1}^{N} x_i e_i\right)$ approaches zero, the random variable $\sum_{i=1}^{N} x_i e_i$ converges in a certain sense to a deterministic constant of zero and thus can be ignored.

The rest of our analysis thus assumes that $\sum_{i=1}^{N} x_i e_i = 0$ and therefore that a portfolio is only characterized by the vector

$$(a(x), a_1(x), \ldots, a_s(x)). \tag{12}$$

An intuitive explanation of the APT is provided next. The Appendix explores a more rigorous explanation.

The Intuition Behind the APT

Let us take a look again at the return process stipulated by the APT.

$$R_i = a_i + \sum_{j=1}^{s} a_{i,j}\ F_j + e_i, \quad i = 1, \ldots, N. \tag{13}$$

As explained above from a technical point of view, the e_i's are ignored. Intuitively these residuals play the same role as the non-systematic risk in the CAPM, since they can be eliminated by holding a well-diversified portfolio. Thus, the meaning of the equation above is that risk in the economy comes from s sources or is captured by s sources, $F_1, \ldots, F_s$.

In contrast to the CAPM where the source of the risk is one, the market portfolio, here there are a few sources of risk. In the CAPM, a risk that does not originate from the market portfolio, is a non-systematic risk and no compensation is offered for it. Here risk that is not captured by the s sources is a residual risk for which no compensation is offered. Like in the CAPM, investors would take risks only if they are compensated for them and thus they should be compensated for bearing risks if their source is one of the s factors.

In the CAPM, there is only one source of risk and portfolios differ from one another by the magnitude of this risk. The larger the proportion invested in the market portfolio, the larger the risk. Here however the environment is much richer. There are a few types of risk and the factors $F_1, \ldots, F_s$ comprise the 'risk menu' available in the economy.One may think about the securities in the market as recipes composed of different quantities of basic ingredients. The basic ingredients are the F's and different mixtures of these F's will produce different risk profiles.

In the CAPM, the risk profile of a portfolio or a stock is given by its standard deviation, and the compensated risk measured by beta. Here the measure of the risk implicit in a security or a portfolio is no longer a scalar but a vector. The different securities have different risk profiles since they have different combinations of the F's. The risk profile of security i is given by $a_{i1}, \ldots, a_{is}$ where a_{ij} represents the "quantity" of risk of type j implicit in security i. Thus, the risk profile of a portfolio is given by the vector $(a_1, \ldots, a_s)$ where the a_j is the weighted average of the a_{ij}'s of the securities in the portfolio, i.e., $\sum_{i=1}^{N} x_i \cdot a_{ij}$. Like in the CAPM where σ (or β) measures the risk and portfolios with the same σ (β) have the same risks, here portfolios that have the same value of $\sum_{i=1}^{N} x_i \cdot a_{ij}$ have the same quantity of risk of type j. Thus as in the CAPM, portfolios are identified by their risk profile, the vector $(a_{i1}, \ldots, a_{is})$. The composition of the portfolios, x, is suppressed and the risk is measured by $(a_{i1}, \ldots, a_{is})$ which of course is a function of x much the same way as σ was a function of x in the CAPM. As in the CAPM also here there could be two portfolios with different compositions that have the same risk profile.

The compensation for bearing risk is given in terms of the rate of return. Thus, holding security i, one should receive an expected rate of return consisting of the risk-free rate plus a compensation for bearing its risks.The compensation, in terms of the rate of return, for holding one unit of risk of type j is not explicitly seen in the economy. However, we are given the expected rate of return offered by each security and we try to uncover the portion of this return that is attributed to holding risk of type j.

Assume that the expected rate of return one receives in compensation for holding one unit of risk of type j is λ_j. Thus, the compensation, $E(R_i) - R_f$, for holding a security with a risk profile of $(a_{ij}, \ldots, a_{is})$ should satisfy the equation:

$$E(R_i) - R_f = \sum_{j=1}^{s} a_{ij}\, \lambda_j. \tag{14}$$

Suppose we have $N(N > s)$ securities in the market, and assume that a_{ij} and $E(R_j)$, $i = 1, \ldots, N$ $j = 1, \ldots, s$ are known or estimated. We therefore have a system of equations

$$E(R_i) = R_f + \sum_{j=1}^{s} a_{ij}\lambda_j, \quad i = 1, \ldots, N \tag{15}$$

in the unknown λs, the prices of a unit of risk j in terms of expected rates of return, from which the value of the λs can be solved for. These λs are not explicitly seen in the market but they are implicit in the rate of return of the securities and risk profiles. They do exist in the shadow (indeed they are intimately related to shadow prices and Lagrangian multipliers for a specific optimization problem).

Once the λs are solved for, one can use them to 'price' (determine) the excess return over the risk-free rate a security k with a risk profile of $(a_{kj}, \ldots, a_{ks})$ should offer. This is done in a linear fashion by simply calculating the value of $\sum_{j=1}^{s} a_{kj}\lambda_j$. Geometrically, $\sum_{j=1}^{s} a_{kj}\lambda_j$ describes a hyperplane or a line in a two-dimensional space. The geometric meaning of our intuitive explanation is thus easy to visualize in the case of only two F's.

It says that the excess return of each security in the market plotted against its risk profile, generates a hyperplane. The following graph assumes that there are two factors in the economy and that $\lambda_1 = 2$ and $\lambda_2 = 5$. Hence, the excess rate of return over the risk-free rate of a security (or portfolio), that has a_1 as its quantity of risk type 1 and a_2 as its quantity of risk of type 2, will be $a_1\lambda_1 + a_2\lambda_2$. Note that here $(a_1\, a_2)$, the risk for which investors are compensated for, is the counterpart of β in the CAPM. The three-dimensional graph in the following is the counterpart of the SML.

```
> plot3d(2*a1+5*a2,a1=0..10,a2=0..10,axes=frame,
  labels=["a1","a2","E(R)-Rf"], orientation=[9,46],
  style=PATCH,axes=boxed);
```

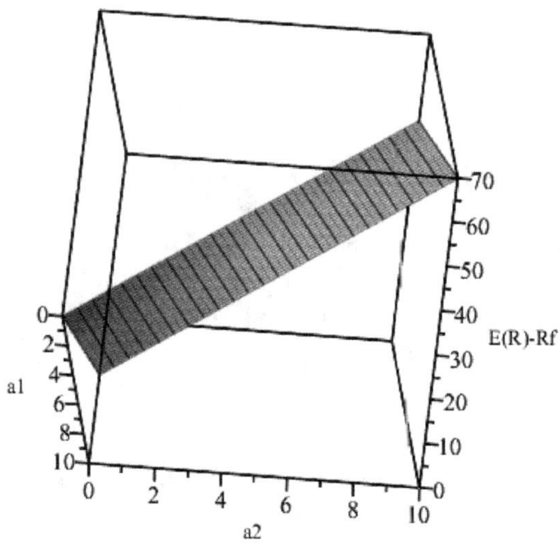


```
>
```

This linearity of $E(r) - R_f$ in a_1 and a_2 is supported by arbitrage arguments. Consider two securities in the market with a risk profile of $(a_{11}, \ldots, a_{1s})$ and $(a_{21}, \ldots, a_{2s})$ and expected values of $E(R_1)$ and $E(R_2)$. It is easy to verify, as we did at the very beginning of this chapter, that a linear combination of these securities will generate a third portfolio, with a risk profile which is the same linear combination of the risk profiles of the given securities. Also the expected rate of return of this portfolio $E(R_3)$, will be the same linear combination of the expected rates of return of the securities in the portfolio. Let α and $1-\alpha$ denote the linear combinations of security 1 and 2, respectively. The linear relationship implies that the expected return of the so generated portfolio must satisfy:

$$\alpha(E(R_1) - R_f) + (1-\alpha)(E(R_2) - R_f) = E(R_3) - R_f. \quad (16)$$

Assume to the contrary that the two securities and the portfolios do exist in the market as primary securities, and that

$$\alpha(E(R_1) - R_f) + (1-\alpha)(E(R_2) - R_f) < E(R_3) - R_f \quad (17)$$

or

$$E(R_3) - R_f < \alpha\,(E(R_1) - R_f) + (1-\alpha)(E(R_2) - R_f). \quad (18)$$

This must cause arbitrage opportunities. Two portfolios with the same risk profile are equivalent (and indistinguishable) and must also have the same rate of return. If they do not have the same rate of return, then arbitrage opportunities exist in the market. Taking short positions in the portfolio with the lower rate of return and a long position in the one with the higher rate of return, will generate portfolios with zero risks, zero net investments, and positive rates of return. Our assumption is therefore that arbitrage opportunities do not exist in the market. The Appendix explores the arbitrage in the APT using Linear Programming and the Lagrange function. It shows, what is considered the main conclusion of the APT, that arbitrage opportunities are absent if and only if there exists a set of λ's such that

$$E(R_i) - R_f = \sum_{j=1}^{s} a_{ij}\lambda_j, \quad \text{for } i = 1, \ldots, N. \quad (19)$$

Examples

Let us look at an example of a market with three securities, one of which is a risk-free security. Assume that the rates of return of the securities are given by:

$$R_0 = 2 + 0 \cdot F_1 + 0 \cdot F_2$$
$$R_1 = 9 + 2 \cdot F_1 + 4 \cdot F_2 + e_1$$
$$R_2 = 1 + 8 \cdot F_1 + 6 \cdot F_2 + e_2 \quad (20)$$

Recall that the risk profile of a security in this market is the vector of the coefficients of the factors. Consequently, it is clear that R_0 is the risk-free rate since it has no risks — the coefficients of F_1 and F_2 in the representation of R_0 are 0. Thus, the risk profile of R_0 is the vector $(0, 0)$.

Assume also that $E(F_1) = 1$, $E(F_2) = 0.5$, $E(R_1) = 13$, and $E(R_2) = 12$. Hence to confirm that, indeed, the expected value of R_i $i = 1, \ldots, 2$ is consistent with the numerical values above, we execute the following:

For R_1, we need to confirm that the following equation is correct:

```
> is(13=9+2*1+4*0.5);
```

$$true \quad (21)$$

and for R_2 we need to confirm the following equation is correct:

```
> is(12=1+8*1+6*0.5);
```

$$true \quad (22)$$

Note that we omit the e_i based on the APT assumption of large portfolios for which the average e will be zero, even though our example deals with only two securities.

The risk profile of security one is $(2, 4)$ and of security 2 $(8, 6)$. The optimization problem which maximizes arbitrage profit (in expected value terms) is solved by the following Maple, where x_i stands for the proportion invested in security $i = 0, 1, 2$ and $i = 0$ denotes the risk-free security. The relation $x_1 + x_2 + x_0 = 0$ makes sure that the identified arbitrage portfolio is self-financed.

```
> simplex[maximize](x1*13+x2*12+2*x0,{x1+x2+x0=0,
  2*x1+8*x2=0,4*x1+6*x2=0});
```

$$\{x_0 = 0, x_1 = 0, x_2 = 0\}. \quad (23)$$

Since the optimal solution to the maximization problem is the vector 0, it means there are no arbitrage (NA) opportunities in this market. The set of equations that must be satisfied in the λ's (prices of risks), if there are NA opportunities, are given as follows. Note that each equation states the excess rate of return over the risk-free rate for each of the risky securities. Thus, we have

$$\lambda_1 \cdot 2 + \lambda_2 \cdot 4 = 13 - 2, \quad \text{and}$$

$$\lambda_1 \cdot 8 + \lambda_2 \cdot 6 = 12 - 2$$

for the first and second security, respectively.

These equations are solved as follows:

```
> solve({lambda0+lambda1*2+lambda2*4=13,lambda0+
  lambda1*8+lambda2*6=12,lambda0=2});
```

$$\left\{\lambda_0 = 2, \lambda_1 = -\frac{13}{10}, \lambda_2 = \frac{17}{5}\right\} \tag{24}$$

Having solved for the price of risk we can find the expected rate of return that each security in this market should offer. For example, if in this market a security is introduced with a risk profile of $(3, 3)$, its expected rate of return should be as follows:

```
> -3*13/10+3*17/5+2;
```

$$\frac{83}{10} \tag{25}$$

```
> evalf(%);
```

$$8.300000000 \tag{26}$$

Let us see if when such a security is introduced to the market with the correct expected rate of return, NA opportunities are being introduced. To this end, we solve the optimization problem as follows.

```
> simplex[maximize](2*x0+x1*13+x2*12+x3*83/10,
 {x0+x1+x2+x3=0,2*x1+8*x2+3*x3=0,4*x1+6*x2+3*x3=0});
```

$$\{x_0 = 0, x_1 = 0, x_2 = 0, x_3 = 0\}. \tag{27}$$

Let's see what happens to the arbitrage maximization problem if a security with a risk profile of $(3, 3)$ is introduced with an expected rate of return of $84/10$.

```
> simplex[maximize](2*x0+x1*13+x2*12+x3*84/10,
  {x0+x1+x2+x3=0,2*x1+8*x2+3*x3=0,4*x1+6*x2+3*x3=0});
```

This time the problem is unbounded, since arbitrage opportunities do exist, and thus Maple's output is NULL. In order to find an arbitrage portfolio, we can change the problem as follows. Obviously, the problem was unbounded since unbounded positions were taken in at least some of the securities. Hence, if we restrict the size of the positions, we can have the problem bounded. As a result, an optimal solution would exist and we can see the arbitrage portfolio.

Also in order to be able to read the expected rate of return of the arbitrage portfolio, we add a dummy variable ExpROR and a dummy constraint; ExpROR $= x_1 \cdot 13 + x_2 \cdot 12 + \frac{x_2 \cdot 84}{10}$. Thus, the optimal value of ExpROR will be the rate of return obtained by the arbitrage portfolio.

```
> simplex[maximize](2*x0+x1*13+x2*12+x3*84/10,{x0+x1+
  x2+x3=0,2*x1+8*x2+3*x3=0,4*x1+6*x2+3*x3=0,ExpROR=
  x1*13+x2*12+x3*84/10,x0>=-1,x1>=-1,x2>=-1,x3>=-1});
```

$$\left\{x_0 = -1, x_1 = -\frac{3}{4}, x_2 = -\frac{3}{4}, x_3 = \frac{5}{2}, ExpROR = \frac{9}{4}\right\} \quad (28)$$

We have now identified a (self-financed) arbitrage portfolio: $x_2 = -\frac{3}{4}, x_1 = -\frac{3}{4}, x_3 = \frac{5}{2}, x_0 = -1$, with an expected rate of return of $\frac{9}{4}$.

We therefore have demonstrated the use of the λ in determining the rate of return of a new security that is introduced to the market. We also have explained how to find, in a systematic way, an arbitrage portfolio if the market has arbitrage opportunities.

APT and CAPM

The APT is an elegant theory which, in a slightly different form, powers most of modern finance results. It does not require an assumption on the risk attitude of the investors, like risk aversion in the CAPM.

On the other hand, it does not specify the factors which are the sources of risk in the economy.

To apply the APT, the factors which explain the rate of return of the securities in the market must be identified. This can be done with the principle component statistical procedure. This procedure, when applied to the APT, forms linear combinations of the securities, i.e., indices or portfolios. The procedures suggest the linear combinations and also statistically suggest how many of these indices are needed to explain the rates of return on the securities.

The main result of the APT states that

$$E(R_i) = R_f + \sum_{j=1}^{s} \lambda_j a_{ij} \quad \text{for every } i.$$

When R_i is the portfolio F_j, i.e., one unit of the jth factor and zero of all others, then $a_{ij} = 1$ if $i = j$ and 0 otherwise. Thus, it follows from the APT main result that

$$E(F_j) = R_f + \lambda_j$$

hence, λ_j can be expressed as

$$\lambda_j = E(I_j) - R_f.$$

If the CAPM also holds in the same market that the APT holds, we have

$$(E(F_j) - R_f) = \beta_j(E(R_m) - R_f)$$

where R_m is the rate of return on the market portfolio. Thus, the rate of return R_i of a portfolio i that is characterized by $(a_{i1}, \ldots, a_{is})$, satisfies

$$E(R_i) - R_f = \sum_{j=1}^{s} a_{ij}(E(F_j) - R_f) = \sum_{j=1}^{s} a_{ij}\beta_j(E(R_m) - R_f)$$

$$= (E(R_m) - R_f) \sum_{j=1}^{s} a_{ij}\beta_j.$$

Hence, it is apparent that the APT and the CAPM do not contradict each other since we have that

$$E(R_i) = R_f + b_i(E(R_m) - R_f) \quad \text{for every } i \quad \text{where } b_i = \sum_{j=1}^{s} a_{ij}\beta_j.$$

Thus, the CAPM and the APT can be consistent with each other and thereby the APT offers an alternative to the CAPM with a richer 'menu' of risk that goes beyond the variance as the measure of risk.

WLG the APT Factors can be Assumed to be Orthogonal

It remains to show that WLG factors can be assumed to be orthogonal. This follows from the following argument. Consider a linear relation between a dependent variable and two independent variables. For example,

$$R_i = a_0 + a_1 \cdot \mathrm{In}_1 + a_2 \cdot \mathrm{In}_2.$$

Assume that there is a relation between In_1 and In_2, i.e., $\mathrm{Cov}(\mathrm{In}_1, \mathrm{In}_2) \neq 0$. Hence, if we run a regression of the form

$$\mathrm{In}_2 = c_0 + c_1 \cdot \mathrm{In}_1 + v$$

then the residual v will be uncorrelated with In_2. That is, $\mathrm{Cov}(v, \mathrm{In}_1) = 0$ as was demonstrated and explained in the section Practitioners' Form of the CAPM. Thus, defining $F_1 = \mathrm{In}_1$

```
> F[1]=In[1];
```

$$F_1 = \mathrm{In}_1 \tag{29}$$

```
>
```

and $F_2 = \mathrm{In}_2 - c_0 - c_1 \cdot F_1$, that is F_2 is the residual v in $\mathrm{In}_2 = c_0 + c_1 \cdot \mathrm{In}_1 + v$.

```
> F[2]=In[2]-c[0]-c[1]*F[1];
```

$$F_2 = -c_1\, F_1 + \mathrm{In}_2 - c_0 \tag{30}$$

```
>
```

We now have a second factor that is not correlated with the first.

```
> solve({%},{In[2]});
```

$$\{\mathrm{In}_2 = c_1\, F_1 + F_2 + c_0\} \tag{31}$$

```
>
```

```
> subs(op(%),In[1]=F[1],R[i]=a[0]+sum(a[i]*In[i],
  'i'=1..2));
```

$$R_i = a_0 + a_1 F_1 + a_2(c_0 + c_1 F_1 + F_2) \tag{32}$$

```
>
```

```
> collect(%,F[1]);
```

$$R_i = (a_1 + a_2 c_1)F_1 + a_0 + a_2(c_0 + F_2) \tag{33}$$

```
>
```

```
> collect(%,F[2]);
```

$$R_i = a_2 F_2 + (a_1 + a_2 c_1)F_1 + a_0 + a_2 c_0 \tag{34}$$

```
>
```

We therefore obtained a relation where the two factors, F_1 and F_2, are not correlated. The equation above also shows the factor loading (the coefficient of) of F_1 and F_2, the orthogonal factors, in terms of the factors loading of In_1 and In_2, the original non-orthogonal factors.

If the model has three factors, that is

$$R_i = a_0 + a_1 \cdot \mathrm{In}_1 + a_2 \cdot \mathrm{In}_2 + a_3 \cdot \mathrm{In}_3$$

then a regression of In_3, the third original factor, on F_1 and F_2 is estimated. This regression is done in order to decompose the factor In_3 to a part which is explained by F_1 and F_2 and to a part which is not explained (orthogonal) or not correlated with F_1 and F_2, i.e.,

```
> I[3]=gamma[0]+gamma[1]*F[1]+gamma[2]*F[2]+delta;
```

$$\mathrm{I}_3 = \gamma_0 + \gamma_1 F_1 + \gamma_2 F_2 + \delta. \tag{35}$$

```
>
```

The third orthogonal factor F_3 is defined to be the residual δ in the above regression, that is

```
> F[3]=I[3]-gamma[0]+gamma[1]*F[1]+gamma[2]*F[2];
```

$$F_3 = \mathrm{I}_3 - \gamma_0 + \gamma_1\, F_1 + \gamma_2\, F_2. \tag{36}$$

```
>
```

Applying the same arguments as above proves that δ is orthogonal to both F_1 and F_2.

The parameters of the relation in which the factors are not correlated is obtained following the same guidelines as above. Hence, to generate such a relation, one needs the factor loading of the relation where the factors are not correlated, and then the factor loading of the factors on themselves. Having already developed the relation in terms of F_1 and F_2 that is

$$R_i = a_2\, F_2 + (a_1 + a_2\, c_1)F_1 + a_0 + a_2\, c_0$$

one only needs to add to the right-hand side of the above equation $a_3 \cdot \mathrm{In}_3$ where

$$\mathrm{In}_3 = F_3 - \gamma_0 + \gamma_1\; F_1 + \gamma_2\; F_2.$$

Collecting the terms will generate the required relation, as demonstrated in the following.

```
> subs(In[1]=F[1],In[2]=F[1]*c[1]+F[2]+c[0],
  In[3]=F[3]-gamma[0]+gamma[1]*F[1]+gamma[2]*F[2],
  R[i]=a[0]+sum(a[i]*In[i],i=1..3));
```

$$R_i = F_1\, a_1 + a_2(c_1\, F_1 + F_2 + c_0) + a_3(\gamma_1\, F_1 + \gamma_2\, F_2 + F_3 - \gamma_0) + a_0 \tag{37}$$

```
> collect(%,F[1]);
```

$$R_i = (a_2\, c_1 + a_3\, \gamma_1 + a_1)F_1 + a_2(F_2 + c_0) + a_3(\gamma_2\, F_2 + F_3 - \gamma_0) + a_0 \tag{38}$$

```
> collect(%,F[2]);
```

$$R_i = (a_3\,\gamma_2 + a_2)F_2 + (a_2\,c_1 + a_3\,\gamma_1 + a_1)F_1 \\ + a_2 c_0 + a_3(F_3 - \gamma_0) + a_0 \tag{39}$$

```
> collect(%,F[3]);
```

$$R_i = a_3\,F_3 + (a_3\,\gamma_2 + a_2)F_2 + (a_2\,c_1 + a_3\,\gamma_1 + a_1)F_1 \\ + a_2\,c_0 - a_3\,\gamma_0 + a_0. \tag{40}$$

Appendix: Linear Programming and Arbitrage

Consider a portfolio $x = (x_1, \ldots, x_n)$ such that $\sum_{i=1}^{N} x_i = 0$. Such a portfolio is self-financed. The absolute percentage invested in the short position and in the long position is equal. Hence, the amount invested in long positions equals that in short positions and thus such a portfolio does not require out-of-pocket financing. The arbitrage in this model is in terms of risk and (expected) rates of return.

The premise is that if securities exist such that their expected rates of return do not fully compensate the holder for the risk borne or over compensate for it, a riskless self-financed portfolio with positive (expected) rate of return exists. The existence of such a portfolio means that investors in this market can have an investment instrument that requires no money while producing a positive expected rate of return. Such an opportunity will be exploited by investors. It causes a price pressure that increases the price of the securities that are in a long position in this portfolio and decreases the prices of the securities held in a short position. Consequently prices will adjust such that the opportunity to obtain positive (expected) rates of return with zero money, and no risk-arbitrage opportunities will disappear. Hence, the assumption is that such a portfolio does not exist in the market. The absence of such a portfolio implies the required result.

The identification of such a portfolio can be formulated as a linear programming maximization problem. The objective function is the (expected) rate of return from the portfolio and the constraints ensure the portfolio is riskless and self-financed. Since the optimization problem requires the portfolio to be riskless, its expected rate of return is its deterministic rate of return, and thus we refer to it as (expected) rate of return. Hence, the optimization problem is given by

$$\text{Max}_x \sum_{i=1}^{N} x_i\, E(R_i)$$

$$\text{s.t.} \sum_{i=1}^{N} a_{ij}\, x_i = 0 \quad \text{for } j = 1, \ldots, s$$

$$\sum_{i=1}^{N} x_i = 0.$$

In this problem, we are looking for a portfolio with a risk profile of $(0, \ldots, 0)$.

Each of the j constraints of the type $\sum_{i=1}^{N} a_{ij}\, x_i = 0$ ensures that the portfolio is riskless.

The rate of return of the portfolio is

$$\sum_{i=1}^{N} x_i\, R_i = \sum_{i=1}^{N} x_i\, a_i + \sum_{i=1}^{N} x_i \sum_{j=1}^{s} a_{i,j}\, F_j$$

which, as we explained before, can be written as

$$\sum_{i=1}^{N} x_i\, R_i = a(x) + \sum_{j=1}^{s} a_j(x) F_j$$

where $a_j(x) = \sum_{i=1}^{N} a_{ij}\, x_i$ and $a(x) = \sum_{i=1}^{N} a_i\ x_i$. However, since each of the F_js are multiplied by $a_j(x)$ which is 0, this is a non-risky portfolio (to the extent that $\sum_{i=1}^{N} x_i\, e_i$ is indeed to be zero). Thus, its rate of return, which equals its expected rate of return, since it is a riskless portfolio, is $a(x) = \sum_{i=1}^{N} a_i\ x_i$. Moreover, the constraint $\sum_{i=1}^{N} x_i = 0$ ensures that the cost of this portfolio is zero. If an optimal solution to this optimization problem with $a(x)$ not being zero exists, there exists in this market a self-financed portfolio producing a positive risk-free rate of return.

Let us take a second look at this optimization problem. It is obviously a linear programming problem since all the involved functions are linear. Furthermore, its optimal value can either be zero or it will be unbounded. If a feasible solution for which $a(x)$ is positive (negative) exists, scaling this solution will increase $a(x)$ without bound. If the problem is unbounded, it means that a portfolio whose (expected) return is infinite with no cost and bears no risk, exists in the market. Equilibrium cannot prevail in such a market and hence we assume that such a portfolio does not exist and therefore assume that the optimal value of this problem must be zero. This is the assumption made by the APT, namely the absence of arbitrage opportunities.

The feasible set of the optimization problem consists of all the vectors that are perpendicular to the $s+1$ vectors; the s dimensional vector

$$(1, \ldots, 1)$$

and the s vectors:

$$(a_{11}, \ldots, a_{N1}), \ldots, (a_{1s}, \ldots, a_{Ns}).$$

As we just explained, the optimal value of the objective function, if there are NA opportunities, must be zero. However, this will be the case if and only if vector $(E(R_1), \ldots, E(R_N))$ is in the subspace spanned by the $s+1$ vectors above. That is, there must exist an $s+1$ dimensional vector $(\lambda_0, \lambda_1, \ldots, \lambda_s)$ such that

$$E(R_i) = \lambda_0 + \sum_{j=1}^{s} \lambda_j \, a_{ij} \quad \text{for } i = 1, \ldots, N.$$

This can be proven with the aid of the Lagrangian, which shows that the $(\lambda_0, \lambda_1, \ldots, \lambda_s)$ are the Lagrangian multipliers of the above optimization problem.

The above equation is the multidimensional counterpart of the SML in which a_{ij} plays the rule of β.

The above equation is the multidimensional counterpart of the SML in which a_{ij} plays the rule of β. The price of one unit of risk (the counterpart of $\frac{R_m - R_f}{\sigma_m^2}$) of type j (captured by the jth factor), is λ_j. To reinforce this interpretation, let us see what is λ_0. If a risk-free asset exists in this market, and its rate of return is R_f then $a_{fj} = 0$ for every j and thus

$$E(R_i) = R_f + \sum_{j=1}^{s} \lambda_j \, a_{ij} \quad \text{for } i = 1, \ldots, N.$$

Now it is more apparent that the rate of return on security i is the risk-free rate plus the compensation of λ_j per one unit of risk j. That is, for each unit of factor j that is embedded in security i, the compensation in terms of the rate of return is λ_j and hence for a_{ij} units of factor j the compensation is $\lambda_j a_{ij}$ and the total compensation is $\sum_{j=1}^{s} \lambda_j a_{ij}$.

Similarly, we can present the other λ's in terms of portfolios that are influenced only by one factor. These are portfolios that have risk profiles presented by a vector in the neutral basis. Let us denote by $E(I_k)$ the expected rate of return on a portfolio with a risk profile of $(0, \ldots, 1, 0, \ldots 0)$ where 1 stands at the kth position. That is a portfolio that is sensitive only to the risk of the kth factor, i.e., $a_{ij} = 0$ for all j except for $j = k$, $a_{ik} = 1$. Hence, for such a portfolio, the equation

$$\sum_{j=1}^{s} a_{ij} \lambda_j = E(R_i) - \lambda_0 \quad i = 1, \ldots, N$$

implies that

$$\lambda_k = E(I_k) - R_f.$$

We therefore can state that

$$E(R_i) = R_f + \sum_{j=1}^{s} (E(I_j) - R_f) a_{ij} \quad \text{for every } i$$

which of course resembles the SML where $E(I_j)$ plays the role of the rate of return on the market portfolio.

The Lagrangian and the APT Main Result

The Lagrangian of the optimization problem

$$\text{Max}_x \sum_{i=1}^{N} x_i E(R_i)$$

$$\text{s.t.} \sum_{i=1}^{N} a_{ij} x_i = 0 \quad \text{for } j = 1, \ldots, s$$

$$\sum_{i=1}^{N} x_i = 0$$

is

$$L(x_1,\ldots,x_N,\lambda_0,\ldots,\lambda_s)=\sum_{i=1}^{N}x_i\,E(R_i)-\sum_{j=1}^{s}\lambda_j\left(\sum_{i=1}^{N}a_{ij}\,x_i-0\right)$$
$$-\lambda_0\left(\sum_{i=1}^{N}x_i-0\right).$$

The optimal x^* and λ^* correspond to a saddle point of the Lagrangian and hence

$$\text{Max}_x\,\text{Min}_\lambda\,L(x,\lambda)=\text{Min}_\lambda\,\text{Max}_x\,L(x,\lambda)=L(x^*,\lambda^*).$$

It is also easy to show from first principles that the optimal value of the optimization problem above equals $\text{Max}_x\,\text{Min}_\lambda\,L(x,\lambda) = L(x^*,\lambda^*)$. Hence, if NA opportunities exist

$$L(x^*,\lambda^*)=0=\text{Min}_\lambda\,\text{Max}_x\,L(x,\lambda).$$

The APT main result is a consequence of the first-order condition of $\text{Min}_\lambda\,\text{Max}_x\,L(x,\lambda)$ and of the optimal value of this problem being zero.For a fixed λ, the first-order condition of $\text{Max}_x\,L(x,\lambda)$ are $\frac{\partial}{\partial x}\,L(x,\lambda)=0$ which implies that

$$E(R_i)-\sum_{j=1}^{s}\lambda_j\,a_{ij}-\lambda_0=0\quad\text{for } i=1,\ldots,N.$$

Substituting $\lambda_0+\sum_{j=1}^{s}\lambda_j\,a_{ij}$ for $E(R_i)$ in $L(x,\lambda)$, yields that $L(x,\lambda)=0$. Thus,

$$\text{Min}_\lambda\,\text{Max}_x\,L(x,\lambda)=0$$

if and only if

$$E(R_i)=\lambda_0+\sum_{j=1}^{s}\lambda_j\,a_{ij}\quad\text{for } i=1,\ldots,N$$

and consequently there are NA opportunities in the market if and only if the above equalities are satisfied.

Index

K

L

M

N

O

P

Q

R

www.ingramcontent.com/pod-product-compliance
Lightning Source LLC
LaVergne TN
LVHW010334220926
848484LV00004BB/899
* 9 7 8 9 8 1 1 2 1 9 5 5 9 *